Retirement Planning

by Matt Krantz

for dummies®
A Wiley Brand

Retirement Planning For Dummies®

Published by: **John Wiley & Sons, Inc.,** 111 River Street, Hoboken, NJ 07030-5774, www.wiley.com

Copyright © 2020 by John Wiley & Sons, Inc., Hoboken, New Jersey

Published simultaneously in Canada

For general information on our other products and services, please contact our Customer Care Department within the U.S. at 877-762-2974, outside the U.S. at 317-572-3993, or fax 317-572-4002. For technical support, please visit https://hub.wiley.com/community/support/dummies.

Wiley publishes in a variety of print and electronic formats and by print-on-demand. Some material included with standard print versions of this book may not be included in e-books or in print-on-demand. If this book refers to media such as a CD or DVD that is not included in the version you purchased, you may download this material at http://booksupport.wiley.com. For more information about Wiley products, visit www.wiley.com.

Library of Congress Control Number: 2019956696

ISBN 978-1-119-62757-9 (pbk); ISBN 978-1-119-62758-6 (ebk); ISBN 978-1-119-62762-3 (ebk)

Manufactured in the United States of America

V10016743_010320

Contents at a Glance

Table of Contents

Introduction

Retirement. The word conjures up different things for different people.

You might picture a life of leisure, walking hand-in-hand with your significant other on a beach. Someone else, maybe even your significant other, might dream of opening a flower shop. Some people can't wait to escape their days jobs, while others either love their careers and don't want to stop or want to start a new career — even if they're 70.

You might have heard that you'll have a comfortable retirement if you save a certain amount of money by a certain age. "Just save a million bucks and you're good," such advice goes. Others say you need to max out your 401(k) or give up your daily cup of coffee. Perhaps you're starting to fear retirement planning because you're not doing something that experts say you must do to retire.

This book is different. My guiding principle is that each person's idea of a happy retirement is different. Your goal for retirement is as unique as you. That's why a rule of thumb or guidance for someone else's retirement is not an exact roadmap for your vision of the future.

This realization is both liberating and challenging. It's liberating to know that you can work with your current situation and goals and still find solutions for retirement planning.

So what's the challenge? The tougher part is figuring out what you want your retirement to look like, especially if your retirement is decades away. So if guessing what you want your future to look like is so challenging, why bother? Simply, the sooner you start, the easier the task will be. Time is your greatest ally when preparing for retirement, so don't waste it!

Luckily, many tools are available to help. Think of this book as your guide to mapping out your retirement plan. You discover not only what your retirement goals should include but how to make those goals a reality.

About This Book

Retirement Planning For Dummies will help you picture what you want your retirement to be, determine what you need to do to make it happen, and discover ways to find out if you're on track. I share the tricks, tips, and secrets I've learned from a career writing about retirement for readers just like you. Unlike other retirement books that try to scare you into saving more, this book looks at retirement planning as an exciting way to think about your future.

Foolish Assumptions

No matter your skill or experience level with investing, you can get something out of *Retirement Planning For Dummies*.

I assume that some readers haven't saved a dime and don't know the difference between a 401(k) and a 747. Or maybe you've finally decided that it's time to start thinking about the future. Part 1 is custom-made for both types of readers, stepping through all the key points in plain English. Although I cover all the technical mumbo-jumbo, such as SEP-IRAs and 401(k)s, I do so only to show you how these are just tools to help you get the retirement you want.

I assume also that some armchair quarterbacks might pick up this book, looking to discover a few things. Planning for retirement is like a second job for some people. For these folks, this book describes more advanced topics and provides select online resources that can add new tools to a retirement toolbox.

Icons Used in This Book

REMEMBER

The remember icon highlights information that you should never forget, even when you're getting caught up in the excitement of retirement planning.

TIP

Read the tip sections to quickly pick up insider secrets that can boost your success when planning for retirement.

TECHNICAL STUFF

I use this icon to flag complicated topics, non-essential topics, or both. Feel free to skip these sections. If you do decide to tackle the information, it might be loaded with retirement lingo, so don't be surprised if you need to read the text a second or third time. Hey, you didn't want this book to be too easy, did you?

WARNING

A warning icon signals information that will help you avoid the landmines scattered throughout Wall Street that can decimate your good intentions of building a successful retirement.

Beyond the Book

In addition to the content in this book, I've provided an online cheat sheet. The cheat sheet shows you how to get started with retirement planning in just 15 minutes, offers tips for retiring early, and shows you how long a million dollars would last. To see the cheat sheet, simply go to www.dummies.com and type **Retirement Planning For Dummies** in the search box.

Where to Go from Here

If you're just starting to think about retirement or are about to sign up for your first 401(k), consider starting at the beginning. That way, you'll be ready for some of the more advanced topics I introduce later in the book.

If you've been planning for retirement for some time and have a strategy you think is working for you, you might want to skip to Part 2.

And if you want to know more about a specific topic, simply look it up in the index or check the table of contents and then flip to the appropriate page.

1

Getting Started

Put away your fear of retirement planning and learn to look at it as a positive way to build your future.

Gain a better understanding of your run rate, or how much you spend on a regular basis.

Determine how much you'll need for retirement.

Learn the unique characteristics and benefits of various retirement accounts.

Measure how much risk you can tolerate in your retirement plan.

Chapter **1**

Retirement Planning Is Up to You

I f you're like most people, you want to retire someday. You might love your job and plan to work well into your 70s. Or maybe you're part of the financial independence retire early (FIRE) crowd and want to escape your corporate ball-and-chain at 40 years old. The beauty of retirement planning is that the timing of your retirement could be up to you.

The goal of this book is to help you get excited about retirement planning. All too often, people are fearful of saving and investing for retirement. You might fear that you aren't saving enough or that you've started too late. Fear, I've found, isn't a great motivator. Instead, it causes retirement-planning paralysis.

In addition, some people get so discouraged about being off track with their retirement planning that they just give up. They figure they'll never catch up to where they think they need to be. Cautionary tales of people who have not saved enough only make people more depressed. You can find lots of those stories. Maybe people you know shared their stories with you.

Put the fear and discouragement aside for a minute. This retirement-planning book is different. I want you to embrace, not dread, retirement planning. What better way to plan for the future than picturing what you want it to look like and then making it happen? Expectations must match reality, but you might be amazed at what you can do when you set your mind to a goal.

Retirement planning is an important way to plot your financial course. And the course you set by reading this book will help make sure that your life 20, 30, 40, or 50 years from now is what you think it should be.

In this chapter, you find out why retirement planning is largely an opportunity for you to plan your own future, rather than have it dictated to you by your employer or government. You also see why getting your plan started as soon as possible pays off in a big way.

Blazing Your Own Retirement Plan

Retirement planning is simply about making sure you have resources available when you're no longer generating them from your labor. However, the financial industry hijacked retirement planning, and now it's all about deferred tax accounts, 401(k)s, and mutual funds. It wasn't always that way.

More than a hundred years ago, more Americans relied on direct labor for their basic needs. In the late 1800s, for instance, about half of Americans were involved in farming. Back then, retirement planning was "an heir and a spare." You wanted to make sure that you had enough kids to keep the farm running after you no longer wanted, or were able, to push a plow.

But now, less than 5 percent of the population touches food before it arrives at the grocery store. And people are more mobile, so your adult children are just as likely to live on the other side of the state as in your basement. In addition, birthrates are falling as more people decide against having children.

These shifts have turned money into the currency of retirement planning. Rather than having a house full of children who will take care of you in your grand old age, retirement planning is about having enough money when you can no longer work. Famous investor Warren Buffett addressed the importance of putting your money to work when he said, "If you don't find a way to make money while you sleep, you will work until you die."

Measuring Your Lifespan

Adding to the planning complexity is the fact that Americans are living much longer than they used to, as shown in Table 1-1. That news is great for humans, but it also means retirement planning for most people must stretch an additional 10 years or longer.

TABLE 1-1

Life Expectancy of Americans

Year You Were Born	Life Expectancy (Both Sexes Combined)
1955–1960	69.66
1960– 1965	70.11
1965– 1970	70.36
1970– 1975	71.43
1975– 1980	73.25
1980– 1985	74.37
1985– 1990	75.89
1990– 1995	75.65
1995– 2000	76.47
2000– 2005	77.18
2005– 2010	78.19
2010– 2015	78.94
2015– 2020	78.81

United Nations, Department of Economic and Social Affairs, Population Division (2019). World Population Prospects: The 2019 Revision; custom data acquired via website.

TIP

If you want to slice-and-dice life expectancy data to glean more precise insights about typical lifespans, you're in luck. The United Nations' World Population Prospect data query tool is a treasure trove of life expectancy data. You can see forecasts going out for decades, how females fare compared to men, and the changes to your life expectancy as you get older. Dig into this fascinating data by using the tool at `https://population.un.org/wpp/DataQuery/`.

Time to take a break from the history of retirement planning to answer the question you're probably asking now that you've read this far: How long will you live? I am not getting fatalistic. Knowing how long you can expect to live is a big part of retirement planning. After all, a person who expects to live to 90 will save and work differently than someone likely to die younger.

I cover this topic in more detail later, but now's as good a time as any to think about your lifespan a bit. I keep the discussion optimistic by focusing on how long you'll live (versus when you'll die). In this section I provide my favorite tools to help you make this calculation.

Social Security Administration's Life Expectancy Calculator

The U.S. government has a good idea about how long you'll live. After all, as the largest payer of income to older people, it's in the government's best interest to know this information.

The Social Security Administration's Life Expectancy Calculator at www.ssa.gov/OACT/population/longevity.html looks at your gender and date of birth to estimate how long you'll live.

For example if you're a 40-year-old male in 2019, you would see a table like the one in Figure 1-1 after entering your gender and date of birth. You would be expected to live until 81.7, which means at 40 you'd be just about ready for a mid-life crisis. If you were healthy enough to make it to 67, the Social Security Administration would figure that you would make it to 86.

Bankrate's Life Expectancy Calculator

You probably know that not all 40-year-olds will live exactly 81.7 years. Some lifestyle choices, such as smoking, have a bearing on how long you live. (Let's forget about George Burns, the chain-smoking comedian who lived until 100.)

Bankrate tries to capture that variability in its Life Expectancy Calculator at www.bankrate.com/calculators/retirement/life-age-expectancy-calculator.aspx. You enter not just your age and gender but also personal details: height, weight, whether or not you smoke and drink alcohol, and a little family history.

Let's go back to our 40-year-old male. He's 6-feet tall, weighs 150 pounds, doesn't touch alcohol, but does smoke. With that added detail, his life expectancy is now estimated to be 72.6 years, as shown in Figure 1-2.

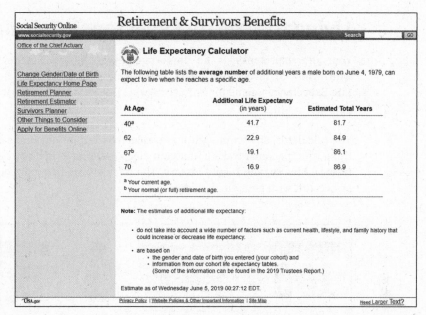

FIGURE 1-1:
Social Security's Life Expectancy Calculator helps you see how your lifespan compares with others.

Social Security Online — Retirement & Survivors Benefits

Life Expectancy Calculator

The following table lists the **average number** of additional years a male born on June 4, 1979, can expect to live when he reaches a specific age.

At Age	Additional Life Expectancy (in years)	Estimated Total Years
40[a]	41.7	81.7
62	22.9	84.9
67[b]	19.1	86.1
70	16.9	86.9

[a] Your current age.
[b] Your normal (or full) retirement age.

Note: The estimates of additional life expectancy:

- do not take into account a wide number of factors such as current health, lifestyle, and family history that could increase or decrease life expectancy.

- are based on
    - the gender and date of birth you entered (your cohort) and
    - information from our cohort life expectancy tables.
    (Some of the information can be found in the 2019 Trustees Report.)

Estimate as of Wednesday June 5, 2019 00:27:12 EDT.

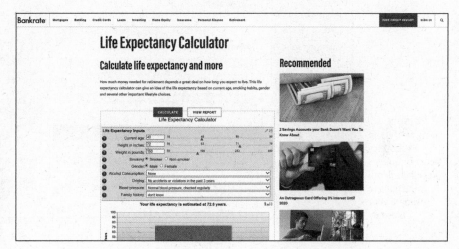

FIGURE 1-2:
Bankrate's Life Expectancy Calculator factors in more details to help you figure out how long you'll go.

REMEMBER

Life expectancy calculators, like many calculators described in this book, provide estimates. Clearly, if you knew exactly how long you'd live, retirement planning would be a lot easier. Unpredictability is a key aspect that makes retirement planning — and life — an imprecise science.

Living to 100 Life Expectancy Calculator

Your life expectancy is an important input in your retirement plan. It's worthwhile to revisit this factor periodically and carefully. The Living to 100 Life Expectancy Calculator at `http://www.livingto100.com` brings rigor to this process.

The calculator, shown in Figure 1-3, asks a battery of questions covering everything from personal traits about your sleep patterns to lifestyle habits, nutrition, medical history, and family history. The calculator is free, but you need to set up an account with your email address.

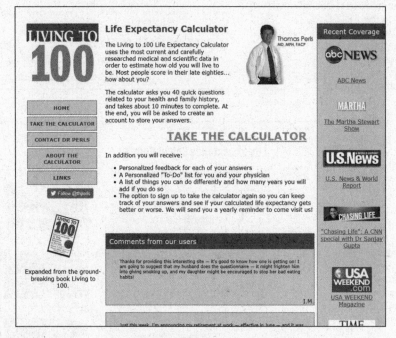

FIGURE 1-3: Living to 100 Life Expectancy Calculator quizzes you with in-depth questions to estimate your lifespan.

Retirement Planning Beginnings: The Pension

As the U.S. industrialized, and farmers hung up their bib overalls and moved to work in factories, a major shift occurred in retirement planning. Workers would sign up with a company and pretty much assume they'd stay their entire careers. Over time, workers counted on their loyalty and decades of service to result in companies providing for them their entire lives — even after they retired.

Given what you know about lifespans, you can see why it wasn't a huge deal for companies to take care of employees for life. Let's say an employee in a steel mill worked until age 65. Look back at Table 1-1 and you'll see that in the mid-1950s and the 1960s, he'd be expected to live only until 70. His company would have to provide retirement income for only five years.

Hence, the pension was born. In a *pension plan*, which is sometimes called a *defined benefit plan*, the employer commits to pay the pensioner a set amount of money each year after retirement. If employees stay with the company, they know how much income to expect.

During an employee's working years, his or her employer would contribute to a fund. It was the company's responsibility to not only add to the fund but also to prudently manage it with investments on the employees' behalf. The company was required to hold and protect sufficient amounts of funds to pay pension proceeds. If the fund got low, typically because money was paid out faster than the fund grew, the company had to use part of its profits to refill the reserves. As you could imagine, investors weren't happy when this happened.

If you've recently joined the workforce, pension plans probably sound strange. But in the 1950s through the 1980s, most employees, especially those working for large companies, expected a pension. Pensions are still common for public employees but have largely vanished for everyone else. As of 2011, only 18 percent of private sector employees participated in a pension plan, according to the Bureau of Labor Statistics. That amount dropped to just 15 percent in 2017, according to an updated estimate from Pension Rights Center (www.pensionrights.org/publications/statistic/how-many-american-workers-participate-workplace-retirement-plans), and to 11 percent in 2018 according to the Employee Benefit Research Institute (www.ebri.org/docs/default-source/ebri-press-release/pr-1244-retplansff-6jun19.pdf?sfvrsn=98a83f2f_4).

So how are you supposed to plan for retirement if you don't have a pension plan? That's where our story takes us next.

Changing Times: The 401(k)

Those of you who were around in 1978 probably recall the debut of the Garfield comic strip. Another big milestone in 1978 was the end of production of the Volkswagen Beetle. But something far more important for retirement planning happened that year: The 401(k) was born.

The 401(k) is practically synonymous with retirement planning now because this plan is the predominant way most people save for retirement, especially those relatively new to the workforce. This popular retirement plan has steadily replaced the pension plan.

REMEMBER

Employer-sponsored defined contribution plans are typically called 401(k)s. But they have close cousins at different employers. Employees at nonprofits access 403(b) plans, government workers have 457(b) plans, and some schools have 401(a) plans. The letters and numbers are different, but the plans are essentially the same as 401(k)s in terms of taxation.

As mentioned, pension plans are defined benefit plans. The plan sponsor, typically the employer, promises the retiree a certain monthly or annual income in retirement. In contrast, 401(k) plans are *defined contribution plans.* The only thing that's set is how much will be contributed to the plan. Typically, employees make most of the contributions. Contributions for standard 401(k) plans are generally made by paycheck deductions using pre-tax dollars; I cover exceptions in Chapter 4. (When you contribute to a 401(k), you lower your tax bill.) Many employers then make additional contributions, usually a matching percentage of what the employee puts in.

REMEMBER

The amount that you will get out of a defined contribution plan is not guaranteed. You can select how your money will be invested, as I describe in later chapters, but you can take out only what's in the account. This is an important difference from defined benefit plans such as pensions.

Why is the traditional 401(k) so powerful? The company match, if available, is great, but the main benefit is the tax-deferred contribution. Suppose you earn $100,000 and elect to contribute $10,000 to your 401(k). The $10,000 would be taken from your paycheck and not immediately taxed. Assuming that you're in the 24 percent tax bracket, you would not pay the $2,400 in tax that would have ordinarily been due the year the money was earned. Instead, the money is taxable in the future when you withdraw it in retirement. This deferral is a powerful tool in retirement planning.

REMEMBER

Contributions to a 401(k) offer tax deferral, not tax elimination. With most traditional retirement plans, you don't pay taxes now, but you do pay taxes eventually. The idea, though, is that when you pay taxes down the road, when you're not working, your tax rate will be lower.

MEET THE FATHER OF THE 401(K)

Not many sections of the Internal Revenue Service's tax code are famous. But the 869-word paragraph k added to Section 401 of the Internal Revenue Code in 1978 is a rock star. And we can thank not a forward-looking Congressperson but a detail-oriented lawyer in Pennsylvania named Ted Benna.

Benna created the first 401(k) plan — and revolutionized retirement planning in the process. He's known as the "Father of the 401(k)." Benna, a benefits consultant, was working with a bank, hoping to find a better way to keep employees that didn't involve handing out fat annual (and taxable) bonuses. The bank wanted a profit-sharing plan that would keep them competitive with other banks in terms of compensation — and give them a tax break on the contributions.

In 1979, Benna knew that IRS code 401(k), passed in 1978, was going into effect in 1980. Although many accountants knew of the provision, they paid little attention to it because it was intended to serve a different purpose. But Benna saw how employees could contribute all or a portion of their bonus into a 401(k) and get immediate tax relief. To sweeten the pot, Benna added a matching contribution option for the bank.

Benna's bank client took a pass on his invention, afraid to do something new and worried that the Internal Revenue Service would reverse it. So Benna created a 401(k) plan for his own company, The Johnson Company (not Johnson & Johnson as widely believed).

Did Benna make a fortune creating this retirement-planning tool? He told me he did fine consulting with firms looking to create 401(k) plans. But since 401(k) is an IRS tax code statue, he couldn't trademark the retirement account structure. It wasn't long before the Fidelities and Vanguards of the world rushed in.

In Benna's book, *401(k) Forty Years Later,* he acknowledges that 401(k)s aren't perfect. He laments the high fees charged by financial companies that administer these plans (this book will help you with those). But he also takes issue with the idea that pensions were better. "There is a widely held myth that we once had a wonderful retirement system that is now corrupted," he writes in his book.

He points out several problems with pensions, most of which 401(k)s solved or at least addressed:

- **Restrictive inclusion rules:** Many pension plans would not allow you to participate until you were 30 or older. This restriction delayed the accrual of benefits to workers when time was on their side. 401(k) plans are typically open to employees after a month or a year at the longest.

(continued)

(continued)

- **Onerous vesting rules:** In many pension plans, you had to stay at the company until you reached 60 before you vested. Leave before then and you got nothing. Some employers would try to dump employees before they vested, saving them a pension liability. 401(k) plans vest, too, but employees are always entitled to the funds they contributed. Employers can hold back employees' access to only the matching funds. Typically, vesting happens gradually, with a maximum holding period of six years.

- **Limited availability:** Benna says only a third of non-farm workers in the private sector had access to a pension plan. Employees at large companies had pensions, but they were rare in smaller firms. Lower costs of 401(k)s make them much more feasible for more companies.

- **Risk of failure:** For many years, the rules were lax as to how fully companies needed to keep pension plans funded. Many companies simply didn't put the necessary funds in the pension, so retirees couldn't collect the money they thought was coming. 401(k)s are filled with actual contributions, not promises of future payments. Employees can always check their 401(k) balances and see how much they have.

"The truth is that the private pension system of the 1960s was far different than the image that is commonly presented today. It was far from ideal and may have, in fact, been much worse than what we have today," Benna writes.

TIP

If you think your tax rate will be higher when you retire, consider a Roth IRA or Roth 401(k) plan. These plans tax your retirement contributions immediately, but you take out already taxed money later. For more on these Roth plans, see Chapter 4.

The rise of defined contribution plans changed retirement planning forever. Employers shifted to employees the responsibility of generating and providing future retirement income.

Although employees take on more risk and responsibility, they also gain some freedom. They can decide how much, if any, to contribute to the plan. They're also less beholden to their employer. If they get another job offer, they're free to pick up their 401(k) and go elsewhere. They can *roll over*, or transfer, their 401(k) to a personal retirement account or to their new employer's 401(k) plan. The only catch is that employees can tap only the part of the 401(k) that they contributed or is vested. *Vesting* is described later in this book, but for now just know that employers can hold back some of their contributions to a 401(k) if the employee doesn't stay a certain number of years.

Behold the power of the 401(k)

To build a nest egg that will help them live the life they want in retirement, most people take advantage of the 401(k). For example, assume that in 1988 you were a 35-year-old worker. You decided to put the maximum allowed into your 401(k) that year and every following year until you turned 65. The money was invested aggressively for the first 10 years, with 80 percent stocks and 20 percent bonds. The risk was dialed back in following decades, with 70 percent stocks and 30 percent bonds from age 45 to 55, and 60 percent stocks and 40 percent bonds going forward. (At this point, don't worry about the mix of stocks and bonds.)

As Table 1-2 shows, you never contributed more than $24,500 to your 401(k). But after more than 30 years of saving, you end up with $1.4 million! Now that was worth the sacrifice, wouldn't you say?

TABLE 1-2

Maxing Out a 401(k)

Year	Age	Contribution Limit (Including Catch Up)	Ending Balance
1988	35	$7,313	$7,313
1993	40	$8,994	$63,243
1998	45	$10,000	$232,431
2003	50	$14,000	$315,963
2008 (U.S. stocks fell 37% this year)	55	$20,500	$459,908
2013	60	$23,000	$937,733
2018	65	$24,500	$1,414,942

Based on actual contribution limits from 1988 to 2018. Stock returns indexed to the Standard & Poor's 500 and bond returns, while 10-year Treasury bond yields used for bond allocation.

TIP

Don't let the fear of market volatility scare you from saving for retirement. As you can see in Table 1-2, some years the market declined and hurt the portfolio's balance, but remaining in the plan and maintaining contributions won out. Also, keep in mind that the government lets you make *catch-up contributions*, or additional money you can put more in your 401(k) after you turn 50.

An opportunity to save

Looking at Table 1-2, you no doubt appreciate why contributing to your 401(k) is powerful. But this contribution is a sacrifice because you need to give up spending now so you can put your money to work for you tomorrow.

Most employees don't contribute the maximum to their 401(k) plans, but they still benefit. During the first quarter of 2019, the average 401(k) contribution from customers at giant asset management firm Fidelity was $2,370, which implies a contribution of $9,480 a year. But by adding the average company match during the quarter — $1,780 — the total yearly contribution becomes $16,600. This amount is an all-time high savings rate of 13.5 percent, says Fidelity (`www.fidelity.com/bin-public/060_www_fidelity_com/documents/press-release/quarterly-retirement-trends-050919.pdf`).

Social Security: The De Facto Safety Net

I cringe when someone says, "Why do I need to plan for retirement? I have Social Security."

Yes, Social Security, the nickname for Old-Age, Survivors, and Disability Insurance (OASDI), is designed to prevent you from ending up on the street after working your entire life. But don't you have higher hopes for your retirement than just scraping by?

Social Security isn't a savings plan. All the money you pay into the system isn't in an account with your name on it, like a 401(k) plan. It's a *pay-as-you-go* system. In other words, the money you pay in as you're working is used to pay income to people in retirement now. When you retire, you don't withdraw the money you paid into the system. Your retirement income will be paid by people in the workforce at that time.

As a general rule, Social Security replaces 40 percent of a retiree's income (`www.ssa.gov/planners/retire/r&m6.html`). The number is lower for wealthier people who need to keep the gas tank full in their yachts.

WARNING

Social Security is a fine safety net, but don't bank a comfortable retirement on it. Your retirement-planning strategy needs to be more than just Social Security for three reasons:

>> **Social Security is just one leg of a four-legged stool for retirement income.** Social Security was designed not to replace your income in retirement but to reduce the odds that you will starve in your old age. Social Security is intended to be accompanied by a pension, if you have one, retirement accounts, and personal savings.

>> **The funding future of the program is uncertain.** The curious structure of the Social Security program — where current workers pay the benefits of current retirees — doesn't leave much room for error. When you have a big wave of retirees, as you do with Baby Boomers retiring now, the system is strained.

Starting in the late 2010s, the cost of Social Security is expected to outstrip its income for the first time since 1982 (www.ssa.gov/oact/tr/2018/tr2018.pdf). Some of the shortfall can be made up with a small amount of reserves. But until the system is reformed, the reserves are forecast to be depleted in 2034, at which point they could pay 77 percent of scheduled benefits. When you hear the word *reform,* that likely means either workers will pay more in or retirees will get less out.

Meanwhile, the full retirement age to get the entire payout from Social Security has changed from 65 to 66 and now to 67, as follows:

Birth Year	Full Retirement Age
1937 or earlier	65
1938	65 and 2 months
1939	65 and 4 months
1940	65 and 6 months
1941	65 and 8 months
1942	65 and 10 months
1943-1954	66
1955	66 and 2 months
1956	66 and 4 months
1957	66 and 6 months
1958	66 and 8 months
1959	66 and 10 months
1960 and later	67

>> **You receive reduced benefits if you retire early.** The earliest you can claim retirement benefits is age 62. But if you do that, your benefit is reduced by 30 percent. Even if you retire at 65, which many people think of as retirement age, your benefit is reduced by 13.3 percent. The following lists the benefit reductions when retiring early.

Retirement Age	Retirement Benefit Reduction
62	About 30%
63	25%
64	20%
65	13.3%
66	6.7%

So you can see why Social Security isn't your ticket to retirement riches. It's up to you to plan for retirement. Now it's time to find out how.

Chapter **2**

Determining How Much You Spend

You might be tempted to jump right into crafting your retirement plan. Wait a second! Let me explain why you need to complete another step first: figuring out your run rate.

Your *run rate* is how much you spend now. You need to understand how much money it takes to maintain your current standard of living before you can calculate how much you'll need when you say goodbye to the 9-to-5.

Some other retirement books teach you to figure out what you want your retirement to look like and then figure out how to reach that number. This approach is frustrating. What if you want to retire off the coast of France, but that goal doesn't match reality?

The biggest determinant of what you need and how much you can save is your current spending. And here's the good news! This key factor is measurable and under your control, unlike many other aspects of retirement planning.

TIP

Are you thinking of hiring a financial planner to build your retirement plan? Calculating your run rate is still worthwhile. Any planner will need to know how much you're spending each year to build a retirement scenario for you.

In this chapter, you examine your spending habits with the goal of figuring out how much money you need to live the way you want. This calculation is critical because it determines how much you need to save before you retire.

Finding Out Where Your Money Goes

Do you ever get to the end of the month and find that you have barely any money left? Or perhaps you're in a different situation, where you're miserable in your high-paying job and not sure if you need the excess money you're earning.

Some of you may already fastidiously track your income and expenses, but most people don't. Fortunately, helpful (and almost automatic) ways exist to figure out where you're spending your money.

Eyeing your expenses

When it comes to tracking your money, you need to know a few things about your expenses:

>> **Category:** Classify what you're spending into groups, such as food, transportation, and housing. Then break down these groups further into subcategories. For example, food is composed of groceries and dining out, and transportation includes gas for your car and bus tickets. Keep in mind, too, that some of your costs are necessities (such as rent and groceries) and others are discretionary (for example, concert tickets and dining out).

>> **Amount:** Tally these costs. Even seemingly small expenses can add up over time.

>> **Frequency:** Some expenses are weekly, such as a grocery store run. Others occur monthly, such as utilities. And still others are due once or twice a year, such as property taxes. You might be feeling rich one month, only to be blindsided by a semi-annual auto insurance bill the next.

>> **Tax deductibility:** Some expenses might be associated with your business or deductible at tax time for other reasons. Keep track of tax-deductible expenses.

>> **Savings:** Okay, so savings isn't an expense, but it's part of your budget. Keeping track of how much you're able to sock away helps you forecast your savings progress.

>> **Taxes:** Keep an eye on how much is withheld, or pulled out of your earnings, each pay period, so you understand how much of your income is going to the tax man.

Tracking your money's every move

You're probably thinking, "How the heck can I track all this with any kind of precision?" After all, if you're like most people, you typically just whip out a credit card when you pay for something, toss the receipt, and worry about the bill later. Or you might be even less actively involved because you set your bills on auto payment and forget about them.

WARNING

Take any expense and divide it by 12 or even 24 and it doesn't seem so bad. You might pause before you pony up $1,000 for a smartphone. But if it's "only" $42 a month (for 24 months), that's not so bad, right? Companies are onto this, and offer monthly fees and subscriptions for almost anything. And many of these fees are automatically billed to your credit card, so you might not even remember you're paying them. These auto charges are like vampires, sucking away money from your retirement plan.

I'm not going to tell you that your monthly Netflix subscription or daily run to Starbucks is a bad idea. Again, the way you use your money is up to you. I will, however, show you how to figure out what these things are costing you. Then it's up to you to decide whether they're worthwhile.

When you track your expenses, know that most fit into one of four main groups:

>> **Overhead:** You need food, clothing, and shelter. These items don't necessarily bring you joy, but they're required to survive. Rent or mortgage payments, groceries, and utilities are the biggest overhead line items.

>> **Taxes:** Another massive line item for people is Uncle Sam's piece. Refer to the tax brackets in Table 2-1 if you need a reminder.

>> **Savings:** As mentioned, you might not think of savings as an expense, but that's how it functions in your budget.

>> **Discretionary money:** After you pay your other expenses, I hope money is left over for you to buy things or experiences you enjoy.

TABLE 2-1 ## 2019 Tax Brackets

Rate	Single Individual, Taxable Income More Than	Married and Filing Jointly, Taxable Income More Than	Head of Household, Taxable Income More Than
10%	$0	$0	$0
12%	$9,700	$19,400	$13,850
22%	$39,475	$78,950	$52,850
24%	$84,200	$168,400	$84,200
32%	$160,725	$321,450	$160,700
35%	$204,100	$408,200	$204,100
37%	$510,300	$612,350	$510,300

Spending guidelines

Following are guidelines on how much you should be spending on the four main expense categories:

» **Overhead:** 50 percent or less of income. Generally speaking, your housing spending should be 30 percent or less of your income. Add insurance, utilities, food, and other necessities, and the total should be about 50 percent or less of your income. If you can spend less on necessities, good for you.

» **Taxes:** 20 percent federal plus state and local. Taxpayers on average paid 20 percent of their income on federal tax (www.irs.gov/statistics/soi-tax-stats-individual-statistical-tables-by-size-of-adjusted-gross-income). State income taxes range from 0 percent in seven states to up to 13.3 percent in California (https://turbotax.intuit.com/tax-tips/fun-facts/states-with-the-highest-and-lowest-taxes/L6HPAVqSF). Good retirement planning can help you lower the slice the taxman takes.

» **Savings:** 10 percent to 15 percent. Most experts recommend socking away for retirement 10 to 15 percent of your *pretax* income. You'll want to save more than that if you're planning a big expense such as college for your kids, a new car, or the down payment on a home. Keep in mind that when you're retired, you no longer need to keep a savings budget.

» **Discretionary:** Whatever's left, which is 15 percent to 20 percent if you follow the other guidelines. After paying everything else, have fun with the remaining money. You should choose what to do with your fun money.

Measuring Your Spending

As mentioned, your run rate is how much you spend now. You can calculate your run rate in several ways:

>> **Paper and pencil:** Yes, you could save your receipts and write down your expenses in a book. If you hate your computer, this method might work for you. But in this book, I skip this dead-tree approach because better ways exist for tracking your money.

>> **Your bank's online resources:** Many banks put a lot of effort into boosting their website's budget feature. For some people, this approach suffices. Later, I show you the best way to use this feature.

>> **Third-party apps and websites:** There's an app for that! You use apps to get from place to place and to order food. Why not control your spending with an app, too? An assortment of apps and associated websites can help you see how much you're spending.

>> **Spreadsheets:** Third-party apps are slick but some come with a catch, charging a monthly fee or sharing your personal financial information. For some people, a good old-fashioned spreadsheet is all they need. I show you how to get started.

Using your credit card company or bank's online resources

Using your credit card company or bank's site to calculate your run rate requires minimal effort. The institution does most of the work for you, if you know where to look.

Plus, many banks and credit card companies are upping their game when it comes to giving consumers tools to track their money. Many will let you tabulate the amount you're spending overall and by category. If you're just jumping onto your credit card company's site to pay your monthly bill, you might be missing out on an opportunity to learn more about your spending patterns.

If you log in to Citibank, a popular bank and issuer of credit cards, you'll see a Spend Summary option. Click it and the screen shown in Figure 2-1 appears. You see the amounts you're spending in specific categories, such as restaurants or entertainment. For most categories, you can drill down and get additional detail. You also see the total amount you spent. Most banks offer similar features.

FIGURE 2-1:
Like most banks and credit card companies, Citibank tracks your spending.

But you're not done. Remember that you have other expenses that may not be picked up by the credit card issuer's site. For instance, if your checking account is elsewhere, checks you write for property tax or insurance aren't included. Remember to include these additional expenses.

When looking at each of your expenses, picture where the expense fits in the major categories. Is it overhead or discretionary?

Some people hold their savings and credit cards at the same bank. If so, you can get summary spending information from the bank's site. Others keep their checking and savings accounts and credit cards with different financial institutions. If that sounds like you, you'll need to consult the online resources of both your bank and credit card company.

If you're going this route to track your run rate, make your life easier by using only one credit card. Remember, if you pay off your credit card in full each month (which you should), you're essentially getting a free monthly loan. Also, you get a more accurate and complete picture of your run rate.

Diving into the world of third-party apps and online tools

If you're like most people, your smartphone is always at your side (or in your pocket). So it's only natural to use this device to monitor your spending. Thanks to your smartphone's capability to send you alerts, it can be a helpful tool in keeping you in close contact with your spending.

In this section, I describe some of the major providers of money-tracking app and websites. If you're interested in a broader view of money-management apps — especially how they can be used to track your brokerage accounts, check out my *Online Investing For Dummies*, 10th Edition (Wiley).

The big daddy: Intuit's Mint

When it comes to an all-encompassing website and app to track your spending, Mint (www.mint.com) is the one to beat. Mint is backed by the deep pockets of Intuit, a firm with many years of experience in financial technology.

Mint is free. Here's how to sign up:

1. **Log in or create an ID.**

   Go to www.mint.com and create an Intuit ID. If you already use TurboTax Online, you can use the same username and password.

2. **Link accounts you want to track.**

   Enter the username and password for your credit card accounts. Mint will then pull in your spending information from those accounts.

3. **Go to the Trends tab.**

4. **Under the During option, select Last 12 Months.**

   Mint summarizes your spending for the past year. You now have your run rate!

5. **Check out your spending by category and your total spending.**

   It's particularly useful to look at spending by category, as shown in Figure 2-2. Knowing that you spend $100 a month at McDonald's is good, but knowing that you spend $1,000 a month going out to eat is valuable information. Tracking your spending by category lets you spot trends, such as an out-of-control addiction buying collectibles or an entertainment budget that's larger than your friends (maybe it's time for them to pick up the restaurant tab sometimes).

Mint has a matching app that you can download for iOS or Android, so you can track your spending and run rate right from your smartphone.

Another way: Quicken

If you're not comfortable sharing your personal information with Mint or you want more control over how to slice and dice your data, try Quicken.

FIGURE 2-2:
Mint.com
provides an easy,
free way to see
where your
money is going.

Quicken is old school, but it's a good option for some people. The Deluxe version costs $50 yearly. Unlike Mint, Quicken stores your data on your computer instead of on a remote server (unless you choose to store it on Quicken's online service) and doesn't pitch financial products.

WARNING

Quicken, like other software companies, moved to a subscription model. When you buy the software for $50, you get only a year of access. After a year, you can still read your data but some of the functions no longer work. Many users find this restriction a turnoff.

To find your run rate, go to the Spending tab. Quicken gives you precise control over time periods and types of spending. The 12-month view, shown in Figure 2-3, provides your run rate.

Using what you have: Microsoft Excel

If you're like most people, every computer or tablet in your house has Microsoft Office. It just so happens that Office's Excel, shown in Figure 2-4, is good at tracking expenses. The benefit is that there's no additional software to buy.

To download free spreadsheets to help you get started, go to Microsoft's Excel template center at https://templates.office.com/. Enter the term *budget* in the search box. One of my favorites is the personal monthly budget at https://templates.office.com/en-us/Personal-monthly-budget-TM04101071.

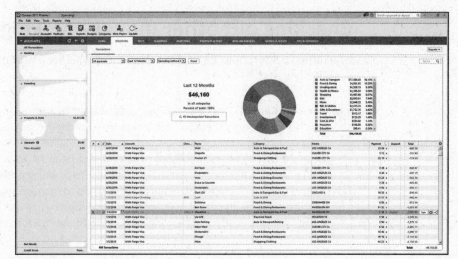

FIGURE 2-3:
You have to pay for Quicken, but it gives you lots of control.

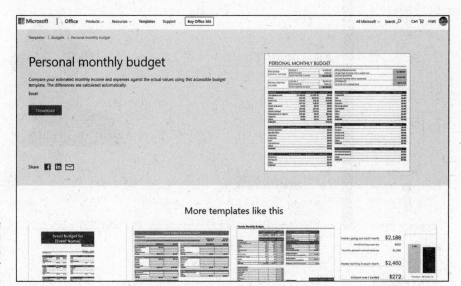

FIGURE 2-4:
Microsoft Excel puts you in control of your budget.

WARNING

Using Excel to tabulate your run rate takes the most time and experience. If you're not familiar with Excel or have little time to spend on this task, another approach will likely be better.

Checking out other money-tracking options

In addition to Mint, Quicken, and Excel, consider whether one of the following fits your lifestyle best:

» **Personal Capital:** This powerful free app and website was built by former Quicken engineers to help you get set up more quickly (no software installation needed). Like Mint, Personal Capital, shown in Figure 2-5, requires you to enter the username and password of each of your financial accounts. The site then pulls in your financial transaction data and helps you see where your money is going. The app also features robust tools to manage your retirement account. More on that later, in Chapter 9. For now, just know that Personal Capital will look at all your spending and calculate your run rate.

FIGURE 2-5:
Personal Capital helps you see where your money is going.

WARNING

Personal Capital is a financial advisory firm. After you sign up for the online budgeting service, you will be contacted by a salesperson who will try to sell you a financial advisory service.

» **YNAB:** An app and website that helps you control your spending, not just track it, YNAB (you need a budget) connects to your bank accounts and downloads your financial transactions. It's up to you to put them into categories. You can manually enter transactions, too.

WARNING

YNAB wins fans but at a cost of $6.99 a month. If you sign up for a year subscription and cancel before the year is up, your refund is prorated. And there's a month-long free trial. But paying money to save money seems a little counterintuitive.

>> **Mvelopes:** Like YNAB, Mvelopes is for the mobile generation. The system pulls in all your bank information (see a trend here?), and helps you see the categories consuming your cash. The system, which is supposed to mimic putting a set amount of money into envelopes, helps you stick to a budget.

Let's say you allow yourself $300 a month for eating out. Mvelopes will monitor your spending during the month and show you how much of your monthly dining out allowance you've used. That way, if you're only halfway through the month and have used, say, 90 percent of your $300 allowance, you'll know you should skip the steak dinner your friends are planning (or talk them into pushing the event back a month).

Mvelopes isn't free. The Basic version costs $4 a month and provides the reports you need to calculate your run rate. You can get tips from a financial trainer every quarter for $19 a month or monthly for $59 a month. Again, paying money to save money is hard for me to justify.

Doing something with all this data

What good are all these technical tools? How does raw financial data help you plan for your retirement? Well, you're accounting for your money to see your financial needs and wants — your run rate.

Nearly all retirement-planning tools start with your run rate. You use this number to build retirement savings and investment plans. If you don't know how much you're spending now, building a plan is difficult.

Putting Your Spending in Context

Now that you know how much you've been spending, you'll want to put this knowledge into context. Likely you'll want to know the following:

>> How does my spending compare with other people's?

>> Am I making proper use of my money?

>> How will my spending change in retirement?

Answering these questions require a bit a research, as described in this section.

A sure-fire route to unhappiness is comparing your money to that of your friends. "Keeping up with the Joneses" puts many people on a spending treadmill where they buy things to keep up the appearance of success. For that reason, I'm reluctant to show you how much typical Americans bring in and spend. On the other hand, a benchmark can help you understand your spending and start setting priorities.

Using government statistics as a guide

The U.S. Department of Labor's Bureau of Labor Statistics (BLS) provides useful spending data. The data, which is typically released in September, compiles household spending for the previous 12 months. You can find the most up-to-date numbers on the BLS site at www.bls.gov/cex/tables.htm.

It's amazing how much detail the BLS provides. Curious about how much Americans spend on booze, pork, wireless service, or stamps? The BLS knows.

You can look at the data in many ways, but Table 2-2 is a good place to start. In the second col you see what the typical *consumer unit,* or household, spends. A typical consumer unit shown in the table looks like the following:

>> The head of the household is 51 years old.

>> The household contains 2.5 people.

>> The household has an average of 1.3 wage earners and 1.9 cars.

I realize no household has 2.5 people or 1.3 wage earners, or drives 1.9 cars. These are averages of the 130.8 million households that the BLS studies.

Before your eyes start to glaze over looking at all this data, consider the following highlights for the "All Adults" column:

>> **Spending consumes 93 percent of after-tax income.** This benchmark is important. If your income is 20 percent greater than the average, is your spending 20 percent greater? Is it more? If you're spending more than 93 percent of after-tax income, find out why.

>> **Housing costs burn a big hole in budgets.** Shelter, as the BLS calls it, accounts for 19 percent of people's annual spending. That amount includes only mortgage or rent. Then add utilities, which make up 6.5 percent of spending.

>> **Little remains for savings.** The typical American's budget is stretched thin. If you subtract total spending from after-tax income, only $4,808 after-tax dollars remain.

TABLE 2-2

Typical American Budget

Item	Average Annual Amount (% of Spending)	
	All Adults	65-Year-Olds
Income before taxes	$76,335	$50,118
After-tax income	$65,623	$45,463
Total spending	$60,815	$50,178
Food at home	$4,445 (7.3%)	$3,906 (7.8%)
Dining out	$3,424 (5.6%)	$2,607 (5.3%)
Shelter (includes rent or mortgage)	$11,807 (19.4%)	$9,213 (17.3%)
Utilities	$3,956 (6.5%)	$3,714 (7.4%)
Apparel	$1,850 (3.0%)	$1,134 (2.3%)
Transportation	$9,735 (16.0%)	$7,472 (14.9%)
Healthcare	$4,924 (8.1%)	$6,700 (13.4%)
Entertainment	$3,379 (5.6%)	$3,003 (6.0%)
Personal care	$764 (1.3%)	$681 (1.4%)
Education	$1,505 (6.1%)	$388 (0.8%)
Insurance	$6,904 (11.4%)	$3,185 (6.3)

BLS Table 1300. Annual expenditure means, shares, standard errors, and coefficients of variation, Consumer Expenditure Survey, 3rd quarter 2017 through 2nd quarter 2018 (www.bls.gov/cex/22018/midyear/age.pdf).

Seeing how spending changes as you age

You might be wondering, "What does the spending of a typical American have to do with my retirement plan?" After all, if you're like most people, you'll work until you're at least 65, and you assume that your spending habits will be different then.

Won't your need for money decrease over time? Let's fast-forward to your future and see how income and spending changes for households aged 65 or older. Check out the numbers in the "66-Year-Old" column in Table 2-2.

TIP

If all these numbers are wearing you out, here's a rule of thumb: For retirement income, you typically need at least 80 percent of your pre-tax income in your working years. If you're curious how accurate this rule is, read on.

So, how does life look different in retirement for most people? Here's what happens to income and spending for a 66-year-old:

» **Income falls dramatically (more dramatically than it looks at first).** The drop of after-tax income to $45,463 is more jarring than it seems. Keep in mind that average after-tax earnings peak at $86,635 when workers are aged 45 to 54. Seeing income fall to about half that is an adjustment.

» **The mix of income sources changes.** Wages and salaries for people aged 65 and older drops to $17,129 a year. That's down from $59,555 for all households. Meanwhile, Social Security and retirement savings pick up some — but not all — of the slack. People aged 65 and older bring in $25,425 a year from these retirement plans.

» **The 80 percent rule is good (and conservative).** It turns out that our typical 65-plus-year-old's spending totals 66 percent of the typical American's pre-tax income. Remember, the average household brought in $76,335 in pre-tax income. If you plan on spending 80 percent of your income in retirement, you'll be okay in most cases.

» **Housing costs fall (but not as much as you might think).** Annual shelter costs still account for $16,723, or 18 percent of spending for the 65-plus set. You might expect this to be lower because most people at this age have paid off their mortgage. However, although 80 percent of those 65 and older are homeowners, 30 percent are still paying a mortgage. And 19 percent are paying rent. In other words, 49 percent of people at this age are either renting or paying a mortgage.

» **Expenses do fall, but not by a huge amount.** Total spending of the older set falls 17 percent to $50,178. Lower spending on some things, such as food and apparel, cuts spending even as healthcare expenses rise. Entertainment costs tend to be flat.

THE FIRE MOVEMENT CAN HELP

Early retirement used to mean calling it quits when you turn 60. But a rising group of people are hoping to hang up their apron much earlier, at 40 or even younger. What's this heresy? It's called FIRE, or financial independence retire early.

I talk about the FIRE movement several times in this book. The strategy has plenty of holes, but these people are onto something. FIRE advocates throw away the goal of retirement as a time to do no work, and take control of their financial lives as quickly as they can so that they can do what they enjoy now.

Some of the assumptions used in FIRE planning are questionable, but one aspect that makes a lot of sense is spending control. Some FIRE leaders who left the workforce early did so because they had large incomes. Others did it by following the guidance in this chapter but at a higher level. Simply stated, they maximized savings rates to shorten the time needed before being financially independent.

Advocates of FIRE meticulously track where every penny is going. Their goal is to save 70 percent or so of take-home pay, so that they have saved and invested 25 times their annual run rate. If their run rate were $80,000 a year, the FIRE crew would aim to sock away $2 million. That way, they say, they could safely withdraw 4 percent of their portfolio (following the 4 percent rule), or $80,000, a year.

I dig further into the FIRE movement and the 4 percent rule later in the book. But we can all learn from the FIRE philosophy. Two blogs explain FIRE well. Mr. Money Mustache (www.mrmoneymustache.com) pretty much kicked off the FIRE movement with his story of spending 50 percent less than most people. Doing so allowed him to retire at 30. Mr. Money Mustache doesn't disclose how much he earned. But a 2016 New Yorker article shares some income figures (www.newyorker.com/magazine/2016/02/29/mr-money-mustache-the-frugal-guru). Armed with a computer-engineering degree, he earned $41,000 a year in 1997. He then moved to another tech company in 1999, at age 24, and made $75,000. Mr. Money Mustache retired in late 2005 with a $600,000 portfolio and a paid-off house.

The blogger Financial Samurai (www.financialsamurai.com) also saved half his after-tax income and retired at 34. He gives lots of financial details on how he did it, but his high income while he was working certainly helped.

Even if you love your job and plan to work forever, the FIRE movement brings a precision to savings that's worth listening to.

Improving Your Numbers

Now that you've quantified your spending and compared it to the average, you know where you stand. If you're happy where you're at, great! If not, read this section for helpful ways to increase your income and get spending under control.

REMEMBER

The goal is to squeeze the most happiness out of the money you have.

I doubt that you get much joy paying rent, paying taxes, and saving. So the goal is to satisfy those needs in such a way that money is left for fun. People get into trouble when they get this mix wrong. Some overspend on overhead (such as an expensive apartment or a too-big house). Others fail to (legally) minimize taxes. And some overspend on fun stuff while neglecting their savings.

Yes, getting your spending balance right takes some practice. But this section will help you find ideas that work for you. Remember, only you can decide what's important to you.

TIP

If this topic interests you, check out Jonathan Clements, who writes about how to use money to boost happiness. You can find his outstanding blog, HumbleDollar, at `https://humbledollar.com/`.

Figuring out if your latte is ruining your retirement

Most personal finance writers demonize the morning brew from your local coffeehouse. But to me it's a perfect example that pulls together everything you've discovered in this chapter.

Next time you drop $4 on a cup of coffee at Starbucks, consider the following questions, which apply to any type of spending:

>> **Have I taken care of my overhead, savings, and tax?** If you've paid your mortgage (or better yet, paid it off), have maxed out your 401(k), and are paid up with Uncle Sam, a $4 cup of coffee won't hurt you. But if you're behind on any of these, the math changes.

>> **Is this a habit?** Are you buying coffee every day solely out of habit? Routine spending can add up while the happiness you get from it declines. If you spend $4 a day on coffee, that's $1,460 a year. After you calculate your run

rate, decide whether the $1,460 a year translates into that much happiness. Think of another budget item that costs about $1,500 a year. Does that spending make you as happy, or happier, than your coffee habit?

» **Do I understand the total cost and is it worthwhile?** Spending has an *opportunity cost*. For example, you could have saved or invested the $1,460 a year that you're spending on coffee, bringing in even more money.

Here's a fun exercise. Figure out the monthly cost of a discretionary item. Then log in to MSN's Time Value of Money calculator (www.msn.com/en-us/money/tools/timevalueofmoney), put that amount in the Monthly Investment field, and change the Present Value field to 0. Select the Calculate button and look at the results. For example, if you put the monthly amount for morning coffee ($122) into a savings account paying 2.5 percent annually, it would be worth $16,613 over 10 years, as you can see in Figure 2-6.

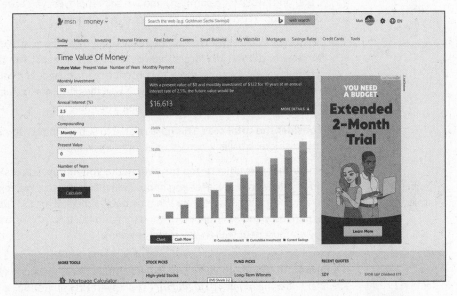

FIGURE 2-6: Calculate how much that daily latte really costs.

And check this out. If you invested the $122 in the stock market and got an 8 percent annual return, you would have $21,208 in a decade.

REMEMBER

Again, I'm not here to tell you to skip your morning brew. If it gives you joy and your overhead, taxes, and savings needs are taken care of, partake. The key to building a retirement-savings plan is understanding the true cost of things you buy and making sure they're worth it. Only you can decide that.

Finding easy ways to stop wasting money

Few people enjoy saving money, but no one likes to waste money. And if you've followed my advice up to this point, you possess great insight into where your money is going.

But simply not wasting money is just the start to building a much better financial life for yourself. Over the years, I've seen the following easy ways that everyone can improve their financial situation:

>> **Save first.** The easiest and least painful way to stop wasting money is to never see it in the first place. If you work for a company, sign up for a 401(k) immediately, and make sure you have enough taken out of your paycheck to qualify for any company match. The savings contributions will be taken out of your paycheck, and you won't miss what you never thought you had.

If you don't work for a company and are self-employed, you have many options, too. I cover those in more detail in Chapter 6.

>> **Scrutinize subscriptions.** Are you really using three music streaming services, or did you just forget that you're paying for them? Also determine whether you're spending more to subscribe than you would if you bought or rented the object. For example, if you're watching only one movie a month, you're better off just renting than paying a monthly fee.

>> **Consider the total cost.** This tip is related to subscriptions. Companies know big costs look smaller when you pay for them monthly.

>> **Know that few objects you buy will make you happy.** Studies show that buying things rarely makes you happy. Billionaire investor Warren Buffett lives in a home in Omaha, Nebraska that he bought in 1958 for $31,000. Experiences and anticipation of good things in the future bring more lasting joy for most people than any material goods.

TIP

If you want to change the way you look at things, pick up a copy of Marie Kondo's *The Life-Changing Magic of Tidying Up* (Ten Speed Press). Kondo, a Japanese expert at helping people dig out of messy homes, urges you to pick up the things you own and think about the value they bring to your life. If objects don't "spark joy," you should donate, sell, or toss them. If you Kondo your home or apartment, you'll be amazed at how many things go out the door and soon realize how spending money on things rarely makes you happier

Boosting your income with a side gig

Retirement planning is partly about wasting less money so that more is left for you to invest. Another powerful way to boost your retirement it to drive your income higher.

Along with the "saving more" guilt trip, another personal finance saw is to "make more money." But let's face it, not all of us can or are willing to switch jobs or careers just to boost our pay. However, if you're looking for something less disruptive to your life, a side gig can be a powerful way to increase the amount you can save. A side gig is typically

>> **A task you do on the side, preferably something you enjoy:** For example, you might make Halloween costumes and sell them on Etsy or eBay. Or perhaps you take photos that others can purchase to use on websites.

>> **A way to take advantage of an underutilized asset:** Have a beach home? Consider renting it when you're not there. Or why not rent your car when you're not using it? Check out Getaround (www.getaround.com), which handles the insurance details when renting your car.

Side gigs come in many forms, and finding this type of work is easy. Although none of these side hustles will make you rich, added income can turbo-charge your retirement plan. (In Chapter 4, I cover how SEP-IRAs and other retirement plans can help you turn side gigs into a bigger retirement nest egg.)

While you're still working, a side gig enables you to earn more money to pad your nest egg. And your side gig might turn into a profitable activity you can keep doing in your 60s and 70s. According to a 2018 report from the Federal Reserve (www.federalreserve.gov/publications/2018-economic-well-being-of-us-households-in-2017-employment.htm), 31 percent of adults were engaged in some type of side gig, which accounted for 10 percent or less of family income for three-quarters of them.

Next up, advice on finding a side gig.

Freelance pairing sites

For temporary work, dedicated sites that match people with skills are booming. Upwork.com (www.upwork.com), shown in Figure 2-7, and Fiverr.com (www.fiverr.com) are two leading sites that help you find a way to make some extra money.

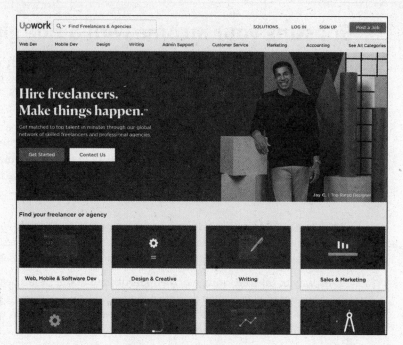

FIGURE 2-7:
Upwork will help you find a side hustle.

TIP

The more specialized the work, the more you'll get paid. For example, rather than offering your services as a consultant, concentrate on an industry such as health-care or finance. Your pool of customers will shrink, but those interested will pay more.

Side gig blogs

Given the rising interest in earning a little extra cash, blogs are cropping up to separate the good side gig opportunities from the bad. One notable source is Side-husl (`https://sidehusl.com/`), run by former Kiplinger's columnist Kathy Kristof. This site helps you find work based on your skill set, ranging from accounting to tutoring. The site also ranks the opportunities based on pay and how well contributors are treated.

The usual places

Companies such as driving services Uber and Lyft, delivery services such as Shipt, and food courier DoorDash rely on side hustlers to get the job done. If you want something fast, these might work. But if you have specialized skills or interests, you can do better.

Chapter **3**

Calculating How Much You Need to Retire

I f you want to accomplish something great, you need to picture it first. Want to land your dream job as CEO? Imagine sitting behind a giant mahogany desk in a corner office. Want to run a marathon? Envision yourself crossing the finish line after 26.2 miles.

Visualizing success is one of the storied approaches taken by effective athletes, executives, and salespeople. Academic research reinforces the power of goal-setting even further. In a noteworthy study (www.dominican.edu/academics/lae/undergraduate-programs/psych/faculty/assets-gail-matthews/researchsummary2.pdf), Gail Matthews, professor of psychology at Dominican University of California, found three techniques successful people used to meet their goals. They wrote down their goals, held themselves accountable in weekly progress reports, and garnered public support for their progress. People who took these steps "accomplished significantly more" than people who didn't, Matthews found.

Let's put this insight to work for you as you plan the ultimate financial goal: retirement. In this chapter, you discover how to visualize your successful retirement. You see how to add numbers when answering the question, "Where do I see myself when I begin retirement?"

Retirement planning at this stage is a numbers game: calculating how much you'll require and what to do to get there. Don't worry, though. Even if you're not a math whiz, after reading this chapter you'll be able to calculate all the necessary numbers.

You find out about the seminal 4 percent rule and how it helps guide retirement planning. The chapter also coaches you on how to use a variety of online retirement calculators. Finally, I show you why time is an asset when trying to reach your retirement goals.

Just remember, retirement is like reaching any important goal: You must know what you're shooting for and how you'll get there.

Getting to Know the 4 Percent Rule

Let's make one thing clear right away. Planning for retirement is imprecise. Who knows what will happen between now and when you retire (or after you retire for that matter)? No one.

Don't fear the uncertainty. Embrace it. Just understand that retirement planning is based on estimates and educated guesses. The role of guesstimates is apparent when answering the top question: "How much do I need to retire?"

You can answer this question in several logical ways. The most widely followed and accepted method is the 4 percent rule.

The *4 percent rule* says that retirees can safely withdraw 4 percent of their portfolio a year, increased annually by the rate of inflation, and be relatively confident that they won't run out of money. For example, if you have $1 million in your retirement account, you can withdraw $40,000 the first year. You can then take out another $40,000 a year, plus the inflation increase, for at least 30 years.

Wait a second. I can hear you questioning my math. How is this possible? After all, if you take out $40,000 a year for 30 years, that would be $1.2 million. How can you take out $1.2 million from an account that you put only $1 million into?

Read on. I'll show you how.

TECHNICAL STUFF

Inflation, or the tendency of prices to rise over the years, is an invisible but insidious reality to consider in retirement planning. Although you may need only $40,000 a year in 2019, that amount will rise over time as prices go up. Curious about inflation? Our friends at the Bureau of Labor Statistics offer an inflation calculator at www.bls.gov/data/inflation_calculator.htm. You'll see that the candy bar you bought for a buck in the year 2000 sets you back $1.52 in 2019.

You've heard of the Riddle of the Sphinx. You're now at the cusp of the Riddle of Retirement Planning. The answer to how you can pull more money out of a retirement account than you put in gets to the core of retirement planning. If you plan properly, you won't be burying your $1 million in the backyard. Instead, you'll invest it.

People usually put 60 percent of their retirement funds in stocks and 40 percent in bonds over their lifetimes. This simple guideline, paired with a prudent retirement and savings plan, causes amazing things to happen, as you'll see.

How the 4 percent rule works

The 4 percent rule isn't just some theoretical pipe dream. It works! In Table 3-1, you can see an actual scenario of a person who retired in 1988 and pulled 4 percent of her portfolio out annually, increased each year by the inflation rate. All the numbers you see are based on actual market returns, which you can download from New York University's Stern School of Business (pages.stern.nyu.edu/~adamodar/New_Home_Page/datafile/histretSP.html).

TABLE 3-1   **The 4 Percent Rule with $1 Million Saved**

Year in Retirement	60/40 Portfolio Return	Beginning Retirement Balance	4% Initial Withdrawal Plus Annual Inflation	Market Return	Ending Retirement Balance
1 (1989)	26.0%	$1,000,000	$40,000	$249,241	$1,209,241
5 (1993)	11.7%	$1,469,643	$47,421	$165,897	$1,588,119
10 (1998)	23.0%	$2,565,435	$54,282	$576,846	$3,087,999
15 (2003)	17.2%	$2,805,149	$60,871	$471,017	$3,215,295
20 (2008)	–13.9%	$3,969,817	$70,153	–$541,698	$3,357,966
25 (2013)	15.6%	$4,616,990	$77,643	$710,191	$5,249,537
30 (2018)	–2.5%	$6,923,272	$82,896	–$171,152	$6,666,224

Based on actual returns of a portfolio that's 60% stocks (Standard & Poor's 500 including dividends) and 40% bonds.

Table 3-1 shows how your money can grow:

» **The 4 percent rule works.** Look closely and you'll see that our retiree not only had plenty of money but ended up with $6.7 million, or nearly seven times more than she started with. Again, this table shows actual results. Remember, too, that the 1989 to 2018 period contained multiple major bear markets, corrections, and even the Great Recession. (A *bear market* is a 20 percent crash in markets from their recent high. A *correction* is a 10 percent to 19.9 percent decline.)

» **Even several horrible years didn't derail the 4 percent rule.** The 4 percent rule held up after significant financial-crisis-related losses in 2008 (–13.9 percent), which shaved half a million from the balance, as well as a moderate loss in 2018 (–2.5 percent). In addition, the back-to-back tech-crash hits in 2001 (–4.9 percent) and 2002 (–7.1 percent) aren't shown in the table but are included in the calculations.

» **Our retiree received a raise every year.** Because she took 4 percent in the first year and 4 percent plus inflation in future years, her purchasing power was preserved. The initial $40,000 withdrawal more than doubled to over $80,000 by year 30 into retirement.

If you start saving for retirement reasonably early and follow the guidelines in this book, reaching a million by retirement is doable. What if you started saving later or don't think you can save a million bucks? Don't worry, the 4 percent rule still holds (as you can see in Table 3-2). You'll just need to make sure that the reduced income that 4 percent provides is sufficient given your run rate.

TABLE 3-2   **The 4 Percent Rule With Less Than $1 Million Saved**

Year in Retirement	60/40 Portfolio Return	Beginning Retirement Balance	4% Initial Withdrawal Plus Annual Inflation	Market Return	Ending Retirement Balance
1 (1989)	26.0%	$500,000	$20,000	$124,620	$604,620
5 (1993)	11.7%	$734,822	$23,710	$82,948	$794,060
10 (1998)	23.0%	$1,282,718	$27,141	$288,423	$1,543,999
15 (2003)	17.2%	$1,402,574	$30,435	$235,509	$1,607,647
20 (2008)	–13.9%	$1,984,909	$35,077	–$270,849	$1,678,983
25 (2013)	15.6%	$2,308,495	$38,822	$355,095	$2,624,769
30 (2018)	–2.5%	$3,461,636	$41,448	–$87,076	$3,333,112

Based on actual returns of a portfolio that's 60% stocks (Standard & Poor's 500 including dividends) and 40% bonds.

The magical power of the 4 percent rule

So, the 4 percent rule works. But what does this mean for you and your retirement plan? Specifically, how can you use the 4 percent rule to determine how much you need to retire? You'll see that the rule is magical.

Middle school math turns the 4 percent rule into a great retirement goal-setting guide. Intrigued? Simply flip 4 percent on its head, by taking the reciprocal, and you'll see what I mean. Here's how:

1. **Convert 4 percent to a decimal.**

Percent means per 100, so 4 percent is 4 per 100, or 4/100. Divide 4 by 100, which gives you 0.04.

2. **Take the reciprocal of 0.04.**

Divide 1 by 0.04. Some calculators have a 1/x button that will do this for you. The answer is 25.

Now let's say that after reading Chapter 2, you determine that your run rate is $60,000 a year after taxes. Let's also say that you figure Social Security will cover $20,000 a year. That means you need to come up with $40,000 a year.

Here's the magical part. Multiply the $40,000 you need annually by 25 and you get $1 million. According to the 4 percent rule, this means you need to have a million bucks after taxes (remember, when you pull money out of some retirement accounts, you owe tax on it. I complicate things with taxes later). To check your math, apply the 4 percent rule. Multiply $1 million by 4 percent (or 0.04) and you get $40,000, which is the income you're shooting for.

The long-term solvency of the U.S. financial safety-net program is constantly debated, and Social Security was never designed to be your primary retirement plan. When looking at retirement planning, it's often useful to leave Social Security out of the equation at first. Doing so helps creates a more conservative retirement plan — and if Social Security is still available when you retire, the money would be a welcome addition. (For details on Social Security, see Chapter 10.)

Shortcomings of the 4 percent rule

The 4 percent rule is so elegantly simple that it's widely followed and debated. Financial planner Michael Kitces put the 4 percent rule through its paces and showed how even if a worker retired at a bad time, when markets crashed in 2008 or 2000, the rule still worked (www.kitces.com/blog/how-has-the-4-rule-held-up-since-the-tech-bubble-and-the-2008-financial-crisis).

Even so, some people take issue with the rule and caution that it's not conservative enough. These critics insist that withdrawing 3 percent is a better idea:

>> **Some retirement plans need to last longer than 30 years.** The 4 percent rule is primarily focused on a typical retirement at 65 that lasts through age 95. Some people may choose to retire younger (or have the decision made for them due to a disability or layoff).

>> **Future market returns may be subpar.** Doubters of the 4 percent rule think that market returns in the future may be lower than they have been in the past. Some also fear an unforeseen market shock that could hurt investment returns.

>> **Unfortunate events happen.** Life can throw us curveballs, such as an unexpected medical emergency. When it does, expenses are usually involved.

>> **Some investors will invest too conservatively.** The 4 percent rule is based on a moderate portfolio of 60 percent stocks and 40 percent bonds. If investors play it safer, their returns may fall short.

If you fear that any of these scenarios might occur, you can adjust the 4 percent rule appropriately. In Table 3-3, you'll see what percentage of your portfolio you can safely withdraw by retirement age if you expect one of the following scenarios:

>> **Best-case scenario (1):** You think that the critics of the 4 percent rule are worried about nothing. This scenario tells you how much you can withdraw if all goes swimmingly in your future and historical investment returns continue.

>> **Good-case scenario (2):** You think that the 4 percent rule is a good guide but that critics make some valid cautionary points. You assume that historical investment returns will continue and that you'll experience an unforeseen financial shock.

>> **Bad-case scenario (3):** You agree with critics that investment returns will be lower in the future, but you don't see a financial shock in your future.

>> **Worst-case scenario (4):** You think that investment returns will be lower in the future and an unforeseen financial shock will occur.

Note that in Table 3-3 that *shock* refers to an unexpected cost of 20 percent to the portfolio at age 75.

If you want to convert these adjusted withdrawal rates into retirement goals, you'll need to take the reciprocal.

Again, for people who plan to work until 60 or older, the 4 percent rule is a good one. People who are looking at unique retirement plans may want to consider Table 3-3.

TABLE 3-3   **Adjusting the 4 Percent Rule, Based on Retirement Age**

Retirement Age	Historical Returns Continue with No Shock (1)	Historical Returns Continue with Shock (2)	Lower Future Returns with No Shock (3)	Lower Future Returns with Shock (4)
35	3.27%	3.23%	2.73%	2.66%
40	3.38%	3.31%	2.82%	2.79%
45	3.48%	3.42%	2.98%	2.86%
50	3.68%	3.51%	3.12%	3.01%
55	3.85%	3.66%	3.36%	3.11%
60	4.13%	3.85%	3.64%	3.32%
65	4.53%	4.08%	4.02%	3.60%

Capital Group (www.thecapitalideas.com/articles/retire-at-40). Based on a 95% confidence of money lasting until age 95.

What do I mean by *unique retirement plans*? Remember the financial independent retire early (FIRE) movement discussed in Chapter 2? These people think retiring at 65 is a prison sentence and want to spring out early. If you're a 40-year-old who wants to retire and expects the worst-case scenario, you might look at Table 3-3 and plan on taking out only 2.79 percent a year. Taking the reciprocal of 2.79, you need to save 35.8 times your run rate. Using the previous example, if you need $40,000 a year in retirement, you need to save $1.4 million ($40,000 x 35.8).

Note the following in Table 3-3:

>> **The 4 percent rule looks solid for normal circumstances.** In the best-case scenario, the 4 percent withdrawal rate works not only for a 65-year-old but also for a 60-year-old.

>> **Planning for a worst-case scenario is tough.** If you're forced out of the workforce much earlier than you expected, investment returns are disappointing, and you suffer a shock, your retirement-planning numbers can change for the worse.

>> **Retiring early is possible.** Don't listen to those who say retirement is only for people in their 60s. If early retirement is your goal, you just need to look at the numbers. Applying these numbers to your own savings amounts and retirement goals will tell you whether you can call it quits early.

ORIGIN OF THE 4 PERCENT RULE

The 4 percent rule is practically gospel in retirement-planning circles. It's arguably the most influential piece of retirement-planning advice ever devised. Where did the rule come from?

The 4 percent rule traces back to an unassuming paper called "Determining withdrawal rates using historical data" published in 1994 in the *Journal of Financial Planning*. William Bengen, a financial planner based in El Cajon, California wrote the article based on his extensive mathematical training. He did the analysis by studying decades of actual investment returns. Tol read the modest paper that changed retirement planning forever, visit www.retailinvestor.org/pdf/Bengen1.pdf.

Bengen, retired since 2013, isn't just an average financial planner. He was trained as an aeronautics and astronautics engineer at Massachusetts Institute of Technology. To give you an idea of the brainpower I'm talking about, Bengen had previously co-authored the MIT Press paper, "Topics in advanced model rocketry" in 1973. Wonder if there's a *Dummies* version of that?

Bengen switched to financial planning later in his career. After graduating from MIT, he worked at his family's soft-drink bottling company in the New York area. The family sold the business in 1987, after which Bengen moved to Southern California and hung out his shingle as a financial planner.

Amazingly, Bengen's work on the 4 percent rule has largely held up to all its challenges. During market rallies, many people say the 4 percent rule is too conservative. When markets swoon, some claim it's too generous and that safe withdrawal rates should be lower, 3 or even 2 percent.

But the definitive reinforcement of the 4 percent rule came in 1998 with the Trinity Study. Three finance professors from Trinity University stress-tested Bengen's findings and came back with the same verdict: A 4 percent initial withdrawal plus an annual inflation adjustment is likely to never drain a retirement plan.

In fact, in his original paper, Bengen addressed criticism that he seemed to anticipate. He found that for people who want their portfolios to last 50 years or longer, a 3 percent withdrawal holds up and in most cases a 4 percent withdrawal rate does, too. He cautioned, though, that a 4.25 percent withdrawal rate could "exhaust a portfolio in as little as 28 years."

So if you want someone to thank for an easy-to-follow but rock-solid retirement-planning rule of thumb, thank Bengen.

Using Online Retirement Calculators

The 4 percent rule is a powerful tool that holds up remarkably well. And for that reason, applying it to your run rate can quickly tell you how much you may need to retire.

But it's a rule of thumb. You might want to measure your needs more precisely. Or you might have a special financial situation and want to personalize your retirement plan.

I'm a big fan of several online retirement calculators that make this important calculation a little more detailed. If you supply a few variables, in just a few minutes these calculators can give you a good idea of how much you need to retire.

WARNING

The quality of online retirement calculators varies; some are much more accurate than others. If you run your numbers with several of them, don't be surprised if you get different answers. That's why I highlight the best ones here. Also, if you put bad information into the tool, you'll get inaccurate results out. For instance, if you understate what you require in retirement, the calculator will likewise understate your retirement needs. Similarly, if you say that you can handle moderate risk, but in reality you want to play it very safe with your investments, the tool will understate what you need to retire.

Getting started

Nearly all the retirement calculators out there will do the math for a retirement plan. In just minutes, they'll tell you how much you need to save to retire and let you know if you need to save more to reach your goal.

But they all need some basic information from you to do their thing. Nearly all online calculators require that you gather the following details before you can use them:

>> **Age:** Provide your and your spouse's current age and the age you both plan to retire.

>> **Run rate:** Determine how much you typically spend each month or year. If you're not sure how to calculate your run rate, flip back to Chapter 2 for details.

>> **Current level of savings:** Log into your savings, brokerage, and retirement accounts and add up your balances. Keep in mind that some calculators ask you to separate your retirement accounts from your regular accounts.

>> **Asset allocation:** Your *asset allocation,* which is your mix of stocks, bonds, and cash, determines the growth and riskiness of your portfolio. (For details, see Chapter 5.) Table 3-4 shows you roughly how these different types of investments, or *asset classes,* do over time.

TABLE 3-4

No Pain, No Gain

Investment	Average Annual Return	Relative Risk
Stocks	10.0% (based on S&P 500 since 1926)	Riskiest
Corporate bonds	6.0%	Moderately risky
Treasury bills (short-term loans to the U.S. government)	3.4%	Least risky

Morningstar through 2018

TIP

If you have only one retirement account, getting your asset allocation is simple. For instance, you can obtain it from your 401(k) provider (as you discover in Chapter 7).

If you have multiple financial accounts, adding up your total asset allocation is a little trickier but doable. Several of the online tools mentioned in Chapter 2 to measure your run rate, such as Mint, Quicken, and Personal Capital, can also calculate your asset allocation.

For example, if you're using Quicken, click the Investing tab. Next, choose Reports⇨Investment Asset Allocation. A pie chart like the one in Figure 3-1 appears, showing you which asset classes you own.

TECHNICAL STUFF

Some retirement calculators will ask you what kind of returns you expect your portfolio to generate. This might seem like an odd question at first. How are you supposed to forecast how your portfolio will do in the future? But it turns out that you can calculate your portfolio's *expected return* based on estimates of how much components in your portfolio are expected to grow.

If you're not sure how to calculate your portfolio's expected return, start with your asset allocation. A bit of math is required, but don't worry. The next set of steps shows you how.

Let's say Quicken, Mint, or your brokerage statement says that your portfolio is 60 percent stocks and 40 percent bonds. You can calculate your expected return as follows:

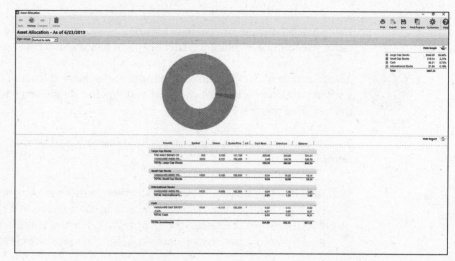

FIGURE 3-1:
Use Quicken to quickly size up your asset allocation.

1. **Multiply the weighting of the first asset class by its historic return.**

   In the example, 60 percent of your portfolio is in stocks. As shown in Table 3-4, the historic return for stocks is 10 percent a year. So multiply 60 percent (0.60) by 10 percent (0.10), and you get 0.06.

2. **Multiply the weighting of the second asset class by its historic return.**

   Here, 40 percent (0.40) of your portfolio is in bonds, which returned 6 percent annually (0.06). Multiply 0.40 by 0.06 and you get 0.024.

3. **Repeat Steps 1 and 2 for any additional asset classes in your portfolio.**

4. **Add the results from Steps 1 to 3 and adjust to a percentage.**

   Add 0.06 (from Step 1) to 0.024 (from Step 2), which is 0.084. Multiply that answer by 100 to convert it to a percentage, which is 8.4. That's your expected return.

TIP

Does this look like too much multiplying? Just choose a retirement calculator that doesn't require an expected return.

Exploring retirement calculators from mutual fund companies

Investment companies are competitive. If you consider the trillions of dollars that Americans pour into retirement accounts, you can see why money-management firms want a piece. One method they use to attract dollars is to provide a whiz-bang retirement calculator.

Several fund companies have excellent online retirement calculators. Vanguard's Retirement Nest Egg Calculator (https://retirementplans.vanguard.com/

VGApp/pe/pubeducation/calculators/RetirementNestEggCalc.jsf) is especially streamlined, making it a friendly place to stop for a first opinion.

WARNING

Always run your numbers through multiple retirement calculators. Just as you get a second opinion even when you trust your doctor, do the same when diagnosing the health of your retirement plan.

To run your numbers in Vanguard's Retirement Nest Egg Calculator, enter the following:

» **How many years your savings should last:** You need to know how many years you think you'll be retired and when you plan to retire. Refer to Chapter 1 if you need help calculating your life expectancy. For this example, let's say you are 65 years old, plan to retire tomorrow, and think you'll live for 30 more years.

» **Your savings balance:** Again, using the same tools discussed in Chapter 2 to measure your run rate, you should have a good idea of how much money you've banked for retirement. For this example, let's say you've put away $500,000.

» **How much do you spend each year:** This amount is your run rate, which is how much you spend in a year. Review the tools in Chapter 2 to help you measure your run rate. For our example, let's say you spend $50,000 a year.

» **How your savings are allocated:** Tell the retirement calculator your mix of stocks, bonds, and cash. Let's say your portfolio is 60 percent stocks and 40 percent bonds.

After you enter all the variables, click the Run Simulation button and Vanguard will tell you how likely it is that your money won't run out. As you can see in Figure 3-2, using our example data, the Vanguard calculator pegs the odds of a successful retirement at just 6 percent. Those aren't great odds. Something has to change: Spend less, work longer, save more, or roll the dice and own more stocks (which have higher expected returns).

WARNING

Look closely at the results. The Vanguard Retirement Nest Egg Calculator shows that you're spending 5 percent of your savings. That violates the 4 percent rule. No wonder it fails! The 5 percent doesn't appear in the figure, but you can see it online when you use the tool.

Vanguard has other useful retirement calculators, including the following:

» Retirement Income Calculator at https://retirementplans.vanguard.com/VGApp/pe/pubeducation/calculators/RetirementIncomeCalc.jsf: Tell this tool how old you are, your run rate, your expected return, your salary, and how much you're saving. The calculator will tell you if you're saving enough.

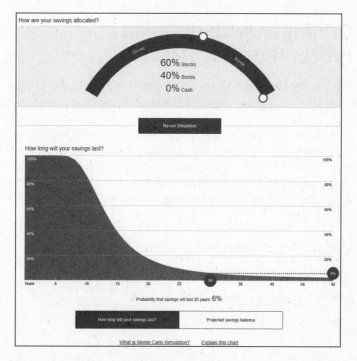

FIGURE 3-2:
Vanguard's
Retirement Nest
Egg Calculator
keeps things
simple.

>> Save for Retirement tool at `https://vanguard.newkirkone.com/plansavings/?cbdForceDomain=true#`: Enter how much you're saving along with your age, salary, expected retirement age, expected portfolio return, and current savings. The tool then tells you how much monthly income you're likely to have when you retire.

Vanguard is by no means the only mutual fund company offering free and excellent retirement calculators. Check out the ones from the following companies:

>> **Fidelity** (`www.fidelity.com/calculators-tools/retirement-calculator/overview`) is a huge mutual fund company. Not surprisingly, it offers tools to help you plan various aspects of your retirement.

>> **T. Rowe Price's Retirement Planner** (`https://www3.troweprice.com/ric/ricweb/public/ric.do`) takes almost a TurboTax-like approach. The site asks you questions and then generates a retirement overview.

>> **American Funds** (`www.americanfunds.com/individual/planning/tools/retirement-planning-calculator.htm`) offers a Retirement Planning Calculator center with two choices. You can take a four-question test in five minutes or a longer and more detailed analysis with 15 questions. The tool studies your situation and tells you how you're doing. If you're not planning to retire at 67, which the quick test assumes, take the detailed analysis.

Drilling in with detailed retirement calculators

Many retirement calculators are designed to keep things simple. But others drill down to get as precise as possible when solving your retirement questions.

In this section, I show you a few retirement calculators that get down to the nitty-gritty. Perhaps the best example is the calculator from NewRetirement (www.newretirement.com/planner/retirement-calculator). This calculator, shown in Figure 3-3, goes to great lengths to understand where you stand and to determine whether you have enough to retire. The main goals of this calculator are to tell you

» What kind of retirement income your plan will generate

» If you'll run out of money

» How much you need to retire

» Ways to improve your plan

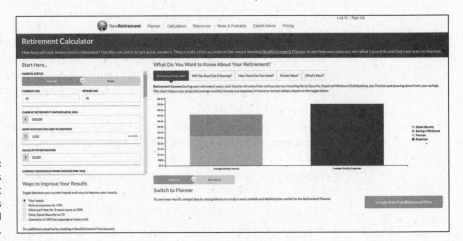

FIGURE 3-3: NewRetirement's Retirement Calculator leaves few financial stones unturned.

These detailed retirement planners can be helpful. Just be aware that they ask more of you. You need to be ready to answer all the questions they request about your retirement and non-retirement account balances, for instance.

These calculators will also ask if you plan to get Social Security and pension benefits. If you choose to enter this information, flip ahead to Chapter 10 to see how to find your Social Security benefit amount. You'll also be asked about your home value and mortgage payment.

The NewRetirement calculator's best party trick is that it offers some suggestions on ways to improve your plan's success. It will show you, in one click, how your retirement plan changes if you cut your run rate by 10 percent, work part time for three more years, or downsize your home.

Again, NewRetirement isn't the only calculator in town when it comes to detailed analysis. A few others worth looking at include the following:

>> **Personal Capital** (www.personalcapital.com): Remember how you used Personal Capital in Chapter 2 to measure your run rate? Personal Capital has a retirement calculator, too. The good news is that if you've already entered your bank and brokerage information, all your data is saved in the tool and you don't have to reenter everything.

>> **DinkyTown** (www.dinkytown.net/retirement.html): Talk about a super-market for retirement calculators. This site has scores of retirement calculators to crunch just about any retirement problem you can throw at it, everything from analyzing your optimal 401(k) contributions to figuring out how long your retirement nest egg will last.

Avoid gambling with retirement: Monte Carlo analysis.

Remember how retirement planning is all about guesses? What if you could make hundreds of guesses — and then figure out which ones are likely to come true? That's the purpose of a Monte Carlo analysis.

In a *Monte Carlo analysis*, a computer models countless scenarios and sees how your retirement plan holds up in each one. You can calculate the percentage of scenarios in which your plan would end up succeeding. The higher the pass rate, the more likely your plan can endure a wide range of events.

REMEMBER

The Monte Carlo analysis isn't used only in retirement planning. It's applied wherever a wide range of outcomes exists. Monte Carlo analysis is commonly used in science, engineering, and even search-and-rescue operations. The idea is that if you run all possible future events, you can figure out what's likely and what's not.

Several retirement calculators described in this chapter use Monte Carlo tech-niques behind the scenes. And if you hire a financial planner to create a plan for you, he or she will use a professional-grade Monte Carlo analysis, too.

A few noteworthy retirement calculators put Monte Carlo front and center, enabling you to see a range of retirement possibilities. One great tool is FireCalc (`https://firecalc.com`). It isn't a particularly detailed retirement calculator, asking only for your spending (run rate), your portfolio size, and the number of years you want to analyze.

FireCalc simulates what your retirement account balance could look like after many years of more than a hundred possible market environments, as shown in Figure 3-4.

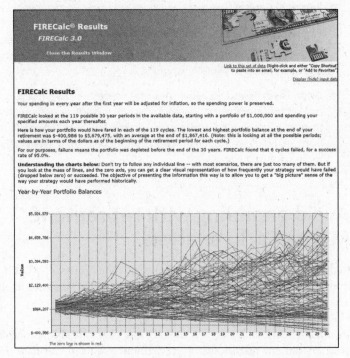

FIGURE 3-4: FireCalc shows you the power of a Monte Carlo retirement analysis.

The calculator doesn't tell you the likelihood of any of these scenarios. After all, it doesn't know (nor does anyone else). But eyeballing the resulting chart can be insightful. If most of the lines end up above the $0 horizonal line, the money invested will most likely last. Also, the text above the chart tells you the odds, in percentage terms, that the retirement plan will be successful.

Recall our original case of a 30-year retirement, spending $40,000 a year (adjusted annually for inflation), and $1 million saved in the plan? FireCalc tested the plan in 119 market cycles. The plan succeed 95 percent of the time, which is a level at which you can feel confident. FireCalc also found, on average, that $1.9 million would still be in the plan at the end of 30 years.

Understanding Why Starting Early Is Important

If all this work with online retirement calculators shows you anything, it's that you're wise to plan now. One of the overriding lessons of these calculators is that retirement planning is easier the sooner you start. Aren't you glad you bought this book now!

Compounding: The most powerful force in the universe

When you start retirement planning early, you put a powerful force in your corner: time. The longer your money is invested, the more time it can compound. *Compounding* occurs when you earn a return on returns. Albert Einstein is believed to have said that compounding is the most powerful force in the universe. And even if he didn't say it, the words are still true.

Think of it this way. Suppose you put $1,000 into an investment that pays 5 percent interest a year. In the first year, you get 5 percent on your initial investment of $1,000, or $50. But in year two, you get interest of $52, not $50. Why? You didn't put any more money in the account. Well, in year two, you earned money on the interest from year one. Repeat this, and before long the return on past years' returns becomes significant.

Inspiration to start retirement planning now

All this talk of Einstein and the universe might be getting too cosmic for a retirement book. Let's bring it back to earth.

When you start planning for retirement early, compounding does much of the work for you. You wind up with more money — even after contributing less from your salary.

For example, consider Early Earl and Late Larry. Early Earl, when just 25 years old, appreciated the value of retirement planning and started socking away $5,000 a year. Let's assume he has a conservative investment plan that generated an average return of 6 percent a year. Earl keeps this plan going until retiring at 65.

Late Larry thinks Earl is a stick-in-the-mud. He figures that retirement planning is something he can catch up on later. After all, he's not old. Late Larry saves nothing in his 20s, 30s, and 40s, but gets serious when he turns 50. At that point, Larry invests $13,000 a year, or more than twice what Earl has been putting away. Both get the same market return: 6 percent a year.

Who ends up better off? You might have a good guess, given where this section of the book is going. Take a look at Table 3-5 first, and then I'll point out some key findings relevant to your retirement plan.

TABLE 3-5

Start Early When Saving for Retirement

Age	Cumulative Investment		Account Balance	
	Early Earl	Late Larry	Early Earl	Late Larry
25	$5,000	$0.00	$5,300	$0.00
30	$30,000	$0.00	$36,969	$0.00
35	$55,000	$0.00	$79,350	$0.00
40	$80,000	$0.00	$136,064	$0.00
45	$105,000	$0.00	$211,961	$0.00
50	$130,000	$13,000	$313,529	$13,780
55	$155,000	$78,000	$449,449	$96,120
60	$180,000	$143,000	$631,341	$206,309
65	$205,000	$208,000	$874,753	$353,767

I'd like to point out a few things in Table 3-5:

>> **Both Earl and Larry ultimately contributed about the same amount.** Earl put in $205,000 cumulatively, only marginally less than Larry. Note that Larry had to dig nearly three times deeper when he started saving money later in life.

>> **Earl ends up with dramatically more than Larry.** Despite contributing the same amount, Earl's ending balance was $874,753, more than double Larry's retirement nest egg.

>> **Larry needs to make a big sacrifice to catch up to Earl.** Larry must save much more, work longer, or take on more investment risk to try to get a higher return. None of these options is ideal.

The race to $1 million: Doable if you start soon

A million bucks for retirement isn't what it used to be. It's still a lofty goal to shoot for, though. Whether $1 million is enough for you to retire depends on your goals for retirement. But one thing's for sure: The sooner you get started, the greater the odds you'll reach it.

Check out Table 3-6. You'll see how the amount of money you need to save annually to hit a cool million is obtainable the sooner you start. If you wait until you're 65 to start, you'd better hope you have a rich uncle who loves you very much.

TABLE 3-6

Getting to $1 Million by Age 65

Age	Annual Amount to Save
25	$6,462
35	$12,649
45	$27,185
55	$75,868
65	$1,000,000

Assumes a 6% average annual gain

Now you're on your way. After reading this chapter, you know how much money you need to retire and why you want to start ASAP.

In the next chapter, you see how Uncle Sam — yes, the taxman — can help you reach your goals.

Chapter **4**

Choosing the Right Account

Questions are likely filling your head. "Where do I start?" "What's a 401(k) or individual retirement account (IRA) anyway?" "What is the difference between a Roth IRA and a traditional ORA?" "Which one is better?" "What's tax deferral and why does it matter?" "I'm self-employed, what retirement plans can I use?"

If you have questions like these, you've come to the right chapter. Here I show you the different types of retirement accounts along with their advantages and disadvantages. Choosing the right retirement account can help you reach your goals more quickly.

Retirement Planning in a Nutshell

All the retirement-planning mumbo-jumbo you hear is due to one word: taxes. In a world with no taxes (we can only dream), you wouldn't need a 401(k), Roth IRA, or any other special retirement account with a funny name. You'd just put money in a brokerage account, accumulate enough to pay for your run rate (how much you spend), retire, and withdraw money as you need it.

But alas, we live in a world where income is taxable — and the tax bite is significant. Balancing the need to give workers a tax shield while not cutting off tax income resulted in the formation of different types of retirement-planning accounts.

As of 2018, a single worker with no children making an average wage paid 29.6 cents on the dollar to federal income and payroll taxes, according to the Tax Foundation (https://taxfoundation.org/us-tax-burden-on-labor-2019/). That's down from 31.8 cents on the dollar in 2017, due to the Tax Cuts and Jobs Act, but it's still a huge cut. Think of how much faster you could save for retirement if you kept all that money.

REMEMBER

You want to get as much tax relief as you can in your retirement plan. That's where retirement planning comes in. All this effort to understand retirement accounts is primarily about taking advantage of the tax savings legally available to you.

Getting started

I get into the nitty-gritty of retirement accounts shortly. But first, here's a quick checklist of what you should do when you want to set up a retirement plan.

REMEMBER

Many people get sidetracked with the jargon and lose the drive to get a retirement plan in motion. However, any progress toward setting up a retirement savings plan beats doing nothing.

Want to get a retirement plan going? Here are the steps you should follow, in order:

1. **See whether your employer offers a retirement plan.** Most mid-sized and large companies offer some sort of retirement plan. If a pension is available, consider yourself lucky. Typically, employers offer a 401(k) plan or, in the public section, a comparable 403(b) plan. Some 401(k) plans are great, but others are lousy. You see how to size up your 401(k) plan in Chapters 5 and 6.

TIP

For now, concern yourself mainly with one issue about the employee plan. Does the employer match your contribution to the 401(k)? More than 80 percent of large companies offer matching contributions. Find out how much you need to contribute to get the maximum match.

For example, suppose your employer matches 50 cents of every dollar you contribute up to 6 percent of your pay. You should contribute at least 6 percent of your salary into your 401(k). If you don't do this, you're giving up free money. You like free money, don't you?

401(k) plans have a few other advantages over other retirement plans. One of these perks is a relatively high contribution limit. If you're really behind on your retirement plan, you can make up ground fast by maxing out your 401(k) plan. Also, if you're at the peak of your career and pulling in a high salary (and in a high tax bracket), you can get a big tax saving by putting money in a 401(k).

2. **Determine whether an IRA makes sense.** I've seen some lousy 401(k) plans. If your 401(k) has no company match, the fees are high, you've already saved a large amount for retirement, or you've maximized the 401(k) match, consider setting up an IRA. This chapter helps you evaluate whether you're better off with an IRA or with an IRA paired with another plan, such as a 401(k).

3. **Look for self-employed options.** If you work for yourself, your decisions are different. Retirement-planning options such as the SEP-IRA and an individual 401(k) are available. If you run a business, you can skip down to the "Self-Employed Plans" section.

If you're a 9-to-5 employee, don't assume that you can't take advantage of self-employed plans. If you freelance, consult, or work in the gig economy, you can turbo-charge your existing retirement plans by adding a self-employed plan. And if you moonlight, think of that extra income not as money to spend but as an opportunity to boost your retirement plans.

4. **Consider a taxable account.** Still have money to save after taking advantage of your 401(k) and maxing out your IRA? It's time to put more in a taxable brokerage or mutual fund account. Although you won't get the same tax benefits as in a retirement account, you'll get much better returns than letting money sit in a savings account.

You can use online tools to closely control and manage money in a brokerage account. Check out my *Online Investing For Dummies*, 10th Edition (Wiley) for more help in using digital tools to get the most from a taxable account, including choosing individual stocks and mutual funds.

What about pensions and Social Security?

If you take a look at the options, they all require you to open and contribute to special accounts and save money yourself. What about plans such as pensions, where someone else makes the contribution? These defined benefit plans are gradually going away.

A radical shift has occurred in retirement planning toward defined contribution plans such as 401(k)s, IRAs, and self-employed plans and away from defined benefit plans such as pensions. With a *defined contribution plan*, you're responsible for putting money in, for what happens to that money, and for determining whether it will be enough for you to retire. (See Chapter 1 for more on this topic.)

With a *defined benefit plan*, your employer guarantees a certain amount of income after you retired. If you're working at one of the companies still offering a pension to new employees, be sure to read Chapter 14.

What about Social Security? It's a safety net, preventing workers from becoming destitute. Social Security isn't designed to provide for a comfortable retirement, but it is part of the retirement-planning puzzle. Read more about Social Security in Chapter 9.

TIP

Many people lament the replacement of defined benefit plans with defined contribution plans. Knowing that a big multinational corporation will write you a check every month after you retire is comforting. But people forget the downsides of defined benefit plans, notably that you're pretty much tied to staying with the company and counting on the company to make adequate contributions.

Where do most people contribute for retirement and how much do they contribute? As you can see in Table 4-1, the assets saved in U.S. retirement accounts hit $29.2 trillion as of March 31, 2019, according to the Investment Company Institute (www.ici.org/research/stats/retirement/ret_19_q1), which tracks investment accounts. Most of that amount, $9.4 trillion, is in IRAs. It's easy to see why — those accounts are available to anyone. 401(k) plans aren't far behind at $5.7 trillion. They are the go-to plans for workers. Also note that pensions from companies (not the government) are a small piece of the retirement pie at just $3.2 trillion.

TABLE 4-1

Where Americans Put Their Retirement Money

Type of Retirement Account	Dollars Invested
IRAs	$9.4 trillion
Defined contribution plans such as 401(k)s	$8.2 trillion, of which $5.7 trillion is in 401(k)s
Government pensions	$6.3 trillion
Private-sector defined benefit plans (private pensions)	$3.2 trillion
Annuity reserves	$2.1 trillion
Total	$29.2 trillion

Investment Company Institute as of March 31, 2019; www.ici.org/research/stats/retirement/ret_19_q1

Now it's time to find out which retirement plans are best for you.

A Great Place to Start: 401(k)s

The 401(k) is the first stop for many retirement plans — and for good reason. Companies have been shifting more employees to these plans since their creation in the late 1970s.

The moment you start a job, the human resources department will likely hand you 401(k) sign-up documents. However, at many companies, you aren't even asked whether or not you want to participate in the 401(k) plan. More than half of the largest 401(k) plans studied by the Investment Company Institute automatically enroll members.

WARNING

Don't assume that your new employer signed you up for a 401(k) plan. At smaller companies, less than 20 percent of plans automatically enroll members. It's up to you to make sure you're enrolled.

Advantages of 401(k) plans

The popularity of the 401(k) has swelled over the years because the plan makes it simple to start saving. Sign a few papers and you're in the plan. Your employer handles the process of opening the account, pulling money out of your paycheck, and making the contributions.

The low barrier to begin saving is perhaps the biggest advantage of 401(k) plans. You don't have to look for a retirement account provider on your own. Your employer, for better or worse, does that for you.

Other advantages include the following:

>> **Matching contribution:** The matching contribution is a big perk of 401(k) plans. More than 80 percent of large companies put money into their employees' 401(k) plans. Most of these matching amounts are put in relative to an employee's own contribution.

Matching contributions add up over time. Suppose you earn $100,000 annually and contribute 6 percent ($6,000) to your 401(k). Now suppose that your employer adds 50 cents to every dollar you contribute up to 6 percent. That amount adds another $3,000 in your account. If your 401(k) grows by 6 percent annually over 30 years and you and your employer continue the contributions, the result would be an extra $237,000. That's real money! Keep in mind that the amount contributed increases as you get raises and the 6 percent of your salary gets larger.

>> **Automatic saving:** Another big benefit of 401(k) plans is that the money comes straight out of your paycheck. If you're like most people, the moment you see a dollar you're tempted to spend it. But with 401(k) contributions, the money is out of your paycheck and out of your mind. If you're new to saving for retirement, the forced discipline of a 401(k) can help you be more successful.

>> **Higher contribution limit:** If you want to maximize how much of your salary you're putting away for retirement, the 401(k) is your friend. As of 2019, workers can put up to $19,000 a year into a 401(k).

It gets better. The IRS periodically boosts how much you can put in your 401(k) plan (www.irs.gov/newsroom/401k-contribution-limit-increases-to-19000-for-2019-ira-limit-increases-to-6000). And after you hit the big 5-0, you can make an additional catch-up contribution of $6,000 a year. The following table shows how already large 401(k) contribution limits have grown in the past few years.

Year	Contribution Limit	Catch-Up Contribution	Total Contribution
2015	$18,000	$6,000	$24,000
2016	$18,000	$6,000	$24,000
2017	$18,000	$6,000	$24,000
2018	$18,500	$6,000	$24,500
2019	$19,000	$6,000	$25,000
2020	$19,500	$6,500	$26,000

On the other hand, the most you could put in an IRA in 2020 was $6,000. When you turn 50, you can add an extra $1,000 yearly. These limits increase periodically, but will likely never catch up to the 401(k).

>> **Tax deferral during your high earning years:** 401(k)s can help employees shield retirement money from the taxman until they take the money out. Let's say you earn $100,000 a year. If you contribute $10,000 to your 401(k), you reduce your taxable income to $90,000. You don't pay the tax until you withdraw the money.

WARNING

Don't make the mistake of thinking that 401(k)s are tax free. They are tax deferred. When you make your contribution, you reduce your taxable income that year. Meanwhile, as your portfolio grows and pays income such as interest and dividends, you don't pay tax on those gains right away either. But (you knew a *but* was coming), when you take money out of your plan, you pay tax on it. Presumably, you'll be bringing home less money when you're retired, so your tax bill should be less than when you're working.

Drawbacks of 401(k) plans

401(k) plans have a lot going for them. Their simplicity and high limits make them a great option if you just want to get your retirement plan started. The employer matching contributions make them lucrative, too. But they're not without their problems.

TIP

If your company doesn't offer a match or you don't need the higher limits, your decision on whether to participate in your company's plan is more difficult. The IRA's advantages might make it a better choice.

Before automatically assuming that you should join your company's 401(k) plan, consider the following negatives:

>> **Potentially high fees:** 401(k)s may charge fees upon fees, and they can add up, as you discover in Chapter 6. You pay fees on the mutual funds in the plan in addition to fees to administer the plan. The mutual fund industry says fees in most large 401(k) plans are competitive, but your 401(k) may charge higher-than-average fees.

>> **Limited menu of investment options:** When you're in a 401(k) plan, you typically choose from a preset number of mutual funds. Sometimes the plan offers only mutual funds with poor track records, high fees, or both. According to investment-account-tracking firm ICI, large 401(k) plans typically offer 27 investment options, but smaller companies might offer fewer than half that. If you want to invest in a fund that's not in your plan, you're out of luck.

>> **Reduced contribution limits for highly compensated employees:** If you earned $125,000 in 2019 or own 5 percent of the company, your contribution limits might be reduced if non-highly-compensated employees don't participate in the plan.

>> **Limited availability of matching contributions:** Most companies won't release all the money they put in your 401(k) until you vest. These companies have a graduated vesting schedule in which you get 20 percent after working for 2 years, 40 percent after 3 years, 60 percent after 4 years, 80 percent after 5 years, and 100 percent after 6 years. However, the money you contribute is always yours.

WARNING

In general, when you put money in a retirement account, you should plan on keeping it there at least until you're close to retiring (or, better yet, until you need it for retirement). With most retirement accounts, including 401(k) plans and traditional IRAs, if you take money out before turning 59½, you'll have to pay the income tax you deferred plus a 10 percent early withdrawal penalty. As described later, exemptions to the 10 percent penalty cover unusual financial hits.

The Roth: An interesting twist on retirement savings

Up to this point, I've talked about the *traditional 401(k)*. With this type of 401(k), you put untaxed money into the plan and pay taxes when you take the money out. The *Roth 401(k)* turns this on its head. You put taxed money into the plan, so there's no immediate tax break. But here's the cool part: When you take money out of a Roth 401(k), you don't pay tax.

TIP

If your employer offers both a traditional IRA and a Roth IRA, you have a decision to make. If you think you'll be in a lower tax bracket when you're retired, you're better off paying the tax later with a traditional IRA. But if you think you'll be in a higher tax bracket in retirement, pay the tax now with the Roth 401(k). Here's a good rule of thumb: Younger savers early in their careers are wise to stuff their Roth 401(k) before hitting peak earnings (and taxes).

Increasingly, it's a good idea to do both. It's impossible to know where your income or tax rate will be in 5 years, much less 20 or 30. Why not diversify? You can put up to $19,000 a year into a 401(k) plan. Or if your employer offers both options, you can put $9,500 in a traditional 401(k) and $9,500 into a Roth 401(k) plan.

A Roth IRA is also available. I describe the few important distinctions between the Roth 401(k) and the Roth IRA in the next section.

WARNING

Some 401(k) plans offer brokerage capabilities that allow you to choose the investments in your plan. You can even buy individual stocks, not just mutual funds. Just be careful: The fees for these brokerage plans are usually ridiculously high and could erode any benefit from choosing different investments.

IRAs: A Cornerstone of Retirement Planning

401(k)s get a lot of attention, but the *IRA*, or individual retirement account, is a bit of an unsung hero in retirement planning. IRAs hold more retirement assets than 401(k)s do.

TIP

Even if you have access to a 401(k) at work, you might still want to consider adding an IRA to your retirement plan. If you've already contributed enough to the 401(k) to get any company match and you can spare to save more, I see an IRA in your future. Just be aware of the disadvantages, which I describe in this section.

With an IRA, the legwork is up to you. You research where you'd like to open your IRA and what you put in it. If this sounds like a lot of work, fear not. You learn how to do these tasks in Chapter 5.

Advantages of IRA plans

If you're a financial control freak, the IRA could be your dream come true. Sure, 401(k)s are a low-fuss and default way for many to build a retirement plan. You do the saving, but everything else is handled by someone else. If you're willing to spend a bit more time, though, you can usually build an IRA that will outperform your 401(k).

This added control is perhaps the biggest advantage of the IRA. But that's only an advantage if you're willing and able to research IRA providers and investment options. If you are, a host of IRA benefits become available:

TIP

» **Huge availability of providers:** Just about every financial firm you work with offers IRA services. Do you like a particular brokerage firm or a mutual fund company and its products? With an IRA, you can deepen your relationship with the firm.

Having more of your money with a single investment firm can bring not only familiarity but also savings. Some investment companies will lower their fees or offer lower-cost versions of products such as mutual funds if you have more money with them.

» **Wide availability of products:** With an IRA, the investment world is your oyster. Want to buy an unusual mutual fund that invests in environmentally conscious companies? You can. Looking to put your money in a low-cost index fund that buys all the stocks in an index, such as the Standard & Poor's 500? No problem.

In contrast, with a 401(k), the investments are chosen for you.

» **Open to all:** Just about anyone can open an IRA. Even if your employer offers a 401(k) plan, you can open and contribute to an IRA and deduct contributions from your taxable income up to certain income limits, as described in the next section.

» **Good source for college and first-time-home savings:** Typically, you have to wait until you're 59½ to take money out of an IRA — or face an early withdrawal fee of 10 percent. But with an IRA, you can take money out early and not pay the 10 percent fee if you're paying for higher education. First-time home buyers can also take out $10,000 without paying the early withdrawal fee. The next section lists the other exceptions to the 10 percent early withdrawal penalty.

>> **Available in a useful Roth variant:** Like 401(k) plans, you can get a Roth version of an IRA. With a Roth IRA, you don't get a tax break on contributions. But after you put in your taxed dollars, you can withdraw your own money (not investment gains on those earnings) anytime and not pay the 10 percent early withdrawal penalty.

TIP

The Roth IRA is a big gift to many, with several major unsung benefits. Most retirement accounts — including traditional IRAs and 401(k) plans — require you to start taking money out the year you turn 70½. (You can delay the first payment until the April after turning 70½.) This forced withdrawal is called a *required minimum distribution*, or RMD, which the IRS describes here: `www.irs.gov/retirement-plans/retirement-plans-faqs-regarding-required-minimum-distribution`. The RMD could be a disruption for people who don't need the income when they're 70½ or are in a high tax bracket at that time. Enter the Roth IRA. The Roth IRA's original owner is exempt from RMD rules. In fact, you can keep putting money in a Roth IRA after turning 70½.

REMEMBER

You'll encounter the term *traditional IRA* throughout this book and in your research. The IRS defines a traditional IRA as one that is not a Roth IRA or a SEP-IRA. The SEP-IRA is a plan for self-employed persons and is discussed in the "Self-Employed Plans" section.

Drawbacks of IRA plans

As you can see, IRAs have lots going for them. But they're not for everyone or everything. Some of the noteworthy downsides of IRA plans include the following:

>> **Lower contribution limits:** If you're under the age of 50, you can contribute just $6,000 a year to an IRA (as of 2020). If you're 50 or older, you can put in only $7,000. This limitation makes the IRA a good plan to use in addition to a 401(k).

Note that even if you get a 7 percent average annual return on your portfolio and contribute $6,000 a year for 30 years, you'll end up with $566,764. Not bad. Note that the 401(k) will likely allow you to save much more, up to $19,000 a year in 2019 if you're under 50 and $25,000 a year if you're 50 or older.

>> **Income-based limits on deductibility of traditional IRAs:** Just about anyone can contribute the max to an IRA. But not everyone can deduct all their contributions from their taxable income. The amount depends on your modified adjusted gross income (MAGI).

People who don't have access to a retirement plan at work can deduct more than those who do. I've summarized the rules in Table 4-2 for several filing statuses. See the link at the bottom of the table for the rules for other tax situations.

TIP

Some higher earners might think traditional IRAs are out of reach, but that's not true. Remember that anyone can contribute to a traditional IRA. The question is whether or not you can deduct your contributions. Even if you can't deduct contributions due to your income, you might still consider putting money in a non-deductible IRA. You won't get the immediate tax savings, but you can defer the taxes due on any income generated by your portfolio, which can help high-net-worth savers.

>> **Income-based limits on contributions to Roth IRAs:** Although anyone can put money in a traditional IRA, you can't contribute anything to a Roth IRA if you make too much. The income limits for Roth IRAs are shown in Table 4-3. Hit these income levels and the amount you can contribute to a Roth phases out.

TABLE 4-2   **Deductible IRA Contribution Amounts (2020)**

Access to Work Retirement Plan	Filing Status	Your MAGI	Your IRA Deduction
Yes	Single	$65,000 or less	Full deduction
	Single	>$65,000 to $75,000	Partial deduction
	Single	$75,000 or more	None
Yes	Married filing jointly	$104,000 or less	Full deduction
	Married filing jointly	>$104,000 up to $124,000	Partial deduction
	Married filing jointly	$124,000 or more	None
No	Single	Any amount	Full deduction
	Married filing jointly	Any amount	Full deduction
One spouse has a plan at work	Married filing jointly	$196,000 or less	Full deduction
	Married filing jointly	$196,000 up to $206,000	Partial deduction
	Married filing jointly	$206,000 or more	None

Internal Revenue Service (www.irs.gov/retirement-plans/plan-participant-employee/2020-ira-contribution-and-deduction-limits-effect-of-modified-agi-on-deductible-contributions-if-you-are-covered-by-a-retirement-plan-at-work)

TABLE 4-3

Roth IRA Eligibility (2020)

Filing Status	Roth Phase-Out Range
Single	$124,000 to $139,000
Married filing jointly	$196,000 to $206,000
Married, filing separately	$0 to $10,000

A few IRA odds and ends

Is your head spinning with all these IRA rules? I have just a few more aspects of IRAs that are worth thinking about.

Rollover IRAs

When you're working and a 401(k) plan is available, you'll probably participate. However, don't think you're shackled to a 401(k) forever. *401(k) rollovers* allow you to move a 401(k) to an IRA. Typically, you can do this if you leave your employer.

TIP

Rollovers can be a great strategy if you're taking advantage of the 401(k)'s higher contribution limit when you're working. When you retire (or switch to another employer), you can move the money to an IRA and have more choices.

WARNING

When you do a rollover, the money must go straight from your old 401(k) to your IRA, and not to you. The IRS doesn't want you withdrawing money early and will tax you if they think you did.

Roth IRA conversions

Did the Roth IRA look great, but you can't contribute because you make too much? You might consider a *Roth IRA conversion*. Even if your income is high, you can turn a traditional IRA to a Roth by using a back door. However, the process is complicated. To learn more, visit www.irs.gov/retirement-plans/retirement-plans-faqs-regarding-iras-rollovers-and-roth-conversions.

Spousal IRAs

Spouses who don't have taxable income can make up to the allowable household contributions to an IRA.

Self-Employed Plans

People who work for themselves might assume that retirement savings plans are only for corporate folks. However, in some ways, self-employed people — including anyone with freelance income — have more options.

Self-employed plans offer big opportunities, including the following:

>> **Tax deductions:** Retirement plans for small businesses offer tax deductions and access to tax-deferred growth. These features are especially attractive to small-business owners because their income can be unpredictable.

>> **Sizeable contribution limits:** Many IRAs designed for small businesses have much higher contribution limits than the standard IRAs offered to cubicle dwellers.

>> **Lots of control:** The plan is up to the boss — you — so you have the power to not only choose the financial institution where you put the plan but also the investments in the plan.

WARNING

With all this control to build a retirement plan for your company comes great responsibility. It's up to you to choose a solid plan. Most reputable financial firms that run self-employed plans, like the ones you encounter in Chapter 5, do most of the work for you. But it's still your job to find a good plan and choose logical investments to meet your goals.

The spectacular SEP-IRA

If you're looking for an easy plan to set up that will benefit the business owner — and employees — it's tough to beat a *SEP-IRA*. These are great plans for people with side gigs as well.

Usually, contributions to SEP-IRA plans are in two parts:

>> **Employer contribution:** If you're the business owner, this is your contribution. You can contribute up to 25 percent of your employees' pay, including your own, into the plan, up to $56,000 in 2019. If you're self-employed, your contributions for yourself usually end up closer to 20 percent of net income (due to the deduction of self-employment tax). Note that you don't have to contribute every year.

>> **Employee contribution:** Employees can sock away money in their SEP-IRA, in addition to what the employer puts in. The same IRA contribution limits apply (up to $7,000 a year for those 50 and older). Employees must be 21 or older and earn at least $600 during the year to participate.

You don't need employees to have a SEP-IRA. If you have a side hustle, SEP-IRAs are a perfect way to add a little extra to your retirement plan. In effect, you make employer contributions to yourself. Most IRA providers will set up a SEP-IRA for you, as described in Chapter 5. Some firms refer to these plans as a *one-person SEP-IRA*.

The 401(k) for one: A one-participant 401(k)

One-participant 401(k) plans are solid options if you're primarily self-employed or a business partner in a closely held company. These plans are for companies where the only employees are the partners or their spouses. One-participant 401(k)s are also called *individual 401(k)s* or *solo 401(k)s*.

Like the SEP-IRA, with a one-participant 401(k) you can make an employee and employer contribution for yourself, so you can sock away a large sum. Just know that if you, as the employer, contribute to your individual 401(k) account, you must contribute to everyone else's too. No contribution hogging is allowed.

Contributions to individual 401(k) plans come in two parts:

>> **Employer contribution:** For the 2020 tax year, this contribution can be up to 25 percent of compensation but not more than $57,000. These contributions are tax deductible.

>> **Employee contribution:** In 2020, employees can sock away up to $19,500 ($26,000 if they're 50 or older).

As the business owner, your total contribution in 2019 must be less than $56,000 or less than $62,000 if you're 50 or older.

Keeping it SIMPLE

A *SIMPLE (Savings Incentive Match Plan for Employees) plan* is an IRA intended to make things easy for a company with 100 or fewer employees. Because these plans are designed to be off-the-shelf, they're fairly rigid. Even if your business has a bad year, you must still continue making contributions, so companies in less stable industries might prefer another option.

SIMPLE contributions come in two varieties (which aren't simple):

>> **Employer contributions:** You, as the business owner, have two options. You can make a 100 percent match of employee contributions up to 3 percent of workers' pay, and you can cut that to just a 1 percent match in two out of five

years. Or you can contribute 2 percent of employee pay up to $285,000 a year (for 2020). You must contribute annually.

>> **Employee contributions:** In 2020, workers can put up to $13,500 in their account or $16,500 for those 50 and older.

What's the Catch?

If your head's not swimming with all these contribution limits, you might be wondering what's the catch to these retirement plans. After all, why would the government be willing to give up tax receipts in the near term? Is it out of the kindness of our lawmakers? The fact is, these plans have important restrictions.

Tax-deferred isn't tax-free

Many but not all retirement plans defer taxes. *Tax deferral* means the tax bill is delayed, not eliminated.

Even if you fund a 401(k) and get an immediate tax break, Uncle Sam will collect taxes from you eventually. You simply put off the tax collection, allowing your money to compound first. You get a tax break while you're working and your tax rate is presumably higher, and you pay taxes when you take money out in retirement, when you're presumably in a lower tax rate.

TECHNICAL STUFF

The other benefit of tax deferral happens when portfolios generate income. You might collect interest from bonds you own in a retirement plan, collect dividends paid by companies, or incur capital gains if a mutual fund you own sells some winning stocks. *Dividends* are periodic cash payments that a company pays to shareholders when the company has excess profit. Dividends are typically taxable immediately in a regular account. Likewise, *capital gains* are taxable proceeds generated when an investment is sold at a higher price than when it was purchased. Capital gains are taxable, too.

If you own an investment in a taxable account that pays a dividend or triggers a capital gain, you owe tax that year. But in a tax-deferred account, you don't pay tax on any distributions until you take the money out.

WARNING

Not having to pay tax on dividends in the year they're paid sounds great — and it is. But the important catch to tax deferral is that when you take money out, you pay your ordinary tax rate on withdrawals.

Paying your ordinary tax rate is fine when you take out money you contributed because you would have paid ordinary income tax rates on this money anyway. But this catch is unfortunate with other forms of income or gains in your account. In a taxable account, many forms of income generated by stocks (such as dividends) are taxed at a lower rate or even 0 percent. Also, when you sell a stock for a gain in a taxable account you've owned for more than a year, you pay a lower capital gains tax. But when you take out money generated by dividends or capital gains in a tax-deferred account, you pay your ordinary income tax rate, which could be higher.

Beware the 10 percent early withdrawal penalty

Again, when you put money in a retirement account, you should plan on leaving it there until you retire. The IRS says retirement is age 59½ or later. If you take money out of a traditional (non-Roth) IRA, 401(k), or self-employed plan earlier than that, you'll have to pay not only the taxes on the contribution but also a 10 percent early withdrawal penalty.

REMEMBER

As mentioned, the Roth has an edge in that withdrawals for college costs and limited withdrawals for first-time home purchases are exempt from this penalty.

Just to make things even more complicated, the IRS has extended some exceptions to the 10 percent penalty to 401(k) plans and some self-employed plans. Table 4-4 shows some of these exceptions. For a full list, go to www.irs.gov/retirement-plans/plan-participant-employee/retirement-topics-tax-on-early-distributions.

TABLE 4-4   **Some Exceptions to the 10% Penalty**

Exception	Workplace Plan Such as 401(k) Exception?	IRA, SEP-IRA, SIMPLE Exception?
Death	Yes	Yes
Disability	Yes	Yes
Education	No	Yes
Taking out equal payments	Yes	Yes
First-time homebuyer	No	Yes
Medical (with limitations)	Yes	Yes
Separation from service	Yes (55 or older)	No

www.irs.gov/retirement-plans/plan-participant-employee/retirement-topics-tax-on-early-distributions

Don't mortgage your future: Retirement plan loans

You might wonder if there's another way to take money out of a retirement plan before you retire or turn 59½. There is, although it's generally a bad idea — which is why I'm mentioning it at the end of the chapter. Some so-called qualified retirement plans, such as 401(k)s, may allow you to borrow from them.

REMEMBER

Loans are not allowed with traditional IRAs, individual 401(k)s, SEP-IRAs, or SIMPLE plans. And 401(k) plan providers are not required to offer loans.

I could dedicate an entire chapter to explaining all the rules around 401(k) loans. Don't worry — I wouldn't do that to you. Just know that, in general, 401(k) loans are limited to 50 percent of your balance. You can read about additional restrictions at www.irs.gov/retirement-plans/retirement-plans-faqs-regarding-loans.

If you're in a tough spot and your 401(k) is the only place to turn, you might consider a loan. But again, you're much better off not borrowing if you can help it. Some of the major downsides of 401(k) loans follow:

>> **You risk lost market returns.** When you pull out your money, it's no longer working for you. If the market rallies, you're missing the opportunity to make your retirement better in the future.

>> **You have to pay the money back, with interest.** If you don't, your loan is treated as a taxable distribution.

>> **If you leave your job early, you have to repay the loan immediately.** Getting fired is one example of leaving your job early. Having to cough up thousands of dollars could make a bad day even worse.

The IRS isn't a big fan of 401(k) loans either. You can read the Internal Revenue Service's warnings about them at www.irs.gov/retirement-plans/considering-a-loan-from-your-401k-plan-2.

Chapter **5**

Gauging Your Appetite for Risk

Retirement planning requires a careful balance of risk and return. If you play it too safe and don't take enough risk, your results may not be enough to give you the returns you desire. On the other hand, if you take on too much risk, you might suffer more volatility than you can handle.

Getting the right mix of risk and return is a pivotal element of a successful retirement plan. No risk, no gain. But what's the right amount of risk to take? What is a reasonable return? Although much of the future is unknown, especially over a span of 20 or 30 years, a general understanding of the risks and returns associated with different types of investments, or *asset classes*, is important.

Why talk about something as arcane as asset classes before you've even opened a retirement account? Glad you asked! The blend of investments you choose goes a long way in determining how your money grows over time.

In this chapter, you learn enough about asset classes to set up your retirement plan. And although knowing what kind of return to expect is important, you find out a thing or two about yourself in the process, too. (For more on asset classes, see Chapter 12.)

Keep in mind that the goal of a successful retirement plan is to find the right amount of risk for you. If you have a low tolerance for volatility, you'll want a portfolio that gives you the most return for the risk you take.

TIP

If you're a more advanced retirement planner looking to further optimize your accounts and mix of asset classes in an asset allocation, Chapter 12 will help.

Getting a Handle on Your Risk Tolerance

You might have your finger perched over your mouse button, ready to open an account. But you should take two more important steps first: Figure out what type of investor you are and the kind of retirement plan you want to create.

Before you open your accounts, answer the following:

>> **How hands-on do you plan to be?** Different retirement accounts give you more control than others. If you want to run things yourself, you'll choose a different type of provider than someone who'd rather put the plan on auto-pilot.

>> **How much risk can you handle?** Your risk tolerance measures both your degree of panic when markets inevitably crash and your exuberance when markets soar. These emotions will play a role in the retirement accounts you create and the investments you put in them.

>> **How complex a retirement plan do you want?** You can optimize a retirement plan in many ways. For some people, a good plan is good enough.

Determining your investor type

This is a dramatic oversimplification, but investors usually come in two broad varieties, especially when it comes to retirement planning: active investors and passive investors. Which category you are in will in large part steer where you open your retirement account, the investments you choose, and what's important to you.

Take a look at the following to figure out which category you're in:

>> **Active investor's objective:** Beat the market. *Beat* typically means either achieving huge returns or controlling losses for less risk. You beat the market by selecting individual investments you think will meet your goal.

>> **Active investor's investment of choice:** Individual stocks, bonds, or other assets. You might also like actively managed mutual funds, where managers choose individual investments for you. Your objective is a big return, lower risk, or other ways to best meet your goals.

>> **Passive investor's objective:** Keep fees low. You want to capture a majority of market returns and keep your costs down. You think trying to actively beat the market is too difficult or costly

>> **Passive investor's investment of choice:** An asset allocation built of broadly diversified assets you hold in good times and bad. Passive investors typically own low-cost index funds, which hold every stock in an index, such as the Standard & Poor's 500.

TIP

Some crossover can exist in active and passive approaches to investing. You might like to keep part of your portfolio in low-cost investments but take a more active approach in other areas. For instance, you might think passive investing works best with large U.S. stocks such as Microsoft and Apple, which are in S&P 500 index funds, but take a more active approach with your other asset classes.

TECHNICAL
STUFF

Passive investing has revolutionized retirement planning. An increasing number of investors who focus on the fees they're paying choose to buy index funds. These funds don't try to choose the best investments, which requires time, expertise, and money. Instead, index funds buy all investments in an index.

An *index* is a group of stocks selected to represent a market. Perhaps the most famous index is the Standard & Poor's 500, or S&P 500. The S&P 500 is a collection of the 500 most valuable stocks (often called the largest companies) trading on U.S. exchanges. Most retirement plans will offer you an option to buy an index fund linked to the S&P 500.

But the S&P 500 is just one of hundreds of different indexes. Table 5-1 shows you some of the indexes you'll encounter when planning your retirement.

TABLE 5-1 ## Key Market Indexes

Index Name	Asset Class	What It Measures
Dow Jones Industrial Average	Stocks	The 30 biggest industrial companies. When investors hear about "the market," more often than not they think of the Dow.
Standard & Poor's 500 index	Stocks	The 500 largest U.S. companies, including the nation's most well-known stocks. Moves similarly to the Dow, even though it includes more stocks.
NASDAQ composite index	Stocks	Stocks that trade on the NASDAQ stock market. Tends to closely track technology stocks.
Wilshire 5000 Total Market Index	Stocks	The entire U.S. stock market. Contains all significant stocks from the largest to the smallest.
Russell 2000 Index	Stocks	Small-company U.S. stocks. Tends to be more volatile than indexes that track large companies, such as the S&P 500.
MSCI ACWI (All Country World Index)	Stocks	Stocks around the world. Includes shares of big companies in developed parts of the world and small companies in less-developed nations.
Bloomberg Barclays U.S. Aggregate Bond Index	Bonds	A cross-section of the bond market. The bond market is huge, filled with scores of IOUs issued by many borrowers ranging from the U.S. government to companies and home buyers. This index attempts to take a cross-section of this diverse universe. The Agg, as it's often called, acts much in the same way for bonds as the S&P 500 does for stocks.

Many indexes track one of two things:

>> **Stocks:** Stocks, or *equity*, are pieces of ownership in a company. Stocks tend to be volatile because there is no promise of return. But stocks also can generate large long-term results when the company is successful because you own a piece of the upside.

>> **Bonds:** Bonds, or *fixed income*, are IOUs issued by companies and governments. Bonds have been less volatile than stocks. The borrower tells you ahead of time when you'll get your money back and at what rate of interest. Even if the borrower flourishes, you get only the pre-agreed payment.

Understanding risk tolerance

Determining whether you are an active investor or a passive investor will help you figure out what kinds of assets you should buy in your retirement plan. Your risk tolerance is another critical step in determining what you should buy. After all, if you have a low threshold for volatility, you'll want a retirement portfolio that can smooth some of the bumps.

TIP

What determines a person's risk tolerance? To be frank, you won't know for sure until you see how aggressive you are during your first huge stock-market rally or how nervous you are when the market is falling. But typically, the following personal traits factor into a risk-tolerance profile:

>> **Your age:** The younger you are, the more risk you can take. Because retirement is likely far away and it's early in your career, you can withstand a tough market and stick with your long-term plan. Older workers closer to retirement don't have as much time to make up for a hit.

>> **How close you are to your retirement goal:** If you've already saved enough to sustain your run rate for 40 years, why bet the farm? Why take on huge risk with your retirement plan just for the chance of generating large amounts of excess wealth you may not need?

>> **Your comfort level with financial markets:** If you are a grizzled veteran and have survived multiple bear markets, you might have a larger risk appetite than someone new to investing.

REMEMBER

Understanding your risk tolerance is one of the first places to start in building a retirement plan. You're trying to see how much market duress you can take before turning into a white-knuckled, panicked mess.

When panic sets in, people tend to give up on their retirement plans — and that can cost them dearly later. It's better to know the amount of financial ups and downs you can tolerate before you start to worry.

Looking at risk tolerance differently

Every financial market crash is a new opportunity to learn about how people behave during periods of intensified risk. Researchers have noticed that the human taste for risk isn't always logically pegged to age, as is often assumed.

Meir Statman, professor of finance at Santa Clara University, is doing groundbreaking work in the area of real risk tolerance. His findings can help you better understand yourself — and build a portfolio that works for you.

Statman's research (`www.scu.edu/media/leavey-school-of-business/finance-/statman-files/Questionnaire-JIC.pdf`) shows that an investor's tolerance for risk is most closely associated with three traits often left out of many risk questionnaires. Think about your own personality and the following traits:

>> **Regret:** The tendency to look back and second-guess decisions you've made is a key part of your risk tolerance, Statman says. If you tend to have large levels of regret or take too little risk, you might kick yourself later as others make more money in their retirement plans than you do.

Statman says you should answer this question: "Whenever I make a choice, do I feel the pain of regret if another alternative has done better than the alternative I've chosen?" If you say yes, you might not want to entirely dial back risk because you might regret it later.

>> **Overconfidence:** Some investors think they're smarter than the market — so much so that they take on more risk than they should. Statman says you should ask yourself, "Some people believe that they can pick investments that would earn higher-than-average returns. Other people believe that they are unable to do so. What is my belief?" The trouble is that if you're truly overconfident, you might not realize it. Ask someone you trust who knows you.

>> **Exuberance:** Optimism is a wonderful personal trait. But too much optimism about the markets can be dangerous. If you think your portfolio is going to grow at an astronomical level, you may throw caution to the wind and get overly aggressive.

How do you know whether you're exuberant? Ask yourself what you think markets will do in the next 12 months, Statman says. Then compare your expectations for market returns to the historical reality shown in Table 5-2. For instance, if you think stocks will go up 20 percent in the next 12 months — or twice the historical rate of return — suspect that you're exuberant.

TABLE 5-2

Reasonable Investment Expectations

Investment	Average Annual Return	Relative Risk
Stocks	10.0%	Riskiest
Corporate bonds	6.0%	Moderately risky
Treasury bills	3.4%	Least risky

Source: Morningstar through 2018

Using risk-assessment tools

By now, you realize that knowing how much risk you can take is a first step in building a portfolio for your retirement. But how do you figure out your risk tolerance more precisely?

Some good online tools are available to help you figure out how you'll react when the market gets wild. Most risk-tolerance questionnaires are free and don't require you to have an account with the firm providing them. After answering the questions, you get guidance that will help you understand which asset classes make the most sense in your retirement portfolio.

TIP

Although these risk-tolerance tools are good, there's no substitute for experience. It's easy to take an online survey and say you'd be unfazed by a 40 percent decline in stocks. But if you remember suffering sleepless nights as stocks cratered in 2008 and 2009, you were overconfident when filling out the survey.

REMEMBER

Some financial providers who offer retirement accounts administer their own risk-tolerance questionnaires when you open an account. But because your risk appetite is such a big driver in how you build a retirement plan, get a second opinion by using some of the tools in this section.

Some of the risk-tolerance measurement tools I like include the following:

>> **Vanguard's Investor Questionnaire** (https://personal.vanguard.com/us/FundsInvQuestionnaire) does an excellent job focusing on factors that might affect your ability to stick with your retirement plans when turbulence hits the financial markets. Most of Vanguard's questions probe how long you plan to keep your money invested.

This approach makes sense. Most *recessions,* or periods of declining economic activity, last only about a year on average. If investors don't need money for five years or more, they're more likely to be patient and not make knee-jerk decisions because they know they'll have time to recover. If you're retiring next year, it would be harder to watch your nest egg evaporate.

Vanguard asks 11 questions. At the end of the quiz, the tool will tell you how much of your portfolio should be in stocks, bonds, and short-term reserves. The more in stocks, the riskier the portfolio. The more in bonds, the more conservative.

>> **Index Fund Advisors' Risk Capacity Survey** (www.ifa.com/survey/) asks a round of questions to find out how you'd react in a severe market decline. The questionnaire comes in two versions: a short one with 5 questions and a more comprehensive one with 25. At the end of the survey, the questionnaire ranks you in terms of how aggressive (100) to conservative (1) you are. The IFA

survey, like the Vanguard questionnaire, tells you what percentage of your portfolio should be in safer bonds as opposed to riskier stocks.

>> **Charles Schwab Investor Profile Questionnaire** (www.schwab.com/public/file/P-778947/InvestorProfileQuestionnaire.pdf), shown in Figure 5-1, is a form you can print. The questionnaire asks seven questions, including a few about what your current retirement plan looks like. After you've answered the questions, you tally your answers and arrive at a Risk Tolerance Score from 0 (conservative) to 40 (aggressive). You can then see portfolios that show what your retirement plan might look like, including recommended percentages in large-caps, small-caps, international stocks, bonds, and cash that fit your risk profile.

FIGURE 5-1:
Measure your risk tolerance with Charles Schwab's questionnaire.

Again, diving into the nitty-gritty of how to build your portfolio is going a bit further than you need to know right now. You get in the asset allocation weeds in Chapter 12.

REMEMBER

These are just a few tools to help measure your risk appetite. Many IRA and 401(k) providers offer their own risk-measurement tools as well. You'll likely be asked to use them as you set up your account, as described in Chapter 6.

The ABCs of Asset Classes

What is an asset class? I've been trying to spare you this term, but it's so commonly used — and so closely connected with risk tolerance — that now is a good time to give you the basics.

You can invest in countless assets, ranging from shares of Microsoft to junk bonds issued by companies with shaky finances. To organize these assets, they're grouped into categories, or classes. Investments that might find their way into retirement portfolios typically fall into four major *asset classes:*

>> Stocks

>> Bonds

>> Cash

>> Commodities (such as gold or oil)

Assets in these classes tend to have similar traits in terms of risk and expected return. *Expected return* is how much the asset class is expected to appreciate in the future based on its historical track record.

Each of these major asset classes can be further divided. For instance, you might break down stocks into U.S. stocks, foreign stocks, small-capitalization stocks, and large-capitalization stocks.

REMEMBER

Why are asset classes so important? Academic studies show time and again that, over the long haul, the mix of asset classes in your retirement plan is an overriding determining factor of the returns you'll get and the risk you'll endure. That's why with asset allocation, you want to get as close to right as you can.

Putting stocks in a box

All stocks involve partial ownership of a business, whether the stock is for an established multinational corporation, a small, new company, or any type of company in between. Given that you're supposed to put a significant chunk of your wealth in this asset class, how are you supposed to figure out what stocks are right for you?

The good news is many companies are willing to help you categorize stocks, along with some bonds, into categories. One of the more popular companies is Morningstar Research (www.morningstar.com).

Most investors use the popular Morningstar-style boxes shown in Table 5-3 to more precisely define the types of stocks and bonds. You'll encounter these Morningstar-style boxes frequently when you're looking for investments to put into your retirement account, so it's best to get used to them now. As you can see, stocks are categorized by their value and their size. The core category in the table consists of stocks that are somewhere in-between inexpensive value stocks and expensive growth ones.

TABLE 5-3

Popular Ways to Categorize Stocks

Value	Core	Growth
Large value	Large core	Large growth
Mid-sized value	Mid-sized core	Mid-sized growth
Small value	Small core	Small growth

©2019 Morningstar, Inc. All Rights Reserved. Reprinted by permission of Morningstar.

Volumes of academic research show that stocks tend to behave similarly to each other based on their size and value as follows:

REMEMBER

>> **Size:** Stocks are separated by size. Investors define size by how much a stock is worth. *Large-cap stocks* are the most valuable stocks in the world and include companies such as Microsoft, Apple, and Facebook. The definition of a large-cap (capitalization) company varies over time, but as of February 2019, it's a company worth $8.2 billion or more. *Mid-cap stocks* are from companies valued between $2.4 billion and $8.2 billion. Any company under $2.4 billion is a *small cap.*

A company's *market cap,* or market capitalization, is the price investors put on the company. Market cap sounds fancy, but it's simply the company's stock price times the number of shares it's cut into. If an apple pie were cut into eight slices and each slice sold for $5, the pie would have a market capitalization of $40.

Typically, smaller companies are more volatile than large ones because many are not as developed and have shakier business models. And because they're riskier, small-cap stocks tend to deliver higher returns (and more sleepless nights).

>> **Value:** Stocks are classified also by their valuation. A stock can be valued in many ways. If you're interested in how to do that, check out *Investment Banking For Dummies* (Wiley). For our purposes in retirement planning, know that a company is a value stock, a growth stock, or a *core* stock.

A *value stock* is one for which investors pay a relatively small amount relative to its net worth or book value. Investors pay less for a value stock for many reasons, including questions about its capability to grow or even survive. Because value stocks are usually considered riskier, they've generated solid returns over the long haul as a group. In investing, as in most things in life, more risk is more gain.

A *growth stock* is the opposite. These stocks are the darlings of Wall Street that can seemingly do no wrong. Investors pay higher prices for growth stocks. They tend to underperform over the long haul because they're the favorites and therefore investors pay too much for them. It's like betting on the favorite horse at the racetrack. Even if the horse wins, you don't make much money.

A *core stock* has characteristics of both a value stock and a growth stock.

TECHNICAL STUFF

Why do the Morningstar categories matter so much? Again, an investment's category determines your expected risk and return. Table 5-4 shows that U.S. large-company stocks (value, core, and growth) are the least risky of the major subsets of stock. We know this because its standard deviation, a statistical measure of volatility, is the lowest, at 18. But with the lower risk, you get a lower expected return, too. U.S. large-company stocks generated an average annual compound return of 9.3 percent, the lowest on the list.

TABLE 5-4   **Investments that Zig When the Market Zags**

Asset Class	Average Annual Compound Return	Risk (Standard Deviation)
U.S. large-company stocks	9.3%	18.0
U.S. large value-priced stocks	10.6%	21.8
U.S. small-cap stocks	11.0%	24.2
U.S. small value-priced stocks	12.4%	28.3
International value-priced stocks	10.4%	23.0
Emerging markets stocks	12.1%	23.5

IFA.com based on data since 1928 through December 31, 2018

Adding bonds

It's easy to overlook bonds when looking at asset classes, but that would be a mistake. Bonds, especially those issued by the U.S. government or large companies, are the bedrock of a retirement portfolio. When stocks are rising and crashing, bonds tend to rise, albeit relatively slowly.

Adding bonds to a portfolio lowers the return you're likely to get but also lowers your blood pressure. Bonds are IOUs, where the borrower promises to pay you back at a certain rate of interest. That promise, depending on who it's from, can reassure investors.

As you can imagine, the Classifier of the Financial Universe, Morningstar, has a style box for bonds, too, as shown in Table 5-5.

TABLE 5-5   **Popular Bond Categories**

High-quality/limited-rate sensitive	High-quality/moderate-rate sensitive	High-quality/extensive-rate sensitive
Medium-quality/limited-rate sensitive	Medium-quality/moderate-rate sensitive	Medium-quality/extensive-rate sensitive
Low-quality/limited-rate sensitive	Low-quality/moderate-rate sensitive	Low-quality/extensive-rate sensitive

©2019 Morningstar, Inc. All Rights Reserved. Reprinted by permission of Morningstar.

Again, our friends at Morningstar neatly classify the massive bond market into nine boxes. However, the two dimensions that define the bond market aren't size and value (as with stocks):

>> **Quality:** The *quality* of a bond is defined by how likely you are to get repaid. Remember, a bond is just a loan that you're making. If you lend money to the U.S. government, you're pretty sure you'll get repaid, so a government bond is a high-quality bond.

But if you lend money to a shaky cannabis startup company that has never made a profit, that's a low-quality bond. *Credit ratings agencies,* such as Moody's Investors Service and Standard & Poor's Ratings, analyze bonds to determine their quality.

>> **Interest rate sensitivity:** Rising interest rates are like kryptonite to bonds. The reason to own bonds is for the interest rates they pay you. Let's say banks are paying 2 percent interest and you're getting 4 percent from a high-quality bond, which makes you happy. But if banks pay 5 percent interest, your 4 percent bond is no longer looking great. If you try to sell your 4 percent bond, you'll have to cut the price because you're competing with higher rates.

A great deal of overlap exists in indexes and asset classes. That's no mistake. Remember that passive investors love to invest in stocks in indexes. So, if you are a passive investor, like that small stocks tend to have the highest returns, and think you can handle the volatility, you would look to buy an index fund that tracks a small-cap index, such as the Russell 2000.

Including a few other asset classes

Stocks and bonds fall obediently into the nine boxes, but not all asset classes do. Asset classes are still important ingredients to a retirement plan, and the following are a few worth mentioning:

>> **International stocks:** International companies are typically based in developed parts of Europe and Asia.

>> **Emerging markets:** Countries such as China, Brazil, and India are rapidly industrializing and present huge potential returns — and risks — to investors.

>> **Real-estate investment trusts (REITs):** An REIT is a real-estate holding that acts like a stock. You can buy an REIT just like you'd buy any stock. When you do that, you own a piece of the REIT's real-estate portfolio, typically strip malls or apartments. REITs are required to pay out 90 percent of their profits each year to investors.

Seeing how risk tolerance and returns work together

When you pair risk tolerance with asset classes, something interesting happens: You can get the most return from the amount of risk you take. The ramifications for retirement planning are profound.

For instance, let's assume that based on your run rate, your retirement goal is to save $1 million. If you decide that you can accept a moderate amount of risk, you might build a portfolio with a mix of stocks and bonds that generates an expected return of 5 percent a year. If you're 30 years old, you'd need to save $880.21 a month to hit your goal, as shown in Table 5-6.

TABLE 5-6   **Saving $1 Million**

Investor's Age	Monthly Investment with 5% Return	Monthly Investment with 10% Return	Monthly Investment with 15% Return
20	$493.48	$95.40	$15.28
30	$880.21	$263.40	$68.13
40	$1,679	$753.67	$308.31
50	$3,741	$2,412.72	$1,495.87
60	$14,704.57	$12,913.71	$11,289.93

Now let's assume you can stomach more risk and put more of your portfolio into stocks (and include riskier assets such as small caps and emerging markets). In this case, you might get a return closer to 10 percent. If you can handle the volatility and stick with your plan, you could hit your goal by saving just $263.40 a month.

REMEMBER

Don't worry if some of the technical information in this chapter is confusing. At this point, you just need to understand why your risk appetite is important. It's also good to know the term *asset class,* and that some assets, such as stocks, are riskier than others, such as bonds. But because stocks are riskier, they tend to generate larger returns over time.

Chapter **6**

Opening Your Accounts

You might be a 401(k) or an IRA expert — and know every arcane rule and limit attached to retirement accounts. You might be able to recite the IRS code pertaining to retirement word-for-word and impress others at a (boring) party. But knowing about a retirement plan and creating one are different.

If you don't know how to choose an account provider, open the account, fund it, and choose your investments, your retirement plan is just a plan. All that knowledge won't make you a penny richer in retirement unless you act on it. "I'll do it later," is the most dangerous sentence in retirement planning.

Hence, the importance of this chapter. Here you find out the Who's Who of the retirement plan space. You also discover how to choose a provider and set up your account.

This chapter is for people who want to get up and running quickly with their retirement plan. For more details, especially when choosing investments, check out Part 2.

Getting Your 401(k) Up and Running

One of the big advantages of 401(k) plans, as you discover in Chapter 4, is that you don't have to do much to use them. In many ways, where you put your 401(k) isn't your call. Your 401(k) picks you, rather than the other way around.

With that said, you might need to do a few things to get your 401(k) activated. I step through each of your responsibilities here so you can start taking advantage of the magical power of tax-deferred savings.

TIP

Don't assume that your employer will sign you up for your 401(k) plan. Only about a quarter of large 401(k) plans automatically enroll employees, according to the Investment Company Institute (www.icifactbook.org/ch8/19_fb_ch8).

To participate in a 401(k), follow these steps:

1. **Get your sign-up packet from your employer.**

Typically, the packet will be mailed to you after you start the job. If you're lucky, you'll be automatically enrolled and get a notification letter like the one in Figure 6-1. If you're not automatically enrolled, you should receive instructions for signing up.

2. **Choose your savings contribution percentage.**

The 401(k) provider is asking you what percentage of your pre-tax income you want taken out of your paycheck. If you're not sure, review the budgeting and savings guidelines in Chapters 2 and 3.

TIP

Contribute at least enough to take advantage of a company match. For example, if your employer will match up to 6 percent of your pay, put in at least that much. Whether you put in more depends on the quality of the plan and how much you can afford to save. In Chapter 7, you find out how to evaluate whether your 401(k) is better than other available options.

REMEMBER

Aim to save 10 to 15 percent of your gross pay for retirement. If you save only 6 percent in your 401(k), you should save 4 to 9 percent more in an IRA or another plan.

3. **Choose your investment option.**

Tell the 401(k) provider how to invest the money that's being taken from your paycheck.

TIP

When you're just getting things set up, choose the target-date fund closest to the year you plan to retire. *Target-date funds* are premixed collections of mutual funds or other investments designed to match your retirement goal. For example, if it's 2020, you're 30 years old, and you plan to retire at 65, choose the target-date fund for 2055. Keep reading for more on target-date funds and the role they can play in your portfolio.

4. **Pat yourself on the back and get to work.**

VOYA
Voya
PO Box 990067
Hartford, CT 06199-0067

INVESTMENT PLAN AND TRUST

Automatic Enrollment and Automatic Rate Escalator Confirmation

Transaction Date: 05/29/2019
Plan Number:

Welcome to the ⬚ INC. INVESTMENT PLAN AND TRUST.
This statement confirms the details of your recent automatic enrollment in your retirement plan.

> Please review this confirmation in its entirety for important information and disclosures relating to your retirement account, including how to access your account statement.

Contribution Source	Automatic Contribution Rate
Employee PreTax	3.00%
Total:	**3.00%**

Investment Name	Election
6991 Voya Target Retirement 2035 Fund R6	100.00%
Total:	**100.00%**

Below are the details of your Automatic Contribution Rate Escalator. Your contribution election will increase at the frequency elected until your maximum is reached. In the event that your next scheduled increase falls on a weekend or a New York Stock Exchange holiday, your contribution election will be increased on the following business day.

This confirmation contains time sensitive financial information. Please review the confirmation carefully and report any discrepancies or transactions that you did not initiate or request by calling one of our customer service representatives at 1-800-584-6001 within 30 days of the date of this confirmation. Automated Voice Response System is available 24/7. Representatives are available Monday thru Friday, 8 a.m. to 9 p.m., ET or visit our web site at www.voyaretirementplans.com. The Company will investigate any claim and determine, in its sole discretion, whether an adjustment is warranted. Failure to report any discrepancy within 30 days will indicate that you are in agreement with transactions in your account as reported in this confirmation.

The Voya Lifetime Income Protection Program "portfolios" are target date asset allocation models through which amounts are invested in target date funds (the "Funds") and multiple variable annuity contracts (the "Contracts"), each issued by a different insurer. A portfolio's allocation between the Funds and the Contracts is based on the portfolio's glide path, which increases the allocation to the Contracts as the portfolio approaches its target date. A portfolio is not an investment separate from its allocation between the Funds and Contracts, is not an investment company and has not been registered with the Securities and Exchange Commission under the Investment Company Act of 1940. Information shown for each portfolio is a blend of the returns and expenses of the Funds and Contracts, as applicable.

Securities are distributed by or offered through Voya Financial Partners, LLC (member SIPC) or other broker-dealers with which it has a selling agreement.

This confirmation is provided on behalf of Voya Financial Partners, LLC (member SIPC).

Page 1 of 2

FIGURE 6-1:
This letter was sent to a newly hired employee, notifying her that she is part of the company's 401(k).

If all you want to do is take the simplest route to a retirement plan, you're task is finished. Enjoy watching your nest egg grow over time as your money goes to work for you. However, you can also optimize your retirement plan. For details on fine-tuning your retirement plan, see Chapter 9.

Understanding target-date funds

Target-date funds are taking the retirement planning world by storm. Simply stated, a *target-date fund* is made up of a preselected blend of stock and bond funds. These stock and bond funds are weighted to be appropriate for a person aiming to retire by a specific year.

Target-date funds are popular because they're easy. Rather than evaluating all the mutual funds in the 401(k) plan and choosing how much money to put into each one, you can buy a target-date fund that does it for you. Better yet, as you age and near retirement, target-date funds lower the riskiness of the blend by increasing the weight in less risky asset classes such as high-quality bonds and cash. This gradual reduction of risk is called a *glide path.*

Given how easy target-date funds make signing up, it's easy to see why they're so popular. About half the people in 401(k) plans now own target-date funds, as shown in Table 6-1.

TABLE 6-1 **Target-Date Funds Are Catching on Fast**

Target-Date Funds	401(k)s in 2006	401(k)s in 2016
Plans offering them	57%	68%
Participants offered	62%	75%
Participants holding	19%	52%
Fund assets	5%	21%

www.ici.org/pdf/2019_factbook.pdf

WARNING

A warning on target-date funds? Didn't I just recommend that you use one? Yes, a target-date fund is a no-brainer when you're trying to get a 401(k) set up while you're in a savings mood. And it's a great choice if you want to put your 401(k) on autopilot. But it's not necessarily the best choice. The fees can be high and the mix of funds might not be right for your situation. Flip to Chapter 7 when you're ready to learn more about whether a target-date fund is a good fit.

Knowing the people involved in your 401(k)

When signing up for your 401(k), a few terms might be unfamiliar, making the process complicated. Following are the ones to know:

» **Participant:** That's you.

» **Entry date:** Some 401(k) plans require you to wait a few weeks or months before you can participate. The entry date is when you're eligible to participate in the plan.

» **Plan sponsor:** The plan sponsor is the organization that offers the 401(k) and sets many of the rules, such as the company match. Usually, your employer is the plan sponsor, but sometimes labor unions or other non-profit organizations act as a plan sponsor.

» **Plan trustee:** Typically, the plan sponsor will hire another company to handle the nuts and bolts of the plan. The plan trustee helps you sign up, collects and invests your contributions, and shows you how to track your balance. Common plan trustees are Fidelity, TIAA, Voya, Vanguard, and Aon Hewitt.

Getting familiar with your 401(k) plan

When you're signing up for your 401(k) plan, you should get a *summary plan description*, or SPD. This document, usually spanning roughly 30 pages, spells out the basics you need to know.

You don't need to read the SPD from front to back. It's nowhere near as interesting as the book in your hands now. But you might want to pay attention to the following information:

» **Employer contributions:** This tells you how much of your contributions your employer plans to match.

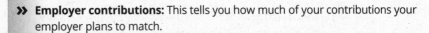

I can't stress this point enough: Find out how much of your contribution your employer will match, and put at least that much in your 401(k).

» **Vesting:** Remember, when your employer puts money into your 401(k), it's usually not yours right away. The *vesting schedule* tells you how long you must stay employed at the company before the matching money is yours to keep.

» **Loan and early distribution rules:** Not all 401(k) plans allow you to borrow from them, but if they do, the details are here. Don't get me started on why borrowing from a 401(k) is a bad idea.

REMEMBER

The SPD is an important document when you're just kicking off your 401(k), but you'll soon need more information when you want to maximize your plan. You need to see Form 5500, a separate document, to get a better understanding of how your plan is operated. More importantly, the 401(k) trustee will have a website to help you keep up on your plan. The 401(k) website allows you to look up your contributions and investment choices, and make important changes to both. You discover how to find and use the Form 5500 and 401(k) website in Chapter 7.

Plugging into Your IRA

One of the great perks of using an IRA is the full control you have over it. You're free to choose the financial firm you'll work with and your investments. But this extra control means you'll have to do some additional legwork to get things set up to your specifications. Don't let the choices stymie you.

Knowing what you'd like to own

It might be tempting to call the usual suspects — the financial firms that always advertise their IRA services during golf matches. But I suggest that you first think a bit about what investments you plan to buy.

The number of financial firms offering IRA services is almost infinite. All the big players and many smaller ones will let you set up an IRA. Most will also waive setup costs just to get you in the door.

IRA providers are distinguished by their investment menus. You'll typically put the following investments in an IRA:

>> **Individual securities:** If you want total control, consider choosing individual bonds or stocks. Rather than owning a mutual fund that holds hundreds of stocks, you might want to own the ten stocks you like best.

>> **Mutual funds:** A mutual fund is the most common investment in IRAs. You put money into a fund that's used to buy individual securities. You then pay a fee. With *index funds*, you own all the securities in an index, such as the Standard & Poor's 500. With *active funds,* you pay fund managers to select the best investments. These funds usually cost more than index funds. Mutual funds are priced at the end of the day.

>> **Exchange-traded fund (ETF):** With an ETF, you own a portion of a basket of investments. Most ETFs are based on indexes and have very low fees. ETFs are priced like stocks, meaning their value changes during the day. ETFs are increasingly popular due to their low fees and no minimum investment.

TIP

If you want to actively trade individual stocks in your IRA, you might not get what you're looking for from a traditional mutual fund company. Consider a discount broker instead. Similarly, if you like the products from a particular mutual fund company, you might want to work directly with that fund company to create an IRA. Keep your investment strategy in mind when you look at IRA providers.

Choosing someone to handle your IRA

The company you choose to house your IRA is important because it will be your financial wingman.

If you call just about any financial firm and ask if they'll take your IRA, the answer will always be yes. IRA customers are dream clients. They invest large sums of money, typically have jobs, and usually don't touch the money for a long time. And many don't pay attention to the fees they're paying.

With that said, most of the firms you'll want to consider for your IRA needs are in one of three main categories: mutual fund companies, traditional and discount brokerages, and robo-advisors.

Robo-advisors are making waves in the IRA business. Originally, robo-advisors were a handful of tech startups with smart people who found a way to make the investing process easier. You'd go to a website and answer a survey, and the site would choose your investments and diversify your holdings. Robo-advisors measured your appetite for risk and spread your money over low-cost investments.

REMEMBER

But the world of robo-advisors has become blurry. Although many firms that are exclusively robo-advisors are still in action, mutual fund companies and brokerages are into the game, too. For example, mutual fund company Vanguard offers one of the most popular robo-advisor services. Keep the changing robo-advisors landscape in mind while considering which route is best for you. If you like your online brokerage, inquire to see if it offers a robo-advisor before moving your money to another firm.

Mutual fund companies

All mutual fund companies are happy to handle your IRA account, and most make the process as simple as possible. However, it's difficult to paint them all with the same brush. For instance, just a few, such as Fidelity, have impressive technology tools. And only some mutual fund companies, Vanguard among them, have adopted innovations such as exchange-traded funds.

If you're interested in using a mutual fund company, you need to understand the advantages and disadvantages it offers for your IRA.

The advantages of mutual fund companies follow:

>> If you buy the company's own funds, you can often avoid paying trading commissions.

>> Customer service representatives have a good understanding of the investments.

>> The companies typically have long track records.

>> These firms are focused on long-term retirement plans. You won't be urged to buy hot stocks or to trade. Some mutual fund companies offer excellent educational materials to help you avoid making short-term decisions that you'll regret later.

The disadvantages of mutual fund companies follow:

>> You're typically encouraged to use the offerings from just one fund family. This restriction might be a problem if you like, say, one fund company for bonds and another for stocks.

>> Mutual fund companies are typically slow to innovate and might not offer some investments you're interested in.

>> Their technology tools can be rudimentary.

>> Popular target-date funds are made up of their own funds, which may or may not be the best for you.

Some of the largest mutual fund players follow:

>> **Vanguard** (www.vanguard.com) is the king of low-cost passive investing. The company's founder, John Bogle, created the company based on the idea that most mutual fund companies spend too much money trying to beat the market, when so few reliably do.

With a Vanguard IRA, you can invest in the fund company's massive suite of best-in-class index funds. You can open an account with an initial deposit of $1,000.

REMEMBER

To buy many of Vanguard's mutual funds, you must invest at least $3,000. There's no cost other than the low Vanguard fund fees. And if you sign up for electronic documents, Vanguard will waive the $20 annual fee.

TIP

Vanguard is a leader in increasingly popular exchange-traded funds (ETFs). You can buy them for no commission at Vanguard, and many ETFs don't have minimum deposits.

» **Fidelity** (www.fidelity.com) shows that a mutual fund company can have major technology chops. The company's website and mobile apps keep up with those offered by brokers and robo-advisors.

Meanwhile, Fidelity is challenging Vanguard on the fees front. Fidelity offers a number of index mutual funds that do not charge an *expense ratio,* which is the annual fee you pay to own a fund and is measured as a percentage of how much you've invested. For example, if you have $10,000 invested and a fund has a 0.2 percent expense ratio, you'll pay a yearly fee of $20.

Fidelity offers the Fidelity ZERO Large Cap Index Fund, which is even less expensive than the rock-bottom 0.05 percent annual fee charged by Vanguard's comparable fund. Fidelity seems aware of its head-to-head competition with Vanguard, as you can see in Figure 6-2.

Fidelity also offers a range of *actively managed mutual funds,* which hire people who try to find stocks that they think will do better than index funds. These funds typically charge more than index funds, up to 1 percent.

» **T. Rowe Price** (www.troweprice.com) is a well-regarded traditional mutual fund company. What makes T. Rowe Price unique is that it focuses on actively managed funds. (It also offers a few index funds, but not as many as Vanguard or Fidelity.) Unlike some other actively managed fund companies, though, T. Rowe Price works directly with investors instead of only through financial advisors. The fees charged by T. Rowe Price funds tend to be higher than the fees for index funds.

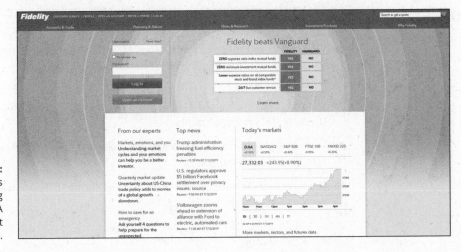

FIGURE 6-2: Fidelity is challenging Vanguard for IRA dollars where it counts — fees.

TIP

Some of the other mutual fund companies that offer IRAs, such as Franklin Templeton (www.franklintempleton.com), work directly with investors to set up accounts. If you're interested in a particular mutual fund company, see if they work directly with individual investors.

Some other large mutual fund companies, such as BlackRock, Invesco, and American Funds, typically work with financial advisors or brokerages. So if you want a BlackRock fund in your IRA, you must hire an advisor to buy it for you or buy it yourself through a brokerage. You see how to do this later in the "Connecting with a Financial Planner" section.

Traditional and discount online brokerages

Sticking with a mutual fund company may be comfortable and convenient, especially if you opened an IRA because your employer doesn't provide a 401(k). But using a mutual fund company for your IRA takes away one of the reasons why you may have opened it: control. Using an IRA allows you to be in the driver's seat of your retirement. Buckle up!

Following are the advantages of an IRA:

>> You're the boss. You can mix and match investment products from different providers.

>> The brokers, especially discount online brokers, usually have best-in-class websites and apps.

>> You have access to brokerage services. Many of these firms started as places to buy and sell stock. If you're interested in online investing, you might want an account here.

>> Many of these brokerages can not only hold your IRA but also help you with checking and savings accounts.

>> Many brokerage firms have branches, so you can head to an office and meet with a person face-to-face.

>> Online brokers are quick to add new features such as ETFs, robo-advisory services, and human help.

Following are the disadvantages of an IRA:

>> Commissions might be charged on investments you could get free elsewhere. This is especially true with some mutual funds.

>> Brokers might steer you toward certain products.

>> Some brokerages are more geared for online trading rather than long-term investing.

Some of the major players are the most popular names in financial services:

>> **Charles Schwab** (www.schwab.com)**:** It's hard to talk about do-it-yourself IRAs without mentioning Chuck. An industry pioneer, Charles Schwab has just about any product you could want. You can buy mutual funds, including thousands with no commission. You can open any type of IRA with no fees and no minimum requirements. The company also offers its own ETFs and provides a robo-advisor, as shown in Figure 6-3.

And if you want to buy or sell individual stocks to avoid annual fees charged by funds, you can do that, too. Schwab used to charge $4.95 a trade. But in late 2019, Schwab, along with most of the major online brokers, cut stock trading commissions to $0. If you buy any of the 500 ETFs in its Schwab ETF OneSource, there's no commission.

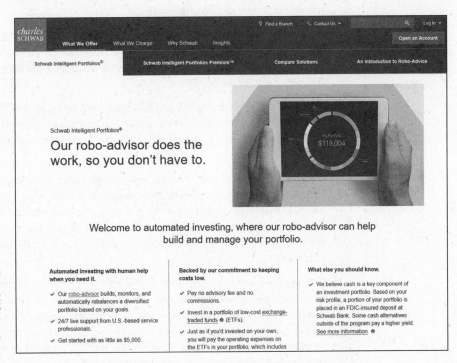

FIGURE 6-3: Charles Schwab offers just about any financial service, including its own robo-advisor.

Schwab also has offerings for people who are not interested in choosing their own investments. Its Schwab Intelligent Portfolios, which is essentially a robo-advisor, will assess your risk appetite and put your money in Schwab ETFs to fit your goals. There's no fee for the service, but there is a $5,000 minimum. You'll also pay the fees on the Schwab funds, which may not be the lowest. If you want a more customized portfolio, you can use Schwab Intelligent Portfolios Premium, which costs $300 upfront and $30 a month thereafter. The minimum deposit is $25,000.

WARNING

Don't be fooled by the so-called free nature of Schwab Intelligent Portfolios. You pay the underlying fees of the ETFs. Also, Schwab will put part of your portfolio in cash. That cash will get next to no return, which costs you in lost interest. For example, suppose Schwab puts $50,000 of your portfolio into cash. If you instead put that money in a savings account at 2 percent interest, you'd get roughly $1,000 a year in interest.

>> **TD Ameritrade** (www.tdameritrade.com): TD Ameritrade is another behemoth in the IRA business. The company, whose roots are in stock trading, is a leader in providing top-notch tools for monitoring your portfolio and the market. They also provide state-of-the-art stock and bond research tools. TD Ameritrade in 2019 cut its $6.95 per stock trade commission to $0. It also has no minimum and no ongoing fees.

If you're looking for more help, check out TD Ameritrade's Essential Portfolios, a robo-advisor that will put your money into low-cost ETFs to match your goals. You pay 0.3 percent a year for Essential Portfolios and up to 0.9 percent for more customized portfolios.

>> **Ally** (www.ally.com): Ally has rapidly grown from being an online bank to a legitimate option for retirement investors. Ally is focused on two types of retirement investors: do-it-yourselfers and those looking for a turnkey solution.

If you're a do-it-yourselfer, you can buy and sell stocks, including ETFs, for no commission. If you're looking for more automated help, Ally offers its Ally Invest Managed Portfolios, a service that is essentially a robo-advisor. You answer questions about your financial goals and Ally puts your money in a number of low-cost ETFs. The service charges a 0.3 percent fee on your balances.

>> **E-Trade** (www.etrade.com): This online brokerage firm has come a long way since its Super Bowl ads featuring a talking baby. Like TD Ameritrade, the company's roots are in low-cost online stock trading, and it offers online stock trades for no commission. E-Trade has since broadened its offerings. In addition to the standard traditional IRA and Roth IRA, it also has an E-Trade Complete IRA that helps you manage withdrawals after you turn 59½.

You can choose from a number of prebuilt portfolios that match your risk tolerance. For an initial deposit of $500, you can build a portfolio made up of mutual funds. If you prefer ETFs, the minimum deposit is $2,500. You do not pay a fee for the portfolio, but you must pay each fund's fee.

For a 0.3 percent annual fee, E-Trade also offers a robo-advisor that is more customized than the prebuilt portfolios. You can choose from five sample portfolios. This option also gives you more control to increase or decrease investments to make your portfolio more or less aggressive.

» **JPMorgan Chase's You Invest** (www.chase.com/personal/investments/you-invest): JPMorgan is competing aggressively with its You Invest offering. If you want to decide which investments you want, you can. The You Invest Trade offering lets you buy stocks and ETFs for $2.95. If you meet certain balance requirements, you may qualify for free trades.

A separate offering called You Invest Portfolios is JPMorgan's robo-advisor. You pay 0.3 percent of your portfolio balance, and JPMorgan puts you into its lineup of ETFs. What's a bit different is that you don't pay any fees for the underlying investments.

For a summary of the offerings described in the preceding list, check out Table 6-2.

TABLE 6-2   ## Five Brokers to Consider for Your IRA

Broker/Bank	Stock Commission	Commission-Free ETFs Available	Robo-Advisor Fee (Annual)
Charles Schwab	$0	All trades free, including ETFs	$0 for basic, $300+$30 a month for advanced version
TD Ameritrade	$0	All trades free, including ETFs	From 0.3% to 0.9% plus investment fees
Ally	$0	All trades free, including ETFs	0.3% plus investment fees
E-Trade	$0	All trades free, including ETFs	0.3% plus investment fees
JPMorgan Chase's You Invest	$2.95 (after the first 100 free trades)	First 100 trades free; some customers get more free trades if they have other relationships with the bank	0.35%

TIP

Most major banks offer their customers IRAs. If you already have a savings or checking account with a bank, see whether an IRA account at the same bank makes sense. You might get additional perks if your balance is high enough.

Robo-advisors

Online shopping has made it easy to get a Bart Simpson chess set delivered to your door the next day. Technology is trying to bring the same convenience to your IRA.

Some financial firms are first and foremost robo-advisors. Betterment and Wealthfront were pioneers in the robo-advisor business, but they broadened their offerings as traditional brokers launched robo-advisory businesses.

Why are online brokers opening their own robo-advisors? For people who don't want to think about IRAs, a robo-advisor can be a good option. Just answer a risk questionnaire, and the system chooses a handful of investments that fit your risk profile. Most robo-advisors charge 0.3 percent or so a year, which is much less than the 1 percent or more charged by human advisors.

To see when a real financial advisor might make the most sense for you, see the "Connecting with a Financial Planner" section, later in this chapter.

In addition to simplicity, robo-advisors offer the following advantages:

>> **Automatic rebalancing:** All robo-advisors, including those from the mutual fund providers listed in the "Mutual fund companies" section and the brokers listed in Table 6-2, handle *rebalancing*. This is the process of shifting money from one asset class to another if one is doing so well you own too much of it.

>> **Automatic tax-loss harvesting:** If you're losing money on an investment and sell it and then wait more than 30 days to buy it back, you might get a tax write-off. Most robo-advisors are smart enough to do this for you.

>> **Instant diversification:** You know to not put too many eggs in one basket. The same is true for investing. You can learn about building an asset allocation in Chapter 12, or you can let a robo-advisor handle it for you.

>> **Dollar investing:** This perk is subtle. If you want to invest a set amount in your robo-advisor account, you can. The robo-advisor handles all the math on how many shares you can buy.

>> **No commissions on transactions:** Typically, after you pay the annual fee, there's no commission when you buy or sell.

Most of these advantages of robo-advisors apply to the robo-advisory businesses of the brokers, too.

REBALANCING: A FREE LUNCH IN INVESTING

What the heck is rebalancing and why is it an advantage with a robo-advisor? Suppose that you're a typical investor who has a moderate appetite for risk. You have a $100,000 in an IRA. You put 60 percent ($60,000) of your portfolio in stocks and 40 percent ($40,000) in bonds. Perfect balance.

Now imagine that stocks go up 25 percent, as they can, and bonds rise 3 percent. Your portfolio is now worth $116,200. What's the problem?

Your stocks are worth $75,000 and your bonds $41,200, so your portfolio is nearly 65 percent stocks and 35 percent bonds. You didn't touch your portfolio, but now it's too aggressive. You're overexposed to riskier stock positions and your safer bond portfolio is too small. If the market declines, you'll get hit harder than you want.

If you were using a regular brokerage account, you'd need to put things back in balance yourself. You'd do that by calculating that your stock allocation, at 60 percent, should be $69,720, or $5,280 less. Then you'd sell enough stocks and buy enough bonds to get back in balance (and perhaps incur commissions in the process).

Robo-advisors know when your portfolio is out of balance and do the buying and selling for you.

Rebalancing forces you to buy asset classes when they're relatively cheap and sell them when they're relatively expensive. Rebalancing has been shown to boost returns and lower risk. If you want to read more, check out Vanguards' opus on the topic at www.vanguard.com/pdf/icrpr.pdf.

Following are the disadvantages of robo-advisors:

>> **Fees:** All this robo-magic isn't free. You can save money by doing everything the robo-advisors do, including rebalancing. A 0.3 percent fee might sound small, but it adds up fast. The fee is $300 a year on a $100,000 portfolio. If you don't trade much, a broker might cost less.

>> **Little to no control:** If you want any say in what you're buying, a robo-advisor might frustrate you. Some robo-advisors allow you to customize what you're buying, but fees might rise.

>> **Difficulty seeing what you're buying:** Robo-advisors can be a black box. You might know only that you're buying a stock ETF or a bond ETF, not that you're buying an ETF from BlackRock, Vanguard, or State Street, or another provider.

If you're looking to team up with a pure-play robo-advisor, consider the following:

>> **Betterment** (www.betterment.com/): When you get to Betterment's site, shown in Figure 6-4, you immediately get a sense of its mission: simplicity. The site breaks down the three objectives you might have: Getting started for the first time, completely automating your portfolio, and having more of a say.

Unlike some robo-advisors, Betterment gives you more control and lets you tweak its suggestions. Prefer to be 30 percent invested in bonds rather than the 40 percent Betterment recommends? You can change the allocation.

Betterment's basic offering costs 0.25 percent a year, plus the fees of the underlying investments. If you want access to a financial planner, you can get the Premium service for 0.4 percent.

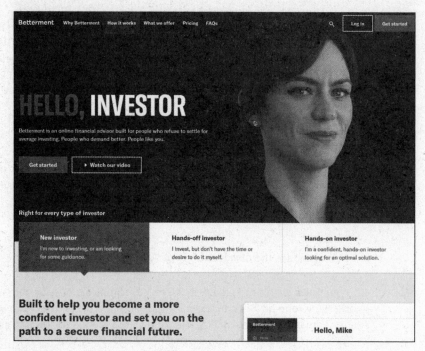

FIGURE 6-4:
Betterment offers robo-advisor services and lets you set the level of automation.

>> **Wealthfront** (www.wealthfront.com): Wealthfront is the chief pure-play robo-advisor rival to Betterment. Wealthfront is more focused on people who want total automation. It also adds some nice banking features. For instance, Wealthfront offers a high-interest savings account where you can put cash you don't want to invest right now. Many brokers pay next to nothing for cash

sitting in your account. The service charges 0.25 percent of the amount in your portfolio, including cash.

>> **Personal Capital** (www.personalcapital.com): At first, Personal Capital looks similar to a money-tracking service such as Mint.com. It has two powerful tools: The financial accounts monitoring tool helps you pinpoint your spending, and the retirement planning tool looks at your balances and tells you how you're progressing toward retirement.

But Personal Capital is also an advisory service, including a robo-advisor. For a 0.89 percent annual fee, Personal Capital will recommend a portfolio of ETFs. Personal Capital also offers live financial planners who will help you online not only with retirement planning but also other goals.

>> **Acorns** (www.acorns.com/): When planning for retirement, you just have to get started — even if you have only a small amount to invest. Acorns takes this theory to the extreme. This robo-advisor lets you save and invest your pocket change.

Acorns offers several services to help you with your spending and investing. And its Acorns Later service can give you a hand planning for retirement. It all starts with an Acorns debit card linked to an Acorns checking account. When you buy goods and services with your Acorns debit card, Acorns will round up the amount and invest the rest. If you buy a can of soda for $1.50, Acorns will round up to $2 and invest the 50¢.

You might decide to put this round-up money to work for retirement. If so, Acorns will recommend the right type of IRA for you. Everything is automatic, and Acorns will spread your money in a variety of ETFs, primarily from Vanguard.

WARNING

The Acorns IRA service is a reasonable $2 a month — until you're a millionaire. Then it's a pricey $100 a month per million invested. Bill Gates, you might want to put your IRA somewhere else.

Table 6-3 compares the major robo-advisors.

TABLE 6-3   ## Comparing Robo-Advisors

Broker/Bank	Account Minimum	Robo-Advisor Fee (Annual)
Betterment	$0 for basic digital and $100,000 for premium	0.25% for basic digital and 0.4% for premium, plus investment fees
Wealthfront	$500 (more for additional services)	0.25% plus investment fees
Personal Capital	$25,000	0.89% for first $1 million invested
Acorns Later	$5	$2 a month with under $1 million invested, and $100 per million a month after $1 million

Connecting with a Financial Planner

If you have the time and the interest, you can build a retirement plan yourself. This book will help. And employer plans, such as 401(k)s, do most of the work for you. In addition, robo-advisors make it easier than ever to set up a savings and retirement plan. All the companies listed in this chapter will practically trip over themselves to help you manage your retirement portfolio.

But in theory, you could fix your plumbing or your car, too. Do you really want to? Do you have the time to learn how?

Retirement planning is such an important financial and personal task that it might be worthwhile to call in a professional. Consider working with a financial advisor to help you build a retirement plan if you

>> **Need a second opinion:** After reading this book, you'll know where you want to open a retirement account, how to set up the account, and what types of investments you want to own. But you might want someone with more experience to look over your decisions and give his or her opinion. Your 65-year-old self might thank you.

>> **Don't have time:** It's sad to see people put off retirement planning when they're young because they're too busy. Time and patience are two of your biggest allies when saving. If you wait until you're 40 to get serious about retirement planning, you will have to make a greater financial sacrifice to reach your goals.

>> **Don't want to learn (or have something more profitable to do with your time):** Some people are simply not interested in learning about asset allocations, asset classes, and IRAs. That's okay. Sometimes it's smarter to pay someone to do something you don't want to do, so you can focus on making money doing things you enjoy.

WARNING

You might be thinking, "Stop right here. You mean I can pay someone to worry about all this for me?" They answer is yes, but the cost is steep. Many financial planners charge 1 percent of your assets (or more) annually to manage your retirement plan. Again, this might not sound like much, but over time, these fees eat away at your returns.

To help you decide whether or not to hire someone, you need to know how much it will cost to get help. Vanguard has a useful tool that shows the cost of advice, as shown in Figure 6-5. To check it out, go to `https://personal.vanguard.com/us/insights/retirement/cost-affect-retirement-spending-tool`. The tool requires Flash, so it might not work on all browsers.

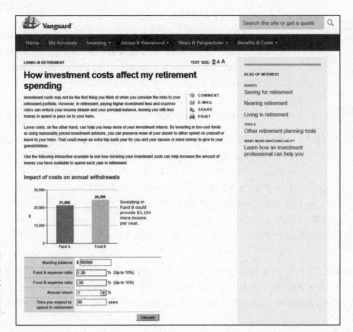

FIGURE 6-5:
Vanguard's
investment cost
tool shows you
the cost of a
financial planner.

Let's say you have a retirement portfolio worth $500,000. If you manage your own portfolio, you could likely do it for 0.35 percent a year (including investing fees). This would provide you with $24,369 in monthly income over a 30-year retirement if you get a 7 percent annual return, says the Vanguard tool.

If you hire someone who puts you in the same plan, your cost could be 1.35 percent. Then you can safely withdraw only $21,265 a year, or $3,104 less a year.

TIP

Some financial planners are worth what they charge and more because they offer tax and estate-planning services as part of their fees. Those services, when bought on their own, are costly. Planners, too, can help you avoid costly mistakes — such as selling in a panic during a market crash.

I'm not saying that planners aren't worthwhile. Just know how much the advice will cost, and then decide.

Finding a financial planner

If you decide that you'd like an advisor to help you with your retirement plan, choose a qualified planner that you trust and feel comfortable with. Referrals from friends are fine, but before hiring a planner, you'll want to do the following:

>> **Check certifications:** A number of organizations require advisors to take tests and stay educated on financial topics. The best-known designation for

advisors is the CFP, or certified financial planner. To get the right to put CFP after their name, planners must demonstrate competence by taking an exam. You can look up advisors to see if they are CFPs at www.letsmakeaplan. org/?utm_source=LMAP&utm_medium=header&utm_content=homepage&utm_ campaign=header&utm_source=LMAP&utm_medium=header&utm_content= homepage&utm_campaign=header

» **Check regulatory paperwork:** Financial advisors are required to be regis-tered. They must either file the proper paperwork with the Securities and Exchange Commission (the federal financial watchdog) or FINRA (an industry body). FINRA runs a site called BrokerCheck (https://brokercheck.finra. org/) where you can look up everything you need to know about a planner. Check out any planner or firm you're thinking about working with, as described next.

BrokerCheck is a one-stop place to search for all the documentation you should consider before working with an advisor on your retirement plan. From the BrokerCheck search screen, you can look up firms or individual advisors.

To look up a firm, do the following:

1. **Go to the BrokerCheck site at** https://brokercheck.finra.org/.

2. **At the top of the page, select the Firm tab.**

3. **Enter the firm's name and click the Search button.**

For example, I typed Fidelity Brokerage Services.

4. **Click the card that shows the firm.**

The summary page shown in Figure 6-6 appears. Make sure that the firm is registered and read any disciplinary actions taken against it.

TIP

When you look up an individual advisor, know that there are two types: brokers and investment advisors. Brokers, who may be paid for selling certain financial products, are regulated by Finra. You'll find complete records about brokers on BrokerCheck. Investment advisors are paid for giving you advice and are regulated by the SEC. If you enter an investment advisor's name in BrokerCheck, you'll be forwarded to their public disclosure with the SEC.

What are you looking for? Basically a clean record: no serious disciplinary actions against the individual or firm. Read any complaints and decide if they're serious. Also, make sure the advisor is registered to work in your state.

The article at www.fool.com/investing/2019/02/17/3-ways-to-avoid-financial-advisors-who-have-scamme.aspx shows you what to look for when examining an advisor.

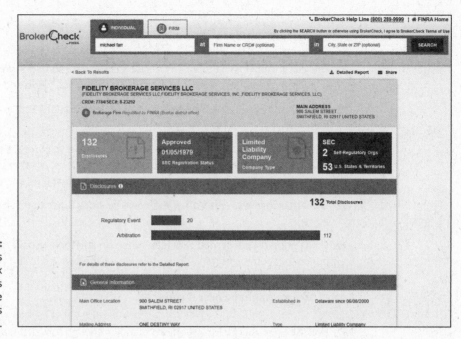

FIGURE 6-6:
Fidelity's BrokerCheck record shows you what the regulator knows about the firm.

WARNING

A bad financial planner can cause enormous damage to your retirement plan. The biggest problem I've seen with some advisors is overpromising. To win your business, advisors might tell you that they can deliver average annual returns of 20 percent. But you know from reading this book that US stock market returns are about 10 percent. So to try to get those returns, the planners might boost the riskiness of your portfolio.

Deciding what is right for you

In many ways, it's a great time to be someone planning for retirement because the options are plentiful — maybe too plentiful. If you're a do-it-yourself investor, online brokerage commissions are low and sometimes even zero. If you'd like a low-cost, easy solution, target-date funds or robo-advisors are great options. And it's easier than ever to find qualified advisors who want to help you out.

If you're willing to put in the time and effort, building your own retirement plan will likely save you money. Plus, by doing it yourself, you can make sure your retirement money works in concert with money you hold in taxable accounts.

People who want to hand over their retirement planning have three main choices now. Do you hire a human advisor, sign up for a robo-advisor, or just buy a target-date fund? The decision is personal, but the following guidelines might help.

An advisor might be best if you

>> Feel comfortable going to an office, sitting down with someone you know, and building a relationship. Many advisors strive to be your friend and confidant.

>> Own a business. Business owners have complex situations that an advisor can help with.

>> Have a complicated estate. If you have trusts, partnerships, real estate holdings, outside taxable brokerage accounts, pensions, or other unusual assets, a specialist might save you money on estate-planning and tax issues.

>> Want to own investments other than passive index funds that sell through advisors.

>> Aren't primarily concerned with fees. A human advisor is usually the costliest option, but you might think it's worthwhile for the peace of mind you get.

A robo-advisor might be best if you

>> Feel like your financial situation isn't complex enough to warrant a human advisor.

>> Hope to hand over the retirement plan, but you want technology tools to see how you're doing and still want to play a role.

>> Would like an easy solution for diversifying an IRA.

>> Don't think your expected retirement date reflects your risk appetite. For instance, you might be 25 years old but can't stomach much volatility. A robo-advisor would let you modify your portfolio's risk level downward.

>> Prefer passive investing and low fees. Most robo-advisors use low-cost ETFs — and your total costs tend to be reasonable.

A target-date fund might be best if you

>> Are investing in an employer-sponsored plan. Many 401(k) plans offer target-date funds but not robo-advisors.

>> Want to own just one investment. The target-date fund is a single financial box that owns multiple investments.

>> Prefer a specific fund company. Many target-date funds are built from mutual funds from one fund family. If you like a fund company and buy their target-date funds, you get their funds plus their portfolio-construction knowledge.

2

Using Online Resources

Chapter **7**

Managing and Optimizing Your 401(k)

Y ou're well on your way with your retirement plan. At this point, you've probably signed up for your company's 401(k) plan, so you can sock away money. Retirement, here you come!

But wait a second. You might be patting yourself on the back for fighting the powerful force of inaction, which is more than half the battle with retirement planning. But if you just follow the automatic sign-up selections for your 401(k), you're not getting the most out of it.

Plans that auto-enroll employees tend to start with low initial contribution rates, often just 1 percent of your pay. And the default choices for your investment options tend to be generic. To get the max from your 401(k), you need to do a bit of research. The process starts with getting registered online with your 401(k) plan provider's website.

After you're online, you'll want to know how much of your pay you're contributing and try to bump it up as much as you can (and certainly enough to get the maximum company match). Next, it's time to look over how your nest egg is allocated to make sure your portfolio matches your goals.

In this chapter, you learn how to research the various options available in your plan. None of this is as difficult as it might sound now. I step you through an example using an actual 401(k) system.

REMEMBER

Most of the examples in this chapter use Voya, a popular 401(k) provider. If your 401(k) is with another provider, the screens will look different but the concepts are the same. If you look around your provider's website, you should be able to find the same options as those on the Voya site.

Getting Online

Many employers tout their 401(k) plans as a job perk. But typically you're on your own when it comes to setting up online access. In some ways, this situation is symbolic of how the responsibility for retirement planning has shifted to employees. Not only do employers want to scale back how much they contribute to your retirement, many don't even want to help you manage the account.

Fear not. That's why I'm here. First, I show you how to register for online access. Then you look at your plan and spot areas that you can improve.

Registering for 401(k) access

Most 401(k)s are established on paper. The paperwork you sign when you join a company opens the account and gives the 401(k) plan administrator the right to take money out of your paycheck.

But you can't do much with the account until you register for online assess with the 401(k) plan site. After that, you can see your balances, make changes, and evaluate how you're doing.

You might be surprised at some of the online tools you can pick up right from your 401(k) plan provider. Nearly all 401(k) sites that I've seen offer useful calculators and information to help you better prepare for retirement.

What kicks off the process of setting up 401(k) account access? Ironically, it's probably snail mail. At some point after starting a job or signing up for a 401(k), you should get a letter in the mail from your 401(k) administrator with your summary plan description. This document, similar to Figure 7-1, lets you know that the account is established and that you can set up online access.

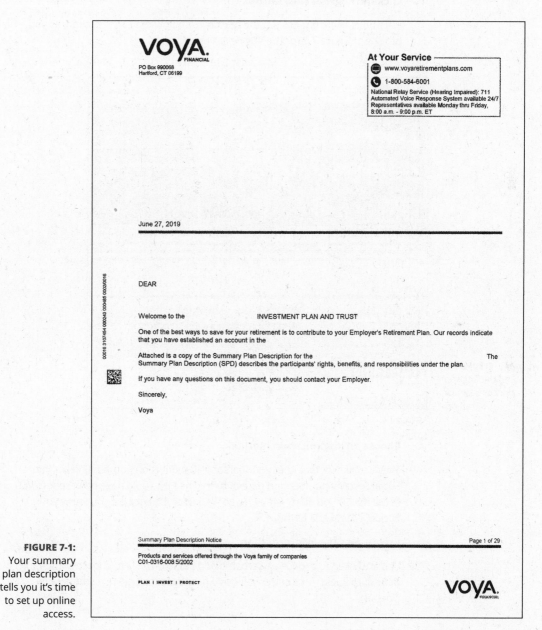

FIGURE 7-1: Your summary plan description tells you it's time to set up online access.

If you look closely, you'll see a website address in the upper-right corner of the summary plan description in Figure 7-1. In this example, it's `www.voyaretirementplans.com`. From here, you'll want to follow these steps to register:

1. **Click the Register Now button.**

   Just about all 401(k) sites put the button just below the Log In section, as you can see in Figure 7-2 for the Voya example.

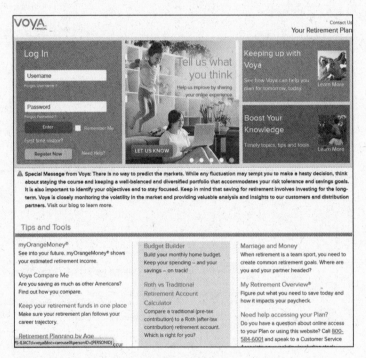

FIGURE 7-2: Find the Register Now or a similar option.

2. **Choose an identification method.**

   Sites usually ask for either your personal identification number (PIN) or your Social Security number and date of birth. The PIN would have been sent to you in the mail. If you didn't get a PIN, go with door #2, because you know your Social Security and birthday.

3. **Create your log-in information.**

   You are asked to choose a username and password. Try to choose something difficult to guess — or better yet, use a password manager (see the nearby sidebar).

TIP

Passwords are getting more complicated in an effort to keep hackers out. Choose a password that's not a real word, and use a string of symbols, numbers, and uppercase and lowercase letters. Try to come up with something only you will know. For example, suppose you're a Star Wars fan. Rather than using *starwars* as a password, use *MT4ceBWY*. (Get it? *May the Force be with you.*)

PASSWORD MANAGERS CAN SAVE YOU HEADACHES

I know what you're thinking. Another hard-to-remember username and password? Yes, our lives are filled with these for bank accounts, streaming video accounts, and online shopping site accounts.

But don't take the easy way out. Although it's tempting to use the same username and password everywhere, doing so is a bad idea. If your password is compromised and obtained by a hacker, an annoying breach can become more serious.

So how are you supposed to remember all these passwords? Consider a password manager, which is an app that stores all your passwords in an encrypted file that only you can view. It also generates passwords that are nearly impossible for anyone to guess.

LastPass (www.lastpass.com) and Dashlane (www.dashlane.com) are two popular password managers. To use them, you visit the websites and sign up. I understand the irony — you're sick of choosing passwords, so I tell you to set up another password.

But this password will be the password to end all passwords. After you open your password manager account, you enter all your account information, including the username and password of each of your accounts. Then, wherever you log in, you'll have ready access to your passwords. You can download password manager apps for Android or iOS, too, and see your passwords on your phone. Or you can download *extensions,* or add-ons, for your computer's browser.

If you're using Microsoft's Edge browser, you can download the LastPass extension from the Microsoft Store in Windows 10, as shown in the figure.

(continued)

(continued)

Password Managers are mostly free — to a point. The free offering from LastPass is comprehensive and syncs passwords over all your devices. If you need tech support or sharing options, sign up for its Premium service at $4.99 a month. Dashlane lets you store 50 passwords on one device for free. If you have more passwords or want to use the app on multiple devices, you pay $4.99 a month for their Premium service.

Getting to know your 401(k) tools

The beauty of 401(k) plans is their hands-off nature. If you're like many 401(k) investors, after you sign up for the plan (see Chapter 6), you don't want to think about it — and you certainly don't want to do is dig around the various features of the 401(k) provider's website.

But you might be surprised at some of the online tools you can pick up right from your 401(k) plan provider. Nearly all 401(k) sites that I've seen offer useful calculators and information to help you better prepare for retirement.

TIP

Using the tools on your 401(k) plan provider's site is helpful because you already have log-in information with them, and many of the tools can be personalized because your details are already there.

A few helpful tools to look for on your 401(k) plan provider's site follow:

>> **Calculators:** Most 401(k) providers will use your account details as inputs for calculators. You'll likely find a contribution calculator that will tell you if you're

putting enough in your 401(k) to meet your full-year contribution goal. This tool is useful if you want to max out your 401(k), putting in the most legally allowed. The tool will also tell you what percentage you should take out of your paycheck to hit your annual contribution target.

Also look for a retirement overview calculator. This tool helps you see how much money you should have when you retire based on your savings rate, income needs, and rate of return.

Lastly, 401(k) providers offer retirement income estimate calculators. These tools look at how much you're saving and your expected returns, and estimate how much income you might expect in retirement.

>> **Investing education:** You'll likely find useful articles and videos to coach you on the importance of diversification and asset allocation. You might also find information on related topics such as estate planning.

>> **Risk questionnaires:** Some 401(k) sites feature basic questionnaires that will help you see how much risk you can handle. You'll be asked how much you know about investing, how much volatility you can handle, and your age.

Some 401(k)-planning sites use this information, paired with what the plan administrator already knows about you, to offer a possible asset allocation, as shown in Figure 7-3. Your *asset allocation* is the mix of asset classes expected to give you the best return for your level of risk.

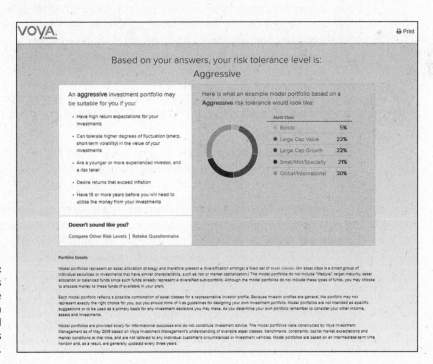

FIGURE 7-3:
Voya's questionnaire recommends a portfolio based on what it knows about you.

Typically, your appetite for risk is a function of how much *volatility,* or ups and downs in portfolio value, you can endure. For example, suppose that the target-date fund for your retirement year suggests a middle-of-the-road portfolio of 60 percent stocks and 40 percent bonds. But after taking the questionnaire, the 401(k) provider's site might suggest a more aggressive portfolio with 70 percent stocks and 30 percent bonds.

Checking your performance

Before you think about making your 401(k) work better for you, it's wise to see how it's doing so far. 401(k) provider sites help you track how much return you're getting on your money.

REMEMBER

Measuring investment performance is important and something you should count on from your 401(k) provider. The results of the calculation tell you if your investment choices are delivering what you need to reach your goals. Performance statistics also tell you if you're getting results that are at least keeping up with the average. If your portfolio returns are less than market returns, or indexes, that's a big sign that you should optimize your 401(k).

Most 401(k) sites will help you see your portfolio performance in two ways:

>> **At the fund level:** Nearly all 401(k) plans have an Investments section. Here you can look up how the funds have performed over various time periods, including short periods (such as a month or year) and longer periods (such as five or ten years). The data is typically shown in a table like the one in Figure 7-4.

TIP

If you own only the 401(k)'s target-date fund, look up your particular fund in the investments list. This might be all the information you need to know how you're doing.

>> **As a personal rate of return:** 401(k) providers don't just tell you how the funds in the plan have performed. They also keep track of how you have done.

What's the difference between the funds' returns and your returns? Keep in mind that some investors spread their portfolios over multiple funds. They might also move money from one fund to another. The timing of your contributions matter, too. The personal rate of return incorporates all these factors to arrive at your total return.

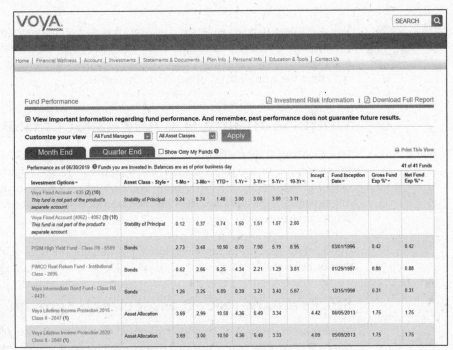

FIGURE 7-4:
The Investments section shows you how each of the individual investments in the plan have done.

Checking Your Portfolio Allocation

The types of investments where you put your money have an enormous bearing on the returns you can expect. It's like cooking a pot of chili. The types of ingredients you use will determine the results. Dump in lots of sriracha hot sauce, and your final dish will sizzle on the tongue and definitely stand out from the bland crowd. You'd better hope you like spicy food. Similarly, if you put beans in your cuisine, that will cool things down. Not much flavor, perhaps. But you might be looking for something to offset the high-octane sriracha.

Your 401(k), believe it or not, is similar. The types of investments you stir into the portfolio pot determine how hot and wild it is. To torture our analogy just a bit more, think of stocks as the sriracha and bonds as the beans.

Typically, most 401(k) plans feature various investments that fall into one of two asset classes: stocks or bonds. Your *asset allocation* is a recipe that tells you how much of each *asset class* you'll own.

Some experts think the asset classes you choose determine 90 percent of your portfolio returns. Others think it's much less than that. But just about everyone agrees that asset allocations are important.

TIP

You don't need to be an asset class mastermind to manage your 401(k). In general, stocks are the riskier part of your portfolio and bonds are the safer part. But the bond world has some caveats that 401(k) investors should know about. You find out about the complexities of bonds in Chapter 12.

Understanding the key asset classes

When looking at asset classes — like flipping through pages of a recipe — you can take precision to the finest degree. For instance, a recipe might call for ground beef. But you might decide that you want 90 percent lean, organic, free-range angus beef. Similarly, rather than just adding stocks to your portfolio, you can add large-company stock.

Again, asset allocations can be detailed, but most of the time you'll be looking at stocks and bonds.

Stocks are the riskiest asset class for growth

The high-octane part of your portfolio will usually be stocks, sometimes called *equity*. With stocks, you're entitled to owning a piece of a company. Your upside is technically unlimited. If the company you own does well, your ownership stake will rise as the company gets more valuable.

TECHNICAL STUFF

Generally, stocks are classified further by size and style as follows:

>> **Size:** The size of a stock is determined by the size of the company. *Large-cap (large-capitalization) stocks* are the most valuable companies, such as Microsoft and Apple. *Small caps* are smaller and typically faster-growing firms. Small-cap stocks are riskier than large-cap, but the expected returns are larger too.

>> **Style:** A stock's valuation determines its *style*. Stocks that are cheap compared to their net worth are considered *value stocks*. The stocks that investors are paying up for are called *growth stocks*.

Bonds add stability to your portfolio

Bonds might seem boring, but what they can do for your portfolio is exciting. Because bonds are IOUs, you know what you can expect to get in return. Unless the borrower defaults, you get your money back plus an agreed-upon interest rate.

Compared to stocks, bonds tend to be the safer asset class because of their rules regarding what you'll get back from the loans you provide. That said, different types of bonds behave differently. The major issuers of bonds follow:

>> **The U.S. government:** The largest seller of bonds is none other than the good old United States. The U.S. government routinely auctions off bonds, which are often called *Treasuries*. The prices that investors pay for these debt securities sets prices for the entire bond market. Treasuries are the safest bonds you can buy because the U.S. government is highly unlikely to default.

WARNING

Investors sometimes refer to treasuries as *risk-free bonds*, but that's misleading. It's true that default isn't likely, but bond investors face other risks — the biggest risk is inflation. If you're getting a 3 percent return from your Treasury when inflation is 2 percent, you'll feel pretty good. Your money is at least growing as fast as prices are rising. But if inflation spikes above 3 percent, you're no longer keeping up. Soon the $25,000 in income generated by your portfolio won't buy the same amount of yearly groceries.

>> **Government agencies:** Separate government agencies, such as for housing loans or small-business loans, issue bonds. These bonds are typically backed by the U.S. government.

>> **Companies:** Building new factories or hiring new people before launching a product requires lots of cash. Many companies will sell bonds to pull off this cash-balancing act. When big companies such as Microsoft or Apple borrow, the bonds are called *investment-grade bonds*. Because default risk with such large companies is low, investment-grade bonds typically have yields only slightly higher than Treasuries.

TIP

The greater the risk you won't get your money back from a bond, the higher the interest rate you should receive.

On the opposite site of the bond spectrum are riskier companies that could very well default. Bonds sold by these less stable companies are called *high-yield bonds* or *junk bonds*.

>> **Cities and municipalities:** When a city wants to build a new stadium or fix roads, they'll often borrow by using *muni bonds*. Interestingly, the interest paid on these muni bonds is not taxable at the federal level and may be free from state tax, too. These bonds tend to be safe because most of these borrowers pay back the debt.

REMEMBER

Bonds issued by cities and municipalities aren't usually a good choice for retirement accounts because these accounts are already tax deferred. And when you take money out of a 401(k), it's taxable, even if it came from a tax-free muni bond.

Looking at your current mix
without using a calculator

Now that you know the importance of asset allocation, it's time to see what yours looks like. Luckily, 401(k) providers will do the work for you.

TIP

Typically, you'll find an Investments Mix or Plan Investment Chart section at the 401(k) provider's site. If you own a number of investments, the site will include all your positions. Your holdings in each asset class will then be divided into your total portfolio balance to get the weightings.

I use Vanguard's 401(k) plan as an example in Figure 7-5. Vanguard shows your total account balance and then breaks it down so you can see the percentage of your portfolio in stocks, bonds, and *short-term reserves* (cash or something like cash). In the example, the investor has 65 percent of the portfolio in stocks and 35 percent in bonds.

FIGURE 7-5:
Vanguard's 401(k) site breaks down all your holdings and shows you the asset allocation.

TIP

If you own target-date funds, 401(k) plans typically handle the asset allocation reporting differently. A pie chart might show that you own a multi-asset fund, which is one fund that holds many types of assets. The Vanguard site features a pie chart showing you where your contributions are being invested. In this example, our saver is investing the entire contribution, 100 percent, in bonds.

Does that mean you're not diversified? Not at all! You just need to dig deeper to see your asset allocation. Click a link or an option labeled Fund Information Sheet or something similar. A summary sheet appears, similar to the one from the Voya plan in Figure 7-6.

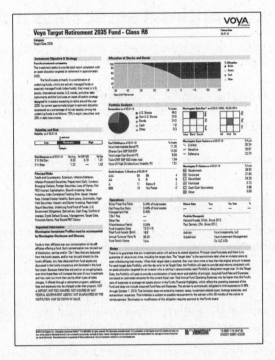

FIGURE 7-6:
Voya's fund
summary page
lets you see the
asset allocation
of your target-
date fund.

Look more closely, and you'll see the following entries:

» **Portfolio analysis:** In the middle of the page is a pie chart that describes your asset allocation. The example target-date fund is 49 percent U.S. stocks, 24.6 percent non-U.S. stocks, 24.5 percent bonds, and 1.9 percent cash and other.

» **Top *five* holdings:** This section provides the names of the most significant investments held in the fund. Although the target-date fund is a mutual fund, it owns a large (10.5 percent) stake in a low-cost ETF, the iShares Core S&P 500.

» **Credit analysis:** This section has details on the types of bonds you own. Bonds rated AAA, AA, A, or BBB are considered investment grade. AAA-rated bonds are typically Treasuries. Bonds rated BB and lower are junk bonds.

» **Expense ratio:** In the Operations section, you find the net expense ratio, which is how much you're paying to own the fund a year. In this example, the person is paying 0.44 percent. So if the person has invested $100,000, he or she is paying $440 a year in fees.

>> **Morningstar Style Box:** Remember the two stock classifications, size and style? In this section, you find out how much of your target-date fund is in each classification.

Finding your optimal asset class mix

You're starting to find information from the 401(k) provider's site that can help you determine whether your 401(k) is as good as it can be.

TIP

Third-party sites can help you further analyze your 401(k) as well as your IRA, usually for a fee. You look at several third-party services in Chapter 9. Here, you focus on tools available from your 401(k) provider.

To figure out how to allocate your portfolio by using your 401(k) provider's site, follow these steps:

1. **Complete the 401(k) provider's questionnaire.**

You are asked a list of questions designed to determine how much of a return you need to reach your retirement goals. Vanguard, for example, asks you 11 questions.

2. **Examine the target allocation.**

Using your answers, the 401(k) provider's site creates a target asset allocation for you, such as the one presented previously in Figure 7-5.

In the example, the 401(k) investor is playing it too safe, with 65.4 percent in stocks versus 76 percent in the target allocation. The investor should make an adjustment by exchanging some bond funds for stock funds.

3. **Examine your target-date allocation.**

If you own a target-date fund, don't assume that the underlying asset allocation is correct for you. After completing the questionnaire, you'll want to look at the investment summary, which will be similar to the one presented previously in Figure 7-6. If the summary doesn't match your target allocation, you might want to buy a target date for a different year.

TECHNICAL
STUFF

A risk questionnaire might select a target asset allocation with different asset classes than you see in the target-date fund's summary sheet. Vanguard's questionnaire calls for a 76.1 percent weighting in stocks. But Voya's target-date fund has stocks broken down by U.S. stocks and non-US stocks; there's no category for just stocks. You can solve this mismatch in two ways. Use a different questionnaire, one that generates asset classes matching what you can buy. Typically, your 401(k) provider's questionnaire matches the asset classes in the plan. (Refer to Chapter 5 for other questionnaires you can take.) The other option is to simply add the US stock and non-US stock allocations and see how the total compares.

4. **Consider fees and returns.**

Look at your portfolio's returns and the fees you're charged. If long-term returns for a fund are lackluster, you might want to take your money elsewhere. It's not only returns that matter. Fees are critical, too.

Try to pay 0.6 percent or less for all fees for investments in your 401(k) plan. Chapter 9 describes some tools that can help you further analyze if you're getting adequate returns.

Changing your asset allocation

Now that you've looked at your asset allocation, you might decide that everything is okay. If you're in a target-date fund and most of your retirement money is in the 401(k), your job is likely finished.

TIP

In most cases, it's tough to beat target-date funds. And some target-date funds contain better investment options than you can buy on your own. For instance, in the 401(k) plan with the target-date fund shown in Figure 7-6, the excellent low-cost iShares ETF could not be bought individually.

If your asset allocation is off, it's time to make some adjustments. You can adjust your asset allocation in three ways:

>> **Change elections:** If your asset allocation is only slightly off, you can adjust slowly by changing your *elections,* which tell the 401(k) provider where to put money taken out of your paycheck.

Suppose that you make $80,000 a year and contribute 10 percent, or $8,000, to your 401(k). You elected to put 65 percent in stocks but need to get your stock positions closer to 76 percent to match your target. You could change your election to stock to 76 percent, and going forward you would work toward that percentage. A more drastic option is to elect to put 100 percent of your future contributions to stocks, which would correct the allocation more quickly.

>> **Transfer funds:** If you want to fix your off-balance allocation right away and have a simple portfolio that needs only a minor adjustment, a fund transfer is a good option. You sell a fund that you have too much of, and move the proceeds of the sale into the fund you need more of. Your future contributions are unchanged because you haven't touched your election.

TIP

In a taxable account, a fund transfer is a big deal. When you sell an investment outside a retirement account, you may owe tax on the gain. In a retirement account, however, you can sell the investment for a profit and pay tax only when you withdraw the money. Pretty sweet.

>> **Reallocate:** To quickly fix a complex portfolio with many asset classes that are off target, it might be time for the reallocate option. Using the reallocate feature on the site, you'll see a list of the percentage weightings of all your current investments. Go through them one by one and choose the percentage weighting you'd prefer. After you approve the reallocation plan, the 401(k) provider figures out how much of each fund must be bought or sold. Most 401(k) sites have similar reallocation screens; Figure 7-7 is the one from Voya.

| More Resources | Message Center | My Profile | Logout |

VOYA FINANCIAL

SEARCH

Home | Financial Wellness | Account | Investments | Statements & Documents | Plan Info | Personal Info | Education & Tools | Contact Us

Reallocate Balances

Certain funds may not be available for reallocation. These funds are not listed below. This transaction will reallocate between the funds that are available but will not touch any existing balance you may have in the funds that are not available for reallocation.

To better understand the investment option information provided to you, please carefully review this additional information about types of investment risks and glossary of terms and statistics found on the fund fact sheets. Documentation will also provide instructions about how to obtain any underlying fund prospectus.

Fund Name	Balance	Amount Available	New %	Estimated Balance After Reallocation
STABILITY OF PRINCIPAL				
4062 Voya Fixed Account (4062)	$0.00	$0.00	%	
BONDS				
2695 PIMCO Real Return Fund Inst	$0.00	$0.00	%	
6431 Voya Intermediate Bond Fund R6	$0.00	$0.00	%	
6589 PGIM High Yield Fund R6	$0.00	$0.00	%	
ASSET ALLOCATION				
2851 Voya Lifetime Inc Protection 2035 II *	$0.00	$0.00	%	
6988 Voya Target Retirement 2020 Fund R6	$0.00	$0.00	%	
6989 Voya Target Retirement 2025 Fund R6	$0.00	$0.00	%	
6990 Voya Target Retirement 2030 Fund R6	$0.00	$0.00	%	
6991 Voya Target Retirement 2035 Fund R6	$120.56	$120.56	%	

FIGURE 7-7: A 401(k) reallocate system enables you to make shifts from different investments, all on one page.

Powering Your 401(k) with Contributions

A 401(k) with a solid asset allocation plan can do remarkable things for your retirement savings. But one input is more important than any other: your contributions.

If you don't put enough into a 401(k), you'll never have much to take out. But unlike market returns, which are difficult to predict, you can control how much you put into your 401(k).

Inspecting your current contribution level

Most paychecks are direct deposited, so you might know only how much you're taking home, not how much is going into your 401(k). This situation is good in a way because you're saving first without thinking about it.

However, you might not be saving as much as you'd like, especially if you were automatically enrolled in the 401(k). To find out what percentage of pay you're contributing, find the contributions area on the 401(k) provider's site. You might see one of two sections:

>> **Change Contributions:** In this section, you can see — and change — the percentage of gross pay that goes into your 401(k) plan. You can also decide how much you'd like to split between the traditional tax-deferred plan and your Roth 401(k) — if one is offered by your plan.

>> **Contribution Rate Escalator:** This section is designed to help you gradually and automatically put more money into your 401(k). You can instruct your 401(k) provider to increase your contribution by a certain percentage over a set period of time, until the contribution reaches a certain level. Voya's Contribution Rate Escalator section is shown in Figure 7-8.

TIP

Don't ignore the Contribution Rate Escalator because it can be a powerful tool. It can add $800,000 to a retirement nest egg pretty easily, according to an analysis by Investor's Business Daily (www.investors.com/etfs-and-funds/retirement/retirement-planning-boosts-nest-egg-800000/). Suppose that a 25-year-old initially earns $50,000, gets a 1 percent annual raise, earns a 7 percent annual return, and contributes 3 percent to a 401(k). The nest egg is $400,338 after 45 years. Now, let's say our saver boosts her contribution rate by 1 percent a year up to 10 percent of pay. This gradual change leaves our now 70-year-old with $1.2 million — or $858,000 more than with the smaller contribution.

Deciding how much to contribute

The sooner you start making meaningful contributions to your 401(k), the better. In previous chapters, you found out how much you can afford to save. You've also seen that trying to sock away 10 to 15 percent of your pay is a good goal and the amount most financial planners suggest.

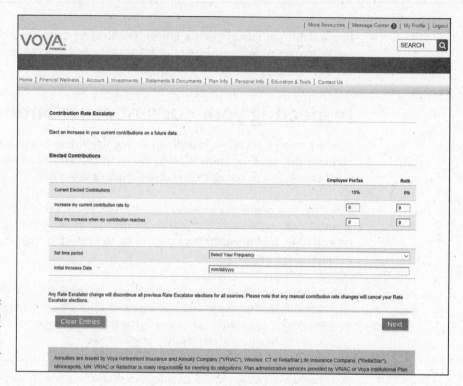

FIGURE 7-8:
A Contribution
Rate Escalator
helps you
automatically
contribute more.

WARNING

Most savers fall short of the 15 percent of pay they should try to contribute. During the first quarter of 2019, employees on average saved 4.7 percent of gross pay in their 401(k)s, according to Fidelity (www.fidelity.com/bin-public/060_www_fidelity_com/documents/press-release/quarterly-retirement-trends-050919.pdf). However, thanks to employer matches, the total savings rate was closer to 13.5 percent, which shows the importance of employer matches.

Another point to consider is how soon you start saving for retirement. The sooner you start, the smaller the contribution you need to make.

Also, be mindful of the limits to how much you can put into a 401(k). The standard 401(k) limit in 2019 was $19,000. So if you're making $200,000 a year, the most you could put in was 9.5 percent. Some plans, too, limit the contributions that higher-paid employees can make.

Finally, keep in mind that when you turn 50, you can contribute an additional $6,000 a year (as of 2019). Read all the details of contribution limits at www.irs.gov/newsroom/401k-contribution-limit-increases-to-19000-for-2019-ira-limit-increases-to-6000.

Seeing the power of putting more away

If you're curious about how much a higher contribution can help you, check out Table 7-1, which was built using data from Fidelity's 401(k) Contribution Calculator (`https://nb.fidelity.com/public/nb/401k/tools/calculators/contributioncalculator`).

TABLE 7-1

Understanding 401(k) Contribution Rates

Salary Contributed	First Year Contribution	Ending 401(k) Balance in 35 Years
1%	$800	$121,477
5%	$4,000	$607,387
10%	$8,000	$1,214,773
15%	$12,000	$1,822,160
20%	$16,000	$2,429,547

Fidelity Contribution Calculator

In this scenario, you

>> Earn $80,000 a year

>> Get an annual 2 percent raise

>> Don't get a matching contribution from your employer

>> Start with no savings

>> Get a 6 percent rate of return over 35 years

Using this setup, look at Table 7-1 to see how an increased contribution can add big time to your retirement fund. If you're able to push toward the 10 percent contribution, you can get into the millionaire club when you're retired. If you stick with the 1 percent contribution, I hope you stayed friends with people who contributed 10 percent.

Discovering Other Nifty Aspects of Your 401(k) Plan Site

Checking and changing contributions and sizing up your asset allocation are the tasks you'll mostly be doing with your 401(k) plan site. But if you dig into the menus, you'll likely find a few other elements worth looking into.

TIP

After signing up for your company's 401(k) and logging in, take the time to look around the site. Many 401(k) providers have turned their sites into valuable, free resources. Try out what your 401(k) site offers before paying for a third-party site.

Locating information on plan loans and withdrawals

One of the so-called advantages of 401(k)s is that you can borrow money from the plan. I use *so-called* because I'm not a big fan of people borrowing money from retirement plans.

A 401(k) loan has strict limits, which I cover in Chapter 8. The IRS also spells out the rules at www.irs.gov/retirement-plans/retirement-plans-faqs-regarding-loans.

Some people borrow money from their 401(k)s for the down payment on a first home, which is a better use than others. However, before borrowing, make sure you've exhausted all your options.

WARNING

If you're borrowing money from your 401(k), you're also borrowing from your future. In addition to having to pay the money back with interest, you're missing out on valuable years in which your money could be invested and grow.

With that said, it's your money. If you decide that you do want to borrow from your 401(k), find the loans section of the 401(k) site, which should tell you the terms of the loan. Figure 7-9 is the loans section of the Voya site.

You'll also find a section that tells you how much you can withdraw from the plan. You may qualify for a withdrawal due to financial hardship or termination of employment. Just know that if you take out money before you turn 59½ when there's no hardship, you'll be hit not only with a tax bill on contributions and earnings but also with the dreaded early withdrawal penalty unless you roll over the money into a qualified plan.

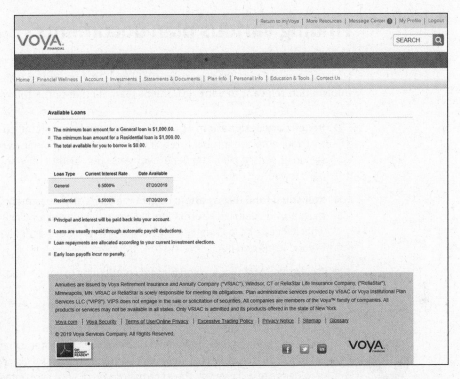

Available Loans

▫ The minimum loan amount for a General loan is $1,000.00.
▫ The minimum loan amount for a Residential loan is $1,000.00.
▫ The total available for you to borrow is $0.00.

Loan Type	Current Interest Rate	Date Available
General	6.5000%	07/20/2019
Residential	6.5000%	07/20/2019

▫ Principal and interest will be paid back into your account.
▫ Loans are usually repaid through automatic payroll deductions.
▫ Loan repayments are allocated according to your current investment elections.
▫ Early loan payoffs incur no penalty.

Annuities are issued by Voya Retirement Insurance and Annuity Company ("VRIAC"), Windsor, CT or ReliaStar Life Insurance Company, ("ReliaStar"), Minneapolis, MN. VRIAC or ReliaStar is solely responsible for meeting its obligations. Plan administrative services provided by VRIAC or Voya Institutional Plan Services LLC ("VIPS"). VIPS does not engage in the sale or solicitation of securities. All companies are members of the Voya™ family of companies. All products or services may not be available in all states. Only VRIAC is admitted and its products offered in the state of New York.

Voya.com | Voya Security | Terms of Use/Online Privacy | Excessive Trading Policy | Privacy Notice | Sitemap | Glossary

© 2019 Voya Services Company. All Rights Reserved.

FIGURE 7-9:
If loans are available from your 401(k) plan, you can find the limits and terms on the provider's website.

WARNING

The withdrawal function can be used if you leave a company or retire, and want to roll over your money to an IRA to give you more control. (See Chapter 8 to read more about IRA rollovers.) When rolling over, the money must go directly to the new IRA provider. If you get a check in your name, the IRS might tax you, thinking you took a distribution. The company where you opened your IRA can help you avoid this mistake.

Know, too, that most employer contributions aren't yours right away. Companies usually have a vesting period, in which you have to wait a certain number of years before this money is yours, or *vested*. This information will be listed on the site.

Digging into the statements

Just like with your bank accounts, your 401(k) provider issues regular statements. These documents show you how much money you contributed to the retirement plan, how much your employer contributed, and how your investments performed.

You might be thinking, "But wait. I can get all that information from the 401(k) website." And you're right. But if you want to print the data — perhaps to share with a financial advisor or banker for a loan — you can.

Finding various plan documents

In the past, you'd get a thick packet of papers to tell you all about your 401(k) plan. Now, of course, that information is online. On the 401(k) website, you'll find information relevant to your retirement plan, including the following:

>> **Beneficiary designation:** Assigning a *beneficiary* is important, so important that your employer probably required you to choose someone when you signed up for the plan. The beneficiary gets your 401(k) if anything happens to you.

>> **Individual fund information:** Each of the funds and investments in the plan must provide detailed information, including the fee the fund charges and what it invests in. In Chapter 9, you discover how to further analyze the funds in your 401(k) and IRA.

>> **Tax forms:** When you're working and contributing to your 401(k), you don't have to worry about taxes. But when you start taking money out of your 401(k), retire, or turn 70½, you must pay the appropriate taxes. The tax forms on the site will help you determine your tax bill.

REMEMBER

You must take a required minimum distribution (RMD) after turning 70½. And when you do this, you most likely will owe taxes. The tax forms on your 401(k) provider's site will give you the information you or your accountant need to pay Uncle Sam.

Chapter **8**

Taking Your IRA to the Next Level

The IRA is the granddaddy of retirement planning. Although 401(k)s get a lot of attention, people count on IRAs for their retirement more than any other kind of account.

It's easy to see why. The IRA has several advantages over other types of retirement savings. The fees can be very low, and the choices of investments are nearly unlimited. But above all, the draw of the IRA is control: You're in charge.

When you have an IRA, you call the shots. You choose the financial companies you deal with. You choose the types of investments you put in the plan. And you can make changes anytime you want.

But this control requires responsibility. To select the best options, you must research investment products. It's also up to you to make sure you're adhering to contribution limits. Above all, make sure that you avail yourself of all the tools your IRA provider offers, online and offline.

If your IRA provider doesn't give you access to top-notch investments and online tools to manage your account, you should pack up your account and take it elsewhere.

In this chapter, you find ways to put your IRA on your desired path. You also learn how to dig into your IRA provider's online tools to help you make decisions.

Getting Online with Your IRA Provider

If you're not online with your IRA provider, it's time you were. If your IRA provider is keeping up with industry trends, you'll be amazed at the digital resources available to you. You just need to know what to look for.

TIP

It might seem tempting to skip the process of registering for online access of your IRA account. If you do that, though, you'll seriously miss out. Yes, you could manage your IRA over the phone and through the mail. But even if you're a hands-off investor, you're much better off doing everything online.

Opening your IRA account

Opening an IRA varies based on the provider, but you can expect a basic script similar to the following, which is the way Vanguard does it:

1. **Go to the IRA provider's website and find the button for opening an account.**

IRA providers make this button easy to find. On most sites, it's in the upper-right corner of the screen.

2. **Choose a new account or a rollover.**

Remember, you can always open a brand new IRA account if you're just getting started. But if you've been saving for retirement somewhere else, you can *rollover,* or transfer, money from a 401(k), another IRA, or sometimes even a pension.

3. **Show me the money.**

The first thing the IRA provider will want to know is how you'll fund the account. You can electronically move money from a checking or savings account. You can also rollover from another plan or transfer securities you own elsewhere. If you're funding your account through your bank, you need your bank account information.

4. **Do one of the following:**

- **If you already have another account with the IRA provider:** You might have an older account with the IRA provider. If you do, sign in. By opening the new IRA with your existing login information, you'll avoid typing lots of information all over again. It's also easier to manage your accounts if they're associated with the same username.

- **If you're opening a first account with the IRA provider:** Be prepared to answer a bunch of questions. You'll need to enter information about yourself, including a Social Security number and address.

5. **Choose the type of account:**

You need to know the type of account you want to open. You'll be asked if the account is for retirement, general savings, or education (as shown in Figure 8-1). If you choose a retirement account, you'll be asked if you want a traditional IRA, Roth IRA, SIMPLE IRA, or SEP IRA. If you're not sure what kind of IRA is best for you, flip back to Chapter 4 to review your retirement account options.

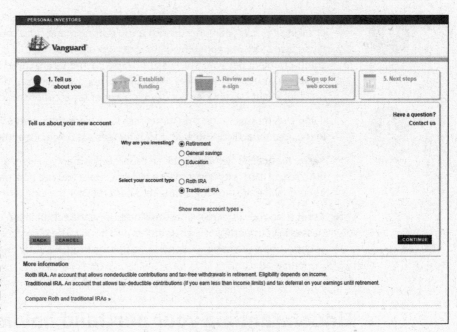

FIGURE 8-1:
Vanguard's online IRA application steps you through opening an account and getting online access.

6. **Answer questions, set up funding, and e-sign.**

You'll be asked to enter the amount of your initial investment. If you're opening an account with this IRA provider for the first time, you'll also need to enter a username and password for online access.

7. **Wait.**

   Some IRA providers will open your account immediately if everything you entered checks out. Others, such as Vanguard, confirm your information, which can take a day or two.

Logging in and looking around

The long road to setting up your IRA is over and you're now an IRA owner. How cool is that? Next, it's time to see what you can find on the IRA provider's site. The list is long:

>> **Account information:** All IRA sites can tell you how much is in your account (your balance) and your investments, or *holdings.*

>> **Account activity:** Any time you put money into (contribute to), your IRA or take money out of (withdraw from), your IRA, the transaction is recorded. Your account activity shows the comings and goings of the money in your account.

TIP

Money can come into or go out of your account, even if you're not putting it in or taking it out. Is your long-lost rich uncle putting money into your IRA? Nope. If you own stock in a company that makes a profit beyond what it needs, the company might pay you, the investor. These payments are called *dividends* and appear in your account activity. What about money coming out? Fees. The IRA provider might take money out of your account for account-servicing costs.

WARNING

If you own mutual funds, the (sometimes large) fees they charge won't appear in the account activity listing. Mutual fund fees are taken out of the fund itself.

>> **Performance:** Remember getting a report card when you were a kid? Your IRA's report card is its performance tracking. Here you see how much your IRA is growing or shrinking during the year and over the long term.

>> **Asset mix:** Your *asset mix,* or asset allocation, is the combination of asset classes in your portfolio, such as stocks and bonds. The more stocks in your portfolio, the riskier your portfolio but the more it's likely to grow in the long term.

Understanding your portfolio holdings

If you want to dig deeper into what you own in your IRA, look for an area called Holdings. In this section, you'll find the following important attributes of the investments in your account:

>> **Summary:** Here you'll find the name of each investment you own and its symbol. Mutual funds and other investment funds are identified by a multi-character abbreviation, or symbol. This symbol is useful if you want to look the fund up using a third-party site, as described in Chapter 9.

>> **Returns:** The amount of money you make or lose from an investment is more than how much its price has changed. It's also a tally of the dividends paid. The Returns section adds all this together. You can find your return on an investment during several time periods, such as one, three, five, and ten years.

>> **Cost basis:** Your *cost basis* of an investment is how much you paid to buy it. If you paid $100 for a share of a mutual fund that's now worth $110 a share, your cost basis is $100. If you sell the mutual fund for $110 a share, you have a *realized capital gain,* or profit, of $10. If you don't sell the mutual fund but hold it, you have an *unrealized capital gain* of $10. Your IRA provider tracks capital gains for you.

REMEMBER

Tracking your capital gains is a big deal with taxable accounts but not with tax-deferred ones such as traditional IRAs. With a taxable account, you pay taxes on only your realized gains. But with an IRA, your entire withdrawal is taxable — even your cost basis because it hasn't been taxed yet.

Checking Your Portfolio Asset Allocation

Your portfolio is only as good as the ingredients that go into it. You might have painstakingly calculated whether a Roth or traditional IRA is better for you. But if your IRA is filled with investments mismatched to your goals, the portfolio is not going to get you the retirement you imagined.

That's why it's important to dig deeper and understand what you own, as you did with 401(k)s in Chapter 7. But the task is all the more important with IRAs because you have much more control and more options. You're making the decisions, not your employer or 401(k) plan administrator.

Understanding correlation

Your asset allocation is a stew of all the asset classes you own in your portfolio. All of these asset classes have attributes that allow them to work together. In previous chapters, you learned how the risk (volatility) and expected returns of your portfolio are largely determined by the asset classes you chose.

Now that you're building an IRA and have unfettered access to any investment, you need to know about another topic: correlation. It's a near-magical property of investments that can help you lower your risk and boost return.

Suppose you have two investments that are equally volatile, with a tendency to drop by 25 percent about 66 percent of the time. However, the two investments tend to suffer these drops at different times. So when one investment is falling, the other tends to stay flat or even rise. In other words, one investment zigs when the other one zags.

This property is called *correlation* and is important when choosing investments. If you find investments that tend to move in different directions, they can work together in a portfolio to smooth out bumps, without cutting your returns.

Table 8-1 shows you what I mean.

TABLE 8-1   Investments That Zig When the Market Zags

Asset Class	Long-Term Return (%)	Correlation with Large U.S. Stocks (S&P 500)	Risk (Standard Deviation)
U.S. large-company stocks	9.3	1	18.0
U.S. large value-priced stocks	10.6	0.94	21.8
U.S. small-cap stocks	11.0	0.89	24.2
U.S. small value-priced stocks	12.4	0.86	28.3
International value-priced stocks	10.4	0.79	23.0
Emerging markets stocks	12.1	0.82	23.5
One-year fixed income	3.78	0.02	1.48
Two-year global fixed income	4.41	0.09	2.92
Short-term government fixed income	4.65	0.08	3.52
Five-year global fixed income	4.76	0.11	3.54
S&P 500	9.71	1.00	18.75

Index Fund Advisors, Inc., www.ifa.com. Time period: 1/1/1928 to 12/31/2018. See disclosures and index descriptions at www.ifa.com/disclosures.

I'll explain correlation by using a classic case: U.S. large-company stocks and international value-priced stocks. International stocks are riskier than U.S. large-company stocks (with a risk of 23 versus 18). And the expected returns of international stocks are only slightly higher than U.S. stocks (10.4 percent versus 9.3 percent). Some investors might think international investing isn't worth the trouble.

So why do most asset allocations recommend that you own international stocks? Correlation. When two investments move in the same direction at the same time, they have a correlation of 1. If the two assets move by the same amounts but in opposite directions, they have a correlation of –1. If two assets move independently of one another, they have a correlation of 0.

As you can see in Table 8-1, international stocks and large U.S. stocks have a correlation of 0.79, which means they don't move in lockstep. That's good. If you own both large U.S. stocks and international stocks, they will work with each other to reduce your volatility.

Correlation is one of the benefits of diversification!

If you'd like to dig further into the idea of correlations, the following sites will show you more details of the interplay between different asset classes:

>> **Portfolio Visualizer** (www.portfoliovisualizer.com/asset-class-correlations) uses a variety of exchange-traded funds to show you how various asset classes work together.

>> **Morningstar Correlation Matrix** (https://admainnew.morningstar.com/webhelp/Practice/Plans/Correlation_Matrix_of_the_14_Asset_Classes.htm) shows you the correlation of dozens of asset classes in one chart.

Viewing your asset allocation on your provider's website

Now that you understand why your portfolio's asset allocation is so important, it's time to use your IRA provider to look under the hood of your portfolio. To see your asset allocation, find an area in your IRA provider's site called Asset Mix or something similar. IRA providers will also show you a *target asset mix,* or what your asset allocation should be, as Vanguard does in Figure 8-2.

Enhancing your asset allocation

How do you decide what your target allocation should look like? If you're like most people, you'll look to your IRA provider for guidance. And if your IRA provider is earning its keep, you'll find features to help you, such as the ones described in this section.

FIGURE 8-2:
Vanguard's asset mix function shows how much of your portfolio should be in stocks and bonds.

Sign-up defaults

Remember when you first opened your IRA account? You answered a number of questions about your financial goals. Most IRA providers use your answers to these rudimentary questions to design a basic asset allocation for you. Typically, these sign-up defaults put you in bonds and stock. Buy two funds, a stock fund and a bond fund, and that's that.

Target-date funds

If you're looking for an easy solution to building an appropriate asset allocation, it's hard to argue with target-date funds. Here, you let the IRA provider do the heavy lifting for you. You tell the IRA provider the year you plan to retire, and they suggest a single mutual fund that owns a basket of investments compiled to match your goals. Better yet, as you approach retirement, these target-date funds shift your assets toward bonds automatically to reduce volatility.

Asset allocation tools

If you're like most IRA owners, a target-date fund from a low-price provider is a great way to go. But if you have a more complicated financial situation, an off-the-shelf allocation might not make sense.

IMPORTANT INFO ABOUT TARGET-DATE FUNDS

Target-date funds are hugely successful in the retirement planning world. Savers love them because they're simple. You make one fairly knowledgeable guess, the year you plan to retire, and the rest is done for you. For that reason, target-date funds from reputable IRA providers like the ones mentioned in this book can be an excellent choice.

But before you blindly pick a target-date fund, relax, and carry on, I urge you to consider a few things.

First, no two target-date funds are the same. Different IRA providers build these funds differently, and the results can vary. Suppose that you're a 50-year-old planning to retire at 65. In the year 2019, that would mean choosing a target-date fund for the year 2035.

If you buy the Vanguard Target Retirement 2035 Fund, your allocation would be 46 percent U.S. stocks, 30.5 percent international stocks, 16.5 percent U.S. bonds, and 7 percent international bonds. Vanguard would put you in 76.5 percent stocks and 23.5 percent bonds. Sounds reasonable.

But over at T. Rowe Price, another big mutual fund company, the mix is slightly different. The T. Rowe Price Retirement 2035 Fund puts you in 51.2 percent U.S. stocks, 27.2 percent international stocks, 12.4 percent domestic bonds, 7.1 percent international bonds, and 2.2 percent cash and other stocks. That's 78.4 percent in stocks and 21.7 percent in bonds.

Why the difference between two target-date funds for the same year? Some target-date funds are designed to get you *to* retirement but not necessarily *through* retirement. Funds designed to adjust to retirement tend to start paring back on stock exposure as you near the target date. Funds managed through retirement leave your portfolio weighted more to stocks even on the day you retire.

Also consider the fees. It's easy for an IRA provider to sell you on the simplicity of a target-date fund, but you should also know what you're paying, all-in, for the fund. You might have to pay a fee for the target-date fund in addition to fees charged by the underlying funds.

The Vanguard 2035 target-date fund, for instance, charges just 0.14 percent a year. The T. Rowe Price version, on the other hand, charges 0.7 percent, or 400 percent more. You'll want to make sure that the T. Rowe Price fund is worth it. You discover how to do this in Chapter 9. For now, know that funds must disclose their performance.

(continued)

(continued)

In the 10 years ending June 30, 2019, T. Rowe Price's target-date funds did pay off, generating an average annual return of 11.69 percent after fees. That topped the Vanguard target-date fund's 10.9 percent return after fees during that period. Why? The T. Rowe Price target-date fund is slightly more aggressive because it holds more stocks than Vanguard.

Will T. Rowe Price's fund keep earning its keep? Will other funds that cost more beat the cheaper Vanguard option? You'll have to decide.

WARNING

Target-date funds build your asset allocation mostly based on your age. The younger you are and the further away from retirement, the more risk you can take. However, if you have a large sum of cash outside your IRA, giving you financial security, you might be able to take more risk in your IRA than others your age.

If you think you might need a more customized asset allocation, you'll find help on your IRA provider's site. Vanguard's Portfolio Watch tool, for example, asks a number of questions about your financial goals and resources. The tool, which is available only to customers, then provides an in-depth analysis of your portfolio — breaking down details of your stock funds, bond funds, and fees, as shown in Figure 8-3. In addition, a Portfolio Tester tool helps you figure out how a proposed change might affect your retirement plan.

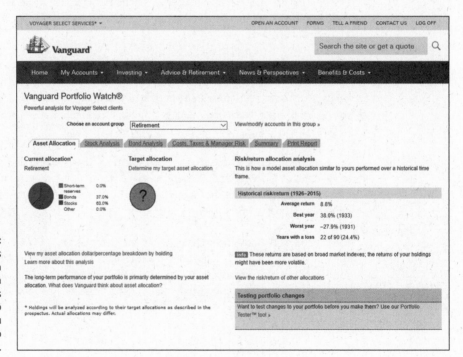

FIGURE 8-3: Vanguard's Portfolio Watch provides an in-depth analysis of your portfolio to help you find ways to improve it.

Robo-advisors

Asset allocation tools, such as Vanguard's, are helpful guides for people who want a more customized portfolio. But these tools still require you to do the work. You need to buy and sell the suggested funds and maintain the correct percentages in the asset classes.

If that sound like a drag, you might like the automatic nature of target-date funds. But what if you want a tailor-made portfolio and don't want to do the work? The major IRA providers hear you loud and clear. They've launched *robo-advisors,* managed portfolios that use algorithms to learn your goals and match you with mostly index funds. A robo-advisor is a good option for people who don't want to deal with choosing an asset allocation and adjusting it as they age.

TIP

Vanguard offers a robo-advisor called Vanguard Personal Advisor Services. For an annual 0.3 percent fee, Vanguard's systems will put you in a low-cost portfolio matched to your goals. It will also handle the buying and selling necessary to keep your portfolio in balance and give you access to a way to reach human advisors over the phone. The catch: A minimum investment of $50,000.

Given Vanguard's high minimum, let's look at another IRA provider who takes a different approach to robo-advising: Wealthfront (www.wealthfront.com/retirement). Rather than starting with a questionnaire, Wealthfront, with your permission, looks at your spending and gets a handle on what your financial needs are and are likely to be. Wealthfront then builds a low-cost portfolio made up of index funds. Wealthfront has resources not just for general investing but also for people planning for retirement, as you can see in Figure 8-4.

REMEMBER

To use a robo-advisor, you pay two levels of fees. With Wealthfront, for instance, you pay the underlying fees of the index funds, usually 0.07 percent to 0.16 percent. You also pay an annual advisory fee of 0.25 percent. You could always save the 0.25 percent advisory fee by choosing the asset allocation yourself. If you're not willing to do that, the robo-advisor is a good option at a reasonable fee. Keep in mind, many human advisors charge 1 percent or more of your assets to manage your account each year.

Self-directed IRA

REMEMBER

Mainstream IRA providers, such as mutual fund companies, online brokers, and robo-advisors, let you invest in all major asset classes, including all sorts of stocks and bonds. In some special cases, you might want to broaden your IRA to include unusual investments, such as an interest in a privately owned business or specialty real estate. *Self-directed IRAs* allow you to create tax shelters for unusual assets.

FIGURE 8-4:
Wealthfront's site and digital app are aimed at people who want more personalization without the added hassle.

WARNING

Self-directed IRAs are not a good idea for most people because the fees can be very high. Most of the big names in IRA planning don't touch them. However, in some cases, they can make sense if you have large real-estate portfolios or complicated business dealings because you'll have more options for putting these unique assets in a retirement plan. Self-directed IRAs are such a specialty that it's best to find a trusted and properly registered advisor to help you. Refer to Chapter 6 for tips on finding an advisor.

Understanding Your IRA Contributions

Getting money into your IRA is where the magic begins. You can't build a portfolio until a source of funds exists. IRAs give you not only big leeway in what investments you buy but also lots of control over how you buy those investments.

Setting up IRA deposits

When you're talking about putting money aside that you can't touch for decades, it's easy to understand why lots of people put off retirement savings. Let's face it, blowing $800 on a new smartphone is more immediately satisfying than putting $800 in an IRA. IRA providers know this, and go out of their way to make it easy for you to get money into your account. You can make ongoing contributions to your IRA in two main ways:

- >> **One-time contribution:** The IRA provider lets you connect multiple checking and savings accounts to your retirement account. You can then tell the provider to digitally pull money from one or more of those accounts as a contribution. Vanguard's one-time contribution screen, shown in Figure 8-5, asks you to choose the investment you want the money to go into. It also tracks your annual contribution to date.

- >> **Automatic contribution:** You can also tell your IRA provider to take money from a checking or savings account, say every month or quarter. This method puts your retirement plan on autopilot.

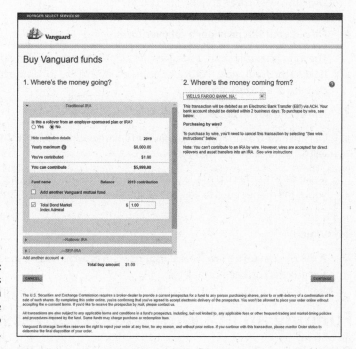

FIGURE 8-5: Vanguard makes it easy to make a one-time contribution to your IRA.

WARNING

It's up to you to make sure your contributions meet the requirements and don't exceed limits. If you're covered by a retirement plan at work, the IRS spells out whether you can deduct your IRA contributions. If you make too much money, the deducible amount of your contribution is reduced or eliminated. In a nutshell, if you made more than $74,000 as a single taxpayer or $123,000 married filing jointly and are covered by a plan at work, you can't deduct IRA contributions. For the details, go to www.irs.gov/retirement-plans/2019-ira-deduction-limits-effect-of-modified-agi-on-deduction-if-you-are-covered-by-a-retirement-plan-at-work.

Roll over Beethoven: IRA rollovers

Another way to fund an IRA is a rollover. You might opt to rollover your old 401(k) from a previous place of employment, which can be a good idea if your old 401(k) has high fees or poor investment choices. You can rollover funds also from one IRA to another, although that process is usually called a *transfer*.

TIP

Generally, it's best to keep your retirement accounts in as few places as possible. Consolidating your retirement funds with one IRA provider helps you qualify for lower-priced investments and makes it easier to keep track of your money.

A rollover involves three steps:

1. **Fill out your IRA provider's rollover form.**

The form is usually short, asking for the account number and the provider holding the funds now. You'll also be asked if you'd like to roll the funds into a new IRA or an existing one.

2. **Notify the 401(k) or IRA provider you're moving from.**

Tell them you're moving the money and where you're moving it. The provider will cut a check for the money.

WARNING

Make sure the check is made out to the firm where the money is going, not to you. If the money goes to you, the IRS might think you took a distribution and hit you with a tax bill.

3. **Wait.**

A rollover can take a few weeks. Your new IRA provider will let you know when the process has been completed.

Funding an IRA with a Roth conversion

With traditional IRAs, you get a tax break now. With a Roth IRA, you pay now but take out the money later free and clear. Guessing which will be best for you is difficult. In general, a Roth is a good idea if you think your current tax rate is lower than it will be when you're retired.

Roth IRAs are preferable also if you think you might need to pull the money out sooner than in retirement, or if you think you won't need the money and want to leave it for a spouse or an heir. Traditional IRAs require you to take money out when you turn 70½. With a Roth, you can leave the money in.

Given all the guesswork in choosing a Roth IRA versus a traditional IRA, you might change your mind about the kind of IRA you want. That's where a *Roth conversion* comes in. You can turn a traditional IRA into a Roth IRA if you pay the taxes now.

WARNING

Converting a traditional IRA to a Roth can make sense. It's also a back door way to open a Roth for people who earn too much to fund a Roth. A Roth conversion has several drawbacks, however. You must wait at least five years after a conversion to take money out of a Roth. The conversion also triggers a tax event — you'll have a tax bill on those tax-deferred contributions.

Does a Roth conversion make sense for you? To answer that question, you can use a variety of online tools, including the following:

» **Schwab IRA Conversion Calculator (**www.schwab.com/public/schwab/investing/retirement_and_planning/understanding_iras/ira_calculators/roth_ira_conversion**):** This tool helps you think about all the important variables that determine whether or not you should convert to a Roth. These variables include the amount of money you'd like to convert and your taxable income.

» **CalcXML's Roth Conversion Calculator (**www.calcxml.com/calculators/roth-ira-conversion-calculator**):** This tool does all the math to see whether a Roth conversion makes sense. The calculator considers the size of the conversion as well as your age and income needs.

Taking Money out of Your IRA

When you turn 70½, you're no longer allowed to contribute to a traditional IRA. You can contribute to a Roth IRA at any age as long as you have earned income below limits dictated by the IRS. Remember that *earned income* is money you make from reportable income-producing activities — in other words, a paying job.

Gearing up to take money out of your IRA requires a change in mindset. Fortunately, your IRA provider can be of help here, too.

Getting money out early: 72(t) distributions

Taking money out of a traditional IRA before you turn 59½ is generally a no-no with retirement accounts because it triggers a bad tax day. You owe not only the taxes on the money you took out but also a 10 percent early withdrawal penalty — unless you know the 72(t) trick. This rule is named after an arcane section of the

IRS code that says you can take money out without a 10 percent penalty if you do so in "substantially equal periodic payments."

TECHNICAL STUFF

You must take out the distributions, in equal amounts, for at least five years or until you turn 59½. You can calculate how much money you must take out in three ways: the required minimum distribution method, the fixed amortization method, and the fixed annuitization method. As you can guess from their names, the calculations are complicated. If you're interested in a 72(t) withdrawal, your IRA provider can help. For more on the topic, visit `www.irs.gov/retirement-plans/retirement-plans-faqs-regarding-substantially-equal-periodic-payments`.

TIP

You can take money out of an IRA before you turn 59½ without paying the 10 percent penalty in a few other ways, without invoking the 72(t). A big exception for the 10 percent penalty is when you're permanently or completely disabled. In that case, you can take money out of both a traditional IRA and a Roth IRA. Also, if you die, your beneficiary can take withdrawals. (I don't recommend this method — I'd rather just pay the 10 percent penalty.) For additional exceptions to the 10 percent early withdrawal penalty, see Chapter 5.

Taking your required minimum distribution

When you blow out a cake with 70 candles, know that in six months you'll be in for a big change with your traditional IRA. That's when Uncle Sam says it's time for your *required minimum distribution (RMD)*. It must be taken out before April 1 of the year after you turn 70½.

The RMD is calculated using a complicated formula based on your life expectancy. You must take your RMD from all of your traditional IRAs. This requirement is another reason to have your retirement money in one place; you'll deal with just one annual check.

As part of their service, most IRA providers will calculate your RMD. Vanguard shows the calculation in its RMD calculator, shown in Figure 8-6 and available at `https://personal.vanguard.com/us/insights/retirement/living/estimate-your-rmd-tool`.

TIP

Don't ignore the RMD. If you don't withdraw the RMD and pay the tax, you'll owe a 50 percent penalty tax on the money you should have withdrawn. Yes, half will be gone in taxes. Most IRA providers calculate your RMD for you and even withhold some of the tax due from what you're paid. IRA providers will even deposit the money into your account electronically — almost like a paycheck.

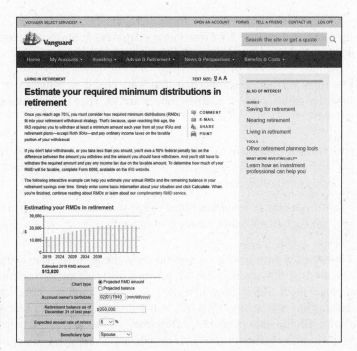

FIGURE 8-6:
Vanguard will calculate your RMD.

Setting up a beneficiary

Your retirement funds are there for you and your spouse, if you have one, or other beneficiary to enjoy later in life. Make sure that your IRA provider knows who to give the money to if you die before your beneficiary. Yes, you could do this in a will, but it's a better idea to set up a beneficiary. Your beneficiary instructions will take precedence over a will.

When you die, the IRA provider knows to shift the ownership of the IRA to your beneficiary. Listing beneficiaries on IRA accounts is so important that many IRA providers won't let you fund an account until you choose a beneficiary.

TIP

If you have a large or complicated estate or unusual wishes for where your money should go when you die, you might want to create a trust. A *trust* is a legal entity that can take ownership of assets and follow your instructions in distributing them. Consult with an estate-planning attorney or pick up *Estate & Trust Administration For Dummies*, 2nd Edition, by Margaret Munro and Kathyrn Murphy (Wiley).

A word about inherited IRAs

Don't keep your IRA a secret from the beneficiary. After you die and your IRA passes to your beneficiary, new rules kick in. The beneficiary will need to contact the IRA provider and let them know you're dead. Most IRA providers require a death certificate.

The rules surrounding inherited IRAs vary based on whether or not the IRA is inherited by a spouse. If spouses inherit an IRA, they have a choice on how to take it over:

>> **Make it their own:** Spouses can choose to take over the IRA in their own name. This allows spouses to contribute or take distributions as if it were theirs in the first place.

>> **Turn it into an inherited IRA:** If you go this route, you'll need to follow rules set out by the IRS, which have many options.

A beneficiary who isn't a spouse has only one avenue: transferring the IRA into an inherited IRA. Again, your IRA provider will help with the details. If you'd like to read more about how inherited IRAs are handled, check out Vanguard's description at `https://investor.vanguard.com/inherit/ira-rmd`. Schwab shows all the inherited IRA rules, too, at `www.schwab.com/public/schwab/investing/retirement_and_planning/understanding_iras/inherited_ira/withdrawal_rules`.

Chapter **9**

Optimizing Your Retirement with Third-Party Offerings

You wouldn't get a major operation without getting a second opinion. You probably wouldn't even agree to a major car repair without first talking to another mechanic.

The principle of double-checking important decisions is called "trust but verify." The same sound advice applies to retirement planning. Even if you think you're happy with your retirement plan and trust the advice you get from your retirement plan provider, checking up on both is a good idea.

In this chapter, you find out how to get a second opinion. You don't have to be a financial planner or mutual fund analyst anymore to pick apart your retirement plan and see if it's worthwhile.

Fantastic online tools can help you examine your retirement account. You can analyze the fees you're paying and determine whether they're worthwhile. You also can discover how to study individual funds that you own and see if they're the best for you. You might also spot ways to improve your retirement plan. The best plan is one that boosts the odds that you can afford the retirement you're picturing.

Above all, I hope this chapter gives you the courage to take your retirement plan into your own hands.

Understanding Fees

Fees are the dirty little secret of retirement plans. IRAs and 401(k)s are designed to help you save and invest as much as you can. But an amazing number of companies and so-called advisors stand between your paycheck and your retirement. They make money by skimming your money.

TIP

Some fees are worthwhile and many are reasonable. But if you don't pay attention to the fees you're paying and who's collecting them, you can end up with much less money than you should for retirement.

Improving success with lower fees

Investment researcher Morningstar has found that the cost of fees is one of the biggest determinants of how an investment will do over time. As Table 9-1 shows, the lower the fees charged by a stock investment (quintile 1, the one-fifth of funds that charge the lowest fees), the higher the odds of investment success. Morningstar defines *success* as an investment that outperformed similar investments.

TABLE 9-1   **Low Costs Equal Higher Investment Success**

U.S. Stocks, Quintile of Expenses	Success Ratio
1 (lowest fees)	62
2	48
3	39
4	30
5 (highest fees)	30

Morningstar data as of December 31, 2015

Knowing the types of fees

As the saying goes, death and taxes are unavoidable. The same goes for retirement account fees. But although fees are part of retirement planning, you should still know what you're paying.

The two major types of fees are advisory fees and fund fees, as detailed next.

Advisory fees

If you hire a financial advisor, sign up with a robo-advisor, or subscribe to an IRA or a 401(k) suggestion service, you'll pay an *advisory fee*. These services add value by suggesting asset classes or investments. Advisory fees can be worthwhile if your portfolio's risk and returns match your goals.

But the advisor fee is taken right off the top of your portfolio. For instance, most financial advisors charge an annual advisory fee of 1 percent. If you have a $300,000 retirement account, for example, you'll pay a $3,000 yearly fee.

WARNING

Some 401(k) plans offer advisory services to members. These services might promote access to a robo-advisor or to an advisor over the phone. Never assume that your 401(k) provider is giving you these programs out of kindness. You pay advisory fees for these offerings.

Fund fees

Whether or not you pay 1 percent to an advisor or 0.4 percent to a robo-advisor, more fees exist. Each mutual fund or exchange-traded fund you own also charges a fee. And some funds charge not just one fee but a handful. Some of the fund fees you might encounter follow:

TIP

>> **Load:** Some funds charge you a lofty *front load fee* simply to buy the fund. Other funds charge you a *back load fee* when you sell them. Such loads can be large, reaching up to 8.5 percent. Front and back loads are a way to pay the broker who sold you the fund.

Loads are an easily avoidable fee. If you can't buy a fund without paying a load, find another fund. Most funds now come in no-load versions.

>> **Management fee:** You pay a *management fee* to the people who decide which stocks or bonds to put into the fund. In general, it's best to keep the expense ratio low. If you pay a high expense ratio, it's even harder for the fund manager to choose investments that not only beat the market but also cover the fee.

>> **12b-1 fee:** A fund company charges a *12b-1 fee* to promote and market its shares. This fee also covers the cost of mailing fund documents. Yes, you pay for that.

>> **Total expense ratio (or expense ratio):** This number is the most important. The fund company must add all the expenses you pay as part of the operation of the fund and provide those costs as a percentage of the fund's assets, or *total expense ratio*. The total expense ratio makes it easy to see what you're paying to own a fund. For example, if the total expense ratio is 0.7 percent and you've invested $1000, you'll pay $7 a year.

>> **Commissions:** If you buy certain investments in an IRA account, you'll pay additional trading commissions. For example, if you buy a mutual fund that's not on the IRA provider's no-commission list, you'll pay the standard commission.

Pay attention to which funds an IRA provider exempts from commissions, and try to stick with that list. If a fund you want to buy isn't on the no-commission list, switch to an IRA that doesn't charge a commission. With 401(k)s, if you stick with their menu of funds, you won't be charged a commission.

The Securities and Exchange Commission's site at `www.sec.gov/fast-answers/answersmffeeshtm.html` further explains the fees you might pay.

Uncovering the shocking truth about fees

The firms charging fees for your retirement accounts are smart. They make the fees seem small, so you'll barely notice them. Who's going to freak out over a 1.25 percent fee? It seems so tiny. The charges are also buried in legal documents you might ignore. This section shows why you should look into the fees you're paying.

Focus on things you can control. That's good advice in life — and in retirement planning. Retirement planning is already based on many hunches and estimates. You don't know how long you'll work or what your returns will be, but you can control the fees you pay. Why buy an expensive fund when lower-cost options are available?

For example, consider Michael, a 25-year-old just starting a 401(k) retirement plan. He plans to

>> Contribute $6,000 a year

>> Work until age 65

>> Build a prudent portfolio that generates an average annual return of 7 percent

Michael could have chosen a lower-cost mix of investments and paid 0.5 percent. But he didn't pay attention and consequently didn't think fees were a big deal.

Just look at Table 9-2 to see what those higher fees cost our saver over time.

TABLE 9-2

Paying More Fees Costs You Dearly

Fee Paid	Amount Saved at 65	Cost of Fee
No fee	$1,197,811	$0
0.5%	$1,053,792	$144,019
0.6%	$1,197,811	$170,481
0.7%	$1,001,597	$196,214
0.8%	$976,573	$221,238
0.9%	$952,238	$245,573
1.0%	$928,572	$269,239
1.5%	$819,633	$378,177
2.0%	$724,799	$473,012

http://401kfee.com/how-much-are-high-fees-costing-you/

Isn't Table 9-2 shocking? Paying a 0.8 percent fee rather than 0.7 percent determines whether or not our saver ends up a millionaire at retirement. And guess who gets all that fee money? Managers of the funds in the plan or the administrators of the plan.

I hope you now see why fees matter.

TIP

No one likes to pay fees. Although fees on retirement plans have been falling, you should still expect to pay them. Larger companies' 401(k) plans typically charge an average expense ratio of 0.4 percent. Smaller company plans might charge 1 percent or higher on average. With an IRA, if you choose your own low-cost investments, you can probably get your annual fees down to 0.4 percent or lower. Make sure you examine all your choices.

Examining Your Portfolio Using Morningstar

Given the near-limitless possibilities of funds to invest in, how do you decide which ones are best? Morningstar should be at the top of your list. The site (www.morningstar.com) offers unrivaled fund data, statistics, and analysis.

And Morningstar can help you if you have an IRA or a 401(k). Much of the information you need to evaluate your retirement plan is free.

Pulling up individual funds that you own

Want to see how Morningstar can help you retire with more money? Use it to analyze the funds in your portfolio. As you might recall from Chapters 7 and 8, you can look up your holdings in your 401(k) or IRA. That's your starting point. Here's a recap:

1. **Log into your IRA or 401(k) provider's site.**

   Navigate until you find an area called Holdings or Portfolio.

2. **Note the symbols and names of your holdings.**

   You should see a list of the funds you own. Each fund has a symbol. If you own a mutual fund, the symbol is five characters long. If you own an exchange-traded fund, the symbol is usually three or four characters long.

3. **Navigate to Morningstar at** www.morningstar.com.

   The main page appears.

4. **In the Search Quotes and Site field, enter the fund's name or symbol and press Enter.**

5. **Start your research.**

After you enter the symbol or name of the fund you own (or are thinking about buying), you'll be surprised at how much information you can find. The analysis is broken down into eight categories, or tabs. Some highlights of the most important tabs follow.

Quote tab

The Quote tab, shown in Figure 9-1, is the main fund page at Morningstar. It's full of analysis and details to help you understand more about what you own in your retirement portfolio.

Following are some of the highlights of the Quote tab:

» **Star rating:** Morningstar is well-known for its Morningstar Analyst Rating (largely because mutual funds that get good ratings often tout them in advertising). This rating, which is at the top of the Quote tab, tells you how good Morningstar thinks a fund is. All sorts of factors, including fees and performance, go into calculating the rating. A five-star rating is the highest.

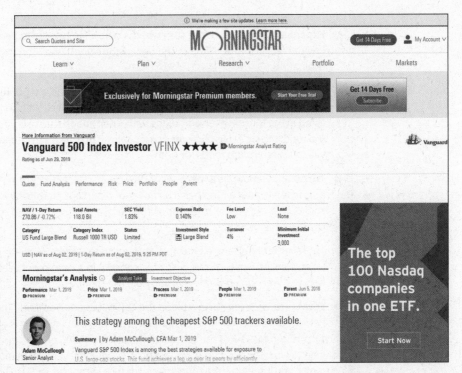

FIGURE 9-1:
Morningstar's Quote tab is stuffed with information pertaining to your mutual or exchange-traded fund.

WARNING

Don't assume that you should buy a fund just because Morningstar gives it five stars. Much of the rating is due to past performance, which may or may not repeat.

>> **NAV (net asset value):** The *NAV* is the price of the mutual fund. It tells you how much you'd get if you sold the fund today or how much you'd pay if you bought it. Mutual funds calculate their NAV once a day after the market closes. Exchange-traded funds update their NAV constantly during the trading day.

>> **Total assets:** The *total assets* number is how much money investors have put into the fund. Why do you care how much other people invested? You want to make sure the fund isn't so small it will be closed and your money returned. On the other hand, if a fund is actively managed, you don't want it to be so large that the manager has trouble finding enough investments to buy. Funds that get too big tend to lag if managers can't find compelling investments.

>> **SEC yield:** The *SEC yield* is how much income the fund pays you a year as a percentage of the fund's NAV. Income includes dividend and interest (from bond funds and exchange-traded funds). For example, if you own a fund with a NAV of $100 that pays $2 a year in income, the SEC yield is 2 percent.

>> **Expense ratio:** If you're not sure whether the all-important expense ratio is low or high, just look a little to the right, where you'll find Morningstar's evaluation.

>> **Investment style:** Your *investment style,* or the size and style of funds you select, largely determines the returns you should expect. Your fund will be listed in the Morningstar box, along with information that tells you whether the fund invests in large or small companies. You'll also see if the fund buys value funds, growth funds, or both.

>> **Turnover:** *Turnover* is a measure of how much change occurs in the portfolio during the year. If a fund has a turnover of 0 percent, nothing was bought or sold during the year. A turnover of 100 percent means the fund sold and replaced everything.

REMEMBER

Turnover is important in a taxable account because lots of selling can trigger a taxable event. But turnover isn't a big concern in a retirement account because you don't pay tax until you take the money out.

>> **Total return:** Scroll down a bit on the Quote tab and you'll find the critical Performance section. After all, getting return is what investing is all about. *Total return* measures the change in the price, or NAV, of the fund plus income paid to you. The fund's returns are broken down by year. Even more importantly, you'll see how the fund's performance compares with that of similar funds and the index against which it's benchmarked. If you're paying a high fee, your fund had better be beating the index by a mile.

Risk tab

Now switch to the Risk tab. Here you'll find out how many sleepless nights you'll need to endure to get the returns you want. Remember, higher returns come with additional risk. Morningstar also shows you several measures of the fund's volatility, as shown in Figure 9-2.

The Risk vs. Category graphic in the upper-left corner is useful. By just glancing at that one chart, you can see whether the risk is paying off.

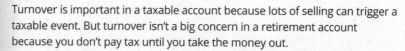
WARNING

If you own a fund with a high risk and a low return, that's a terrible tradeoff. If the risk-reward is out of balance, go back to your IRA or 401(k) provider and see if a better option is available.

Morningstar breaks down your fund's risk further with several measurements, including the following:

FIGURE 9-2:
No pain, no gain? Morningstar's Risk tab helps you see if your returns are sufficient for the risk you're taking.

» **Alpha:** The *Alpha* statistic shows you how much better, or worse, a fund performed than the market after adjusting for risk. If a fund has an alpha of 0, it's not adding incremental value. A small alpha between –0.2 and 0.2 or so means that the fund is essentially doing the same as the market. A large positive alpha or 1 or more indicates that the fund is adding value. Conversely, a large negative alpha means the fund is hurting you. If a fund is expensive, it had better be generating massive alpha.

» **Beta:** *Beta* tells you how volatile the portfolio is compared to the market. If a portfolio has a beta of 1, it tends to move along with the market. A beta of less than 1 means the portfolio has lower volatility than the market. If the beta is significantly higher than 1, the stock or fund tends to be volatile.

» **Standard deviation:** *Standard deviation* is another statistical measure of portfolio or asset volatility. You'll see this measurement in most fund documents. A high standard deviation, say 20 or more, tells you that the portfolio's returns tend to stray wildly from its average return. A portfolio filled with risky technology stocks would have a high standard deviation. An investment that tends to have similar returns year after year has a low standard deviation, one in the single digits.

Standard deviation can tell you how wide a range of returns you might expect from a portfolio. Suppose a portfolio has a long-term average return of 10 percent and a standard deviation of 8 percentage points. With the average return and standard deviation, you can use the following table to get a good idea of what you might expect from the fund in the future.

Number of Standard Deviations	Odds of Occurrence	Amount of Swing	Expected Return (Average Return Plus Standard Deviation)
+1	34.1%	8%	10% to 18%
-1	34.1%	–8%	2% to 10%
+1 to +2	47.7%	16%	10% to 26%
–1 to –2	47.7%	–16%	–6% to 10%

Statistics tell us that there's a 34.1 percent chance the portfolio will rise by one standard deviation in any given year. Therefore, more than a third of the time, the asset will gain somewhere between 10 percent and 18 percent (10 percent plus 8 percentage points). Conversely, 34.1 percent of the time, the asset will return from 10 percent to 2 percent (8 percentage points less than 10 percent).

If your brain hasn't exploded by now, here's another way to look at standard deviation. We know that 68.2 percent of the time, or well more than half the time, the portfolio will rise or fall by one standard deviation, or 8 percentage points. Therefore, 68.2 percent of the time, the asset will rise 18 percent or fall 2 percent (or something in-between).

Precise? No. But it's a decent rule of thumb. I realize this is wonky stuff, but you should be somewhat familiar with standard deviation. Many of the robo-advisors talk about standard deviation, so you'll want to know what it means.

>> **Capture ratios:** Here comes another wonky risk measurement. The *upside capture ratio* tells you how much your asset goes up when the market goes up. If the market rises 9 percent and your investment does too, the capture ratio is 100 percent. *Downside capture ratio* works in reverse. If the market and your investment tank 10 percent, your downside capture ratio is 100 percent. Ideally, you want an upside capture ratio of 100 percent or higher and a downside capture ratio of less than 100 percent.

TIP

Money managers like to say that although they might miss some of the upside in a bull market, they protect you in a bear market. The upside and downside capture ratios will help you see whether that claim is true. If the fund's downside capture ratio is 100 percent or higher, it's not protecting you from downturns.

Price tab

Seeing how important fees are to your results, it's no wonder Morningstar pays so much attention to them. In the Price tab, shown in Figure 9-3, you see in a new light the fees that mutual fund companies are charging.

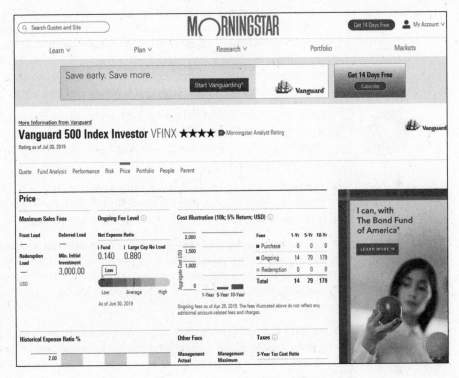

Morningstar's Price tab reveals and explains the fees you're paying.

You'll find answers to questions you should have about the fees you're paying, such as the following:

>> **How do the fees compare?** In the Ongoing Fee Level chart, Morningstar shows you what you're paying for the fund. You can then compare those fees with those charged by other funds in the same category.

>> **What will the fees actually cost?** Most people find that dollars and cents make more sense than an expense ratio. Morningstar, in the Cost Illustration chart, shows you what the fund will cost you on an ongoing basis if you invest $10,000.

>> **How have the fees changed over time?** Fees industrywide are coming down, so yours should be, too. The Historical Expense Ratio % chart shows you whether your fund's fees are falling.

Portfolio tab

When studying an investment at such a bird's-eye level, it's easy to forget that a fund holds underlying assets such as stocks and bonds. The Portfolio tab breaks down what your fund owns, in terms of the following:

>> **Asset Allocation and Stock Style:** In the Portfolio tab, you'll find an Asset Allocation section. If you own a stock fund, you'll want to know how much it owns in U.S. and non-U.S. stock. If it's a balanced fund that owns both stock and bonds, you can see the breakdown in the Asset Allocation part of Morningstar's site. Also, remember the ever-present Morningstar style box, which is in in the Stock Style section of Morningstar's site.

TIP

Look, too, at how much cash the fund is holding. A little bit of cash, less than 2 percent or so of assets, allows the fund to pay people who redeem shares. But a high cash level indicates that the fund isn't doing what you're paying it to do: Invest your money.

>> **Exposure:** The sector breakdown in the Exposure section at Morningstar shows you the industries that the fund is invested in. If you're buying a broadly diversified fund, you'll want to see a wide dispersion between industries.

>> **ESG metrics:** Answering a rising chorus of investors who want to own companies helping the earth, Morningstar added ESG (environmental, social, and governance) measures. *ESG measures* tell you whether the companies owned by the fund are working toward socially conscious objectives, such as reducing toxic emissions and cutting energy use.

>> **Holding summary:** Here you'll find how many investments the fund owns and the concentration of holdings. For instance, what percentage of the fund's holdings are in the top 10? Speaking of the top 10, you'll see which companies have the biggest positions in the fund.

Parent tab

No, the Parent tab isn't a place for your mom and dad. It's where you can learn a bit about the company that runs the fund. You'll find information about the following:

>> **Parent company's size:** Most fund companies run many funds. Here you can find how much money is going into the group's entire family of funds. You can also see how many funds the company runs and how much money is in them.

>> **Fund managers:** The people who select the investments that go into a fund, especially an actively managed fund, determine how well it does. You want to see managers who stick around and invest their own money in the funds they run. All this information is here.

Putting your entire portfolio to the test

Morningstar is a powerful tool for analyzing your individual funds. But looking at individual funds is only part of the job of building a solid retirement plan.

Think of your portfolio as an orchestra, with you as the conductor. You audition the separate musicians and get the very best person in each chair. You assemble top brass players, seat them next to the best percussionists, and throw in some world-class woodwinds, too. But that doesn't mean the orchestra as a whole will sound great.

The same idea applies to your retirement portfolio. You need to consider how all the funds work with each other. As you might imagine, analyzing a portfolio can be complicated, requiring higher-level statistics. Luckily, Morningstar does the work for you. Its Instant X-Ray tool (www.morningstar.com/portfolio-manager) crunches all the data about your portfolio and tells you how you're doing. Here's how:

1. **Log in to Instant X-Ray at** www.morningstar.com/portfolio-manager.

    You may need to create a free Morningstar account to launch Instant X-Ray.

2. **Enter the symbols of the assets in your portfolio, and include the dollar value of each position.**

3. **Click the Show Instant X-Ray button.**

    From there, Morningstar works its magic. You'll see a comprehensive report like the one in Figure 9-4.

Instant X-Ray completely breaks down your portfolio, showing your

>> **Asset allocation:** What you have in cash, U.S. stocks, foreign stocks, and bonds

>> **Stock sectors and holdings:** The industries your portfolio is most concentrated in and the types of stock, such as aggressive growth, you own

>> **Expense ratio summary:** The fees for your entire portfolio

TIP

Instant X-Ray is a great basic and free checkup of your portfolio. But you'll quickly notice some limitations. You must manually type your portfolio each time; you can't save it. Also, to use some advanced tools, such as a more detailed asset class, style, and fee analysis, you must sign up for a Morningstar Premium Membership, which costs $199 a year. If you're interested in managing your own retirement accounts, rather than buying a target-date fund or using a live financial advisor or a robo-advisor, the subscription should be worthwhile.

FIGURE 9-4:
Morningstar's Instant X-Ray tool studies your entire portfolio in depth.

Putting Your 401(k) Under the BrightScope Microscope

It's easy to see why Morningstar is so respected in the retirement-planning industry. Many advisors (and financial journalists) use professional-level versions of Morningstar tools. The first part of the chapter shows you the depth of information you can get from Morningstar.

However, if you're want a simple quick assessment of your 401(k), you'll look forward to performing a Morningstar Instant X-Ray as much as you love getting a real x-ray. For 401(k) investors, the simpler option is BrightScope.

BrightScope is designed to help investors who want a quick way to check on their mutual funds, 401(k) plans, and financial advisors. It's more of a smart summary than a database (although it's powered by a massive database). Enter the name of your mutual fund, 401(k) plan, or advisor, and in minutes you'll have a reasonable idea about whether or not your retirement plan is in good shape.

BrightScoping your 401(k)

Not sure if your 401(k) is any good? BrightScope is about to become your best friend. The service knows how to pull all the needed documents to examine your 401(k).

TIP

It's good to know whether your 401(k) is lousy, riddled with high fees and poor investment choices. If it is, you'll need to decide if you should skip it and simply fund your own IRA account. But the advantages of 401(k) plans make them compelling even if they're just so-so. Remember, contribution limits on 401(k) plans are much higher than traditional and Roth IRAs. Using a 401(k) will allow you to save much more than with an IRA. Also, your company may match your contributions up to a set percentage. Even if your 401(k) isn't great, you'll want to put in at least enough to get the full match. It's hard to argue with free money!

To put your 401(k) through the paces, do the following:

1. **Go to BrightScope at `www.brightscope.com`.**

2. **Choose the Research A 401(k) Plan option.**

3. **Enter the name of your employer.**

   I used Amazon.com's 401(k) plan as an example.

4. **Feast your eyes on your 401(k)'s report card.**

   The BrightScope report gives the 401(k) an overall rating, with 0 the worst and 100 the best. The rating is based on everything from cost to the generosity of the match to the size of the plan (larger plans can get cost breaks). Check out the just-average generosity score of the Amazon plan shown in Figure 9-5. Come on Jeff Bezos!

You'll find all sorts of gems in the BrightScope report. A few highlights (other than the overall rating) follow:

>> **Details of participation:** You can see how many fellow employees and former employees are in the plan. You can also find out how much money is in the 401(k).

>> **How much more you could have if the plan were better:** BrightScope tells you the amount of "lost" savings if the plan is average or poor.

>> **Investment summary:** Curious about how many funds you can choose from in the plan? The answer is in the investment summary. You can also see in which funds most of your fellow employees are putting their money.

>> **How much others saved:** I find the average account balance statistic particularly interesting. You can size up how much you've saved compared with your fellow workers.

FIGURE 9-5:
Amazon.com's 401(k) plan gets a so-so rating from BrightScope.

DIVING INTO FORM 5500

If you want to examine your 401(k) with a fine-tooth comb, it's time to talk about Form 5500, which the IRS requires employee benefit plan administrators to file. These forms aren't page-turners, but they are chock-full of information.

BrightScope, again, makes Form 5500 accessible and readable. Select the Form 5500 Data button at the top of the 401(k) rating page. Be prepared to know more about your 401(k) plan than you ever thought possible.

You'll see when the plan was started and how many retired employees are drawing benefits from it. You'll even see how many beneficiaries of deceased employees are in the plan. Hey, inquiring minds want to know!

Scroll down because there's more. You'll see if any mistakes or delays were made in handling contributions, the service provider (Amazon uses Vanguard), and a full run-down of all funds in the plan. Lastly, you can see the full financial statements of the 401(k) plan, down to its assets and liabilities.

Bottom line: You don't know your 401(k) until you've read Form 5500.

You can read the IRS rules regarding Form 5500 at www.irs.gov/retirement-plans/form-5500-corner.

Learning more about your funds

When it comes to understanding your funds, Morningstar is tough to beat. But BrightScope gives you a quick rundown of the minimum information you really should know.

From the drop-down box at BrightScope.com, choose Analyze a Fund and enter the name of a fund. You'll see a graphical summary of key points, such as the plan's assets, its managers, and the flows into or out of the fund.

The fees area is particularly useful. A graphical display shows you the annual expense ratio versus similar products. You'll also find a colorful performance chart that shows how $10,000 invested in the fund would have performed over various time periods.

Getting to know your advisor

You can save yourself a bundle in advisory fees. But not everyone has the interest or the time to become a retirement-planning expert.

Financial advisors can be great allies in working toward a solid retirement. They spend every day studying retirement planning. Good ones can help you find ways to optimize your situation.

You might hand over the job to an advisor you trust. Another option is to hire an advisor to look over the retirement plan you designed. Either way, you'll want to know that you can trust your advisor. Word of mouth, the way most people find advisors, is a good place to start. But BrightScope can help you double-check.

Again, from BrightScope.com, choose the Evaluate a Financial Advisor option from the drop-down menu. Enter the name of the advisor or the advisor's firm. You'll see a description of the advisor's experience, including at other firms. You'll find out how much money the advisor is managing and how much money each client has.

REMEMBER

BrightScope can be useful to scope out advisors, but the database isn't complete. I couldn't find many advisors in the system. Some details I'd like to see aren't always there, either. I expect BrightScope to get better over time. When sizing up advisors, the most comprehensive information comes from Finra's BrokerCheck at `https://brokercheck.finra.org`. You learn how to use BrokerCheck in Chapter 6.

Grading Your Retirement Plans in Other Ways

Ever wonder how Netflix knows what other movies you'd love? Similarly, Amazon can almost predict what you'd like to buy next. Creepy, eh?

Welcome to the age of artificial intelligence, or AI. The same digital smarts are being applied to the financial world — especially retirement planning. The timing is perfect. With the job of retirement planning being left to workers — many of whom are too busy or not prepared to measure their plans — any extra help is welcome.

REMEMBER

Many robo-advisors are already putting AI-like skills to work in choosing portfolios for clients. The firms mentioned in this section are just examples. In the future, expect much more innovation using AI in portfolio management.

New tools continue to crop up to help time-crunched workers measure their 401(k) plans. Rather than having a person try to determine if your 401(k) is decent, a computer can pull in all the data and tell you.

Expect lots of innovation in this area. More people are aware of the fees eating away at their 401(k) and how much they cost in the long run in general terms. But they just don't know how to measure how much fees are costing them individually in their own retirement plan.

You might think about using AI to help you

>> **See how much you're paying in fees.** This is a recurring theme, if you haven't noticed.

>> **Find potential options that will cost you less.** There's almost always another option.

>> **Fine-tune your asset allocation.** AI can help you find another approach to your mix of asset classes. Remember, your asset allocation is a big factor in the risk you'll endure and the return you'll get.

X marks the spot for a better 401(k)

FeeX (www.feex.com), founded in 2012, is an automated workplace retirement plan analyzer. You can set up a free account with the company at https://401kfeeanalyzer.tdameritrade.com/auth/signup.html.

The company isn't connected with TD Ameritrade, but it teamed up with TD Ameritrade online brokerage to offer the Retirement Plan Fee Analysis tool. After you sign up, you enter your age and the state you live in. You can then enter your 401(k) information manually or give FeeX permission to pull it in for you.

After you get your 401(k) information into the tool, FeeX does its data crunching, figuring out whether you're invested in expensive funds. FeeX will tell you how much you could save with lower-priced funds, and names specific funds that would be similar to what you have but with lower fees.

REMEMBER

FeeX is a great tool and will undoubtably be improved over the years. It currently has several limitations. It works only with workplace retirement plans such as 401(k)s and 401(b)s. So if you have an IRA, it's of no help. Also, with 401(k)s, you can't really get money out until you're retired or leave the company. That means you might not be able to act right away on the suggestions offered by FeeX. Finally, because the free tool is sponsored by TD Ameritrade, you'll see a strong message about the benefits of rolling over your IRA to them.

Getting up close and personal with Personal Capital

Personal Capital (www.personalcapital.com) is difficult to put into a single box. It offers financial tracking like Quicken and budgeting help. It offers a robo-advisor and a solid retirement calculator. Personal Capital will also pair you up with a live financial advisor.

But for our purposes, Personal Capital brings AI to your retirement planning. Following are a couple of tools that can help bring a digital second opinion to your retirement plan:

>> **Retirement Fee Analyzer:** If you choose Retirement Fee Analyzer on the Planning tab, you'll fire up one of the functions that put Personal Capital on the map. After you link to your online 401(k) or IRA plan's account credentials, Personal Capital will pick apart your account. The site will tell you what you're paying in annual fees and how they compare with the benchmark.

>> **Investment Checkup:** In Personal Capital's Planning tab, you'll also find an Investment Checkup option. Again, this function works best if you link your financial accounts and let Personal Capital pull in all your financial account data.

After you link your accounts, Investment Checkup will look over what you own and what you should own. You'll see your asset allocation, as shown in Figure 9-6. Personal Capital tells you whether your mix of stocks and bonds is right for your retirement goals. It also suggests what your target asset allocation should look like, and why.

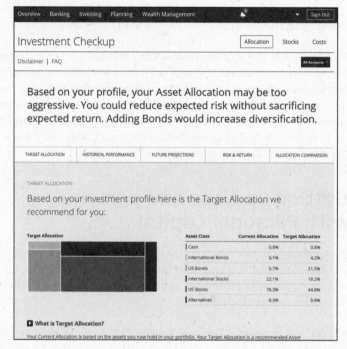

FIGURE 9-6:
Personal Capital's Investment Checkup provides a good reality check on how to improve your asset allocation.

WARNING

AI is so new in retirement planning that I could fill a chapter with cautions and warnings. Instead, I will provide two. First, garbage in, garbage out holds true. If you enter incorrect or inaccurate information about your accounts or retirement goals, the findings will be way off. AI is smart, but it knows only what you tell it. Second, AI bases its assumptions mostly on the past. Although the future usually rhymes with the past, surprises are part of financial markets and retirement planning.

Chapter **10**

Digging into Social Security

M ore than 60 million Americans collect Social Security benefits each year. You're likely to be one of them eventually, which is why it's important to understand this important government program.

Social Security is a much maligned, criticized, and certainly flawed system. But it's also an important one. Americans received nearly $1 trillion in payments from the Social Security Administration in 2018. Many Americans rely on Social Security for all or most of their income, even though it was never intended to be used like that.

In 2018, the typical monthly payment to retired workers was $1,404, or nearly $17,000 a year. And for some people, Social Security is the only thing keeping them out of poverty. Any person age 65 or older is considered impoverished if his or her income is $11,756 a year or less.

The program also offers other types of financial safety nets, including disability and workers compensation benefits.

If you don't understand Social Security or know how to use online tools to maximize it, you're missing out on what's likely to be an important part of your retirement plan. You've come to the right chapter.

Discovering All the Benefits of Social Security

Nobody likes opening their paycheck and seeing 6.2 percent of it removed to cover Social Security tax. The tax is even more painful for self-employed people, who must cover not only the employee's 6.2 percent portion of the tax but also an additional 6.2 percent (which employers pay).

There's also a tax for Medicare, the national healthcare program primarily for retired people. For this tax, you pay 1.45 percent of your salary and your employer pays 1.45 percent. Again, if you work for yourself, you pay the entire 2.9 percent. So all told, you give up 7.65 percent of your paycheck (15.3 percent if you're self-employed) with Social Security and Medicare taxes. And starting in 2013, someone who makes $200,000 or more ($250,000 for married couples filing jointly) pays an additional 0.9 percent for a Medicare tax surcharge.

What exactly do you get for the money you're putting into the Social Security system? The answer is much more than just some extra money in retirement.

Disability coverage (SSDI): The forgotten bonus of Social Security

It's not fun to think about, but disability is common. The Social Security Administration estimates that there's a 25 percent chance that a 20-year-old will become disabled before reaching full retirement age. Those odds are significant.

If you become disabled, your retirement-planning spreadsheets might as well be blown out the window. All the income you thought you'd be using to pay your bills, contribute to your 401(k) plan, and buy a house can quickly vanish if you're not able to work.

That's where Social Security can help. If you can't work due to a medical condition expected to last at least a year or one expected to be fatal, you qualify for *SSDI*, the Social Security disability insurance program.

Qualifying for SSDI

To qualify for SSDI, you must meet the following two tests:

» **Recent work test:** Your eligibility is based on your age when you become disabled. You are exempt from this test if you lose your eyesight. For instance, if you're disabled after you turn 31, you need to have worked five out of the past ten years.

» **Duration of work test:** You need to prove that you worked long enough to earn your entrance into SSDI.

Social Security maintains a table, like the one summarized in Table 10-1, showing how long you must have worked to qualify for benefits at different ages.

TABLE 10-1

Age and Work History Define SSDI Eligibility

Age You Become Disabled	You Must Have Worked
Before age 28	1.5 years
42	5 years
50	7 years
56	8.5 years
60	9.5 years

www.ssa.gov/pubs/EN-05-10029.pdf

Determining whether you're disabled

How do know if you're disabled in the eyes of the government? The Social Security Administration uses five questions to determine whether you're disabled enough to qualify for SSDI. These questions are asked in the following order:

1. **Are you still working?**

If you're still at work, you're not considered disabled.

2. **Are you suffering from a severe disability?**

Your condition must be so debilitating that you cannot lift, stand, walk, or sit for at least a year.

3. **Are you affected by a category of disability that Social Security considers an impairment?**

The impairment must be bad enough to be considered severe.

4. **Are you able to do the work you did before?**

   Does the disability stop you from doing the tasks you did before?

5. **Are you able to do another job?**

   You must show that you're unable to do any job, not just the one you had before.

REMEMBER

Medicare medical coverage kicks in after you've been deemed disabled and received SSDI benefits for two years. Also keep in mind that it can take up to five months after filing for disability for the claim to be processed.

To apply for SSDI, go to www.ssa.gov/benefits/disability/.

It's good to know that disability insurance is there if you need it, but it's just a Band-Aid, not a complete solution for an income shortfall. The average monthly disability payment in 2019 (to roughly 9 million people) was $1,234, or just $12,140 a year.

Social Security has two disability coverages. SSDI is the primary disability coverage from Social Security and the one most people use if they become disabled. The second program is *SSI*, or Supplemental Security Income. SSI, which is a distinct program from SSDI, pays benefits to low-income people who are over the age of 65 or disabled. SSDI is paid for from Social Security taxes; SSI is paid for from general tax revenue. To learn more about SSI, check out www.ssa.gov/ssi/.

Medicare for All

Are you appalled at cost of health insurance? Now imagine how much it would cost if you were 65 instead of a spritely 25. If you could even find an insurer willing to give you a policy at 65, the cost would be out of reach for most people.

Enter *Medicare*, the national health insurance program for people 65 and older. Medicare wouldn't be a respectable government program if it didn't have multiple parts:

>> **Part A:** This is your hospital insurance. If you've ever seen a bill after spending just a day or two in the hospital, you'll appreciate the importance of this coverage. Medicare Part A pays for a portion of your hospital bills.

>> **Part B:** Here's where you get help with your doctor bills. Some medical equipment and home health care are covered as well.

>> **Part C:** Also called Medicare Advantage, Part C allows you to get your Part A and Part B benefits, plus additional benefits from a private insurer. You can read the details at `https://medicare.com/medicare-advantage/medicare-part-c/`.

>> **Part D:** This part is where you get prescription drug coverage.

REMEMBER

Medicare and Medicaid share similar names, but they're different programs. *Medicaid* is a state health insurance program to help low-income people.

If you're eligible for Social Security, you're eligible for Medicare, too. Even if you're not collecting Social Security, you can enroll in Medicare at age 65. The Social Security Administration recommends that you sign up three months before turning 65. For details, go to `www.socialsecurity.gov`.

TIP

In some cases, people can qualify for Medicare before turning 65. Some examples include if you've collected Social Security disability for 24 months, have Lou Gehrig's disease, or have kidney failure.

Medicare rules could fill an entire book. In fact, they do. For more, go to `www.ssa.gov/pubs/EN-05-10043.pdf`.

Survivors benefits

Seeing a family lose the sole breadwinner is difficult. Some families have life insurance to protect them from this unfortunate event. In addition, Social Security offers a bit of extra help for people who find themselves in this situation.

Roughly five million widows and widowers get monthly Social Security benefits. The benefits that survivors get following the death of a spouse, father, or child vary based on how long the person worked and the age of the survivor. To see who is and isn't covered, go to `www.ssa.gov/planners/survivors/onyourown.html`.

Retirement benefits

For most people, Social Security conjures up images of retirement checks. And sending monthly checks is Social Security's primary function. The retirement benefits of Social Security have the following useful features:

>> **Cost-of-living adjustments:** Periodically, Social Security makes a cost-of-living adjustment and bumps up the amount paid to beneficiaries. This adjustment helps payments keep up with rising costs, or *inflation.* In 2019, Social Security raised payments by 2.8 percent.

>> **Delayed benefits advantage:** Social Security has a full retirement age, which is the age at which you'll get your full benefit. If you were born in 1937 or before, your full retirement age is 65. If you were born after 1937, your full retirement age rises. If you were born in 1960, for example, your full retirement age is 67.

If you retire at your full retirement age, you get your full retirement check from Social Security. But if you need the money sooner, you can retire earlier and get a smaller amount. Similarly, if you don't need the money at your full retirement age, you can postpone taking it. When you do take the money later than your full retirement age, you'll get a higher payment.

Let's say your full retirement age is 66. If you wait until age 67 to take benefits, you get 108 percent of the monthly benefit. If you wait until age 70, you get 132 percent of the monthly benefit. There's no added benefit for waiting to collect after you turn 70.

CAN YOU OPT OUT OF SOCIAL SECURITY?

Given the stiff Social Security tax and the fear that Social Security won't be solvent when they need it, some investors would rather keep the money and invest it themselves. But can you opt out of Social Security's FICA (Federal Insurance Contributions Act) tax?

The answer is yes, you can opt out in rare situations. But you probably shouldn't.

To get out of paying Social Security tax, you must be part of a qualifying religious organization. The rules are strict and require you to fill out Form 4361 (www.irs.gov/pub/irs-pdf/f4361.pdf) and Form 8274 (www.irs.gov/pub/irs-pdf/f8274.pdf). You can't just start up a religion and hope to opt out. The religious sect must have existed since 1950 and have a demonstrated track record providing for its aged and disabled members.

Some workers with older state pensions might be able to opt out, too.

Although you probably can't opt out of paying Social Security, that's not a bad thing. Remember that Social Security provides more than just retirement benefits. You also get disability and survivor benefits. Yes, you could buy your own disability insurance, but less than a third of private sector workers do.

The bottom line: You probably can't opt out of Social Security, and even if you can, don't.

Managing Social Security Information Online

Social Security, especially its disability benefits, acts somewhat like an insurance policy. It also behaves a bit like an IRA or pension, due to its retirement benefits. But Social Security is uniquely different from your insurance policies and retirement plans.

How so? Social Security is a pay-as-you-go system. In other words, the money coming out of your paycheck for Social Security tax isn't being held aside somewhere for your future self to spend. The money you're putting into the system now pays the benefits of current recipients. And when you retire, your Social Security benefits will come from workers paying into the system at that time.

Examining what you're paying into Social Security

The U.S. Government is diligent about making sure you pay your share when it comes to Social Security. As soon as you get a job and provide your Social Security number, your employer will make sure you're paying the tax. Your paycheck should look similar to Figure 10-1.

Sample Company LLC
2305 Gruene Lake Drive, Suite C New Braunfels, Texas

EARNINGS STATEMENT

EMPLOYEE NAME			SSN	EMPLOYEE ID	CHECK NO.	PAY PERIOD	PAY DATE
Hidalgo P. Swift			XXX-XX-1234	12345	76612	01/08/19-01/14/19	01/15/19

INCOME	RATE	HOURS	CURRENT TOTAL	DEDUCTIONS	CURRENT TOTAL	YEAR-TO-DATE
GROSS WAGES	24.25	40.00	970.00	FICA MED TAX	14.06	28.12
				FICA SS TAX	60.14	120.28
				FED TAX	117.68	235.36

YTD GROSS	YTD DEDUCTIONS	YTD NET PAY	CURRENT TOTAL	CURRENT DEDUCTIONS	NET PAY
1,940.00	383.76	1,556.24	970.00	191.88	778.12

FIGURE 10-1:
A typical paycheck deducts Social Security and Medicare tax.

TIP

Many people don't take the time to look at their pay stubs. But given how much money is coming out and how important Social Security is, you should check your take-home pay calculations.

TIP

If you're thinking about accepting a new job and curious what your take-home pay will be, check out the ADP Salary Paycheck Calculator at `www.adp.com/resources/tools/calculators/salary-paycheck-calculator.aspx`. The calculator estimates your Social Security, federal, and state taxes.

If you're self-employed, you pay all Social Security and Medicare taxes as part of your annual tax return. If you're curious about how this tax collection process works, check out Schedule SE (Self Employment), which is shown in Figure 10-2. Schedule SE pulls in the profit or loss from your business, which is calculated on Schedule C minus your deductions. That amount is modified and used as the basis for your Social Security tax.

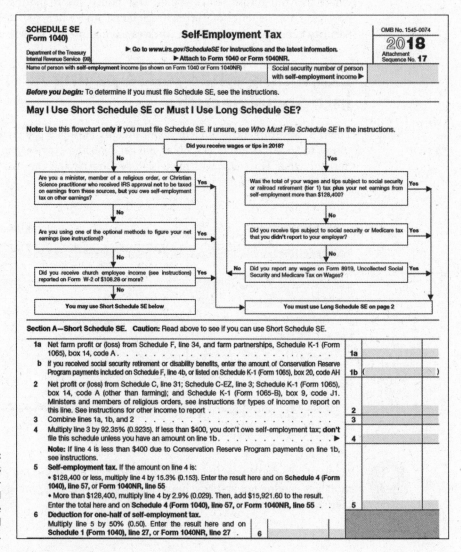

FIGURE 10-2:
Schedule SE is where self-employed people calculate their Social Security taxes.

Let's say your business brings in $100,000 in revenue, but you have $25,000 in deductions and expenses. The net profit of your business is $75,000 (as shown on line 31 of Schedule C). That net profit is then carried over to line 2 of Schedule SE.

The government allows you to reduce your taxable net profit before calculating your Social Security tax. You start with your gross income to calculate your net profit. If your business's adjusted gross income is $128,400 or less in 2019, you multiply it by 15.3 percent, or 0.153. Gross income greater than $128,400 may be reduced by 7.65 percent.

So going back to our example, the profit of $75,000 is less than $128,400, so you multiply by 0.153 to calculate a Self-Employment Social Security tax of $11,475.

Or you could just use tax-preparation software.

Signing up for and accessing Social Security information online

Let's back up for a second. Just because you're paying into Social Security doesn't mean you're getting credit for your contributions. The Social Security Administration deals with millions of people. Mistakes happen. It's your responsibility to catch errors and tell the Social Security Administration to fix them. Fortunately, online tools can help you with this verification process.

Setting up your account

When you're born, you're handed a Social Security number and a Social Security card. Well, your parents are. But it's up to you to get online access for your Social Security account. Don't worry, it's easy:

1. **Head to Social Security Online Services at** https://secure.ssa.gov/RIL/SiView.action.

    This site is where you kick off the process.

2. **Click the Create an Account button.**

    You're reminded of the personal information you need to open an account, including your email address, Social Security number, and U.S. mailing address. You must be at least 18 years old to sign up for online Social Security access.

REMEMBER

After you register for online Social Security access, you'll no longer receive paper account status letters in the mail. You won't miss them.

3. **Fill out your personal information.**

   Enter your name, Social Security number, and other data.

4. **Verify your identity.**

   If you're extra cautious about security, you can choose to get a password mailed to you. Otherwise, you can verify who you are online and choose your own password.

Logging into your account and knowing what to look for

After you have a Social Security account, you're in business. Head over to `https://secure.ssa.gov/RIL/SiView.action` and enter your username and password. The My Social Security screen, which is a launchpad for all your Social Security information, appears as shown in Figure 10-3.

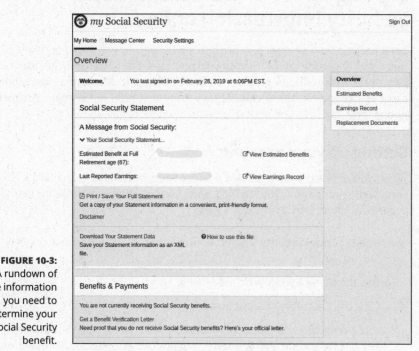

FIGURE 10-3:
A rundown of the information you need to determine your Social Security benefit.

From the My Social Security screen, you can

>> **Discover your estimated benefit at your full retirement age.** The site displays the amount of monthly benefits you can expect when you retire.

>> **Check your reported earnings.** By default, you'll see how much you paid into the Social Security system last year. You can also get a complete record of your contributions going back to your first job. Click the View Earnings Record link to the right of your last reported earnings (refer to Figure 10-3). A complete rundown of your Social Security payments appears. Scroll down and you'll see the total taxes you (and your employers) paid for Social Security and Medicare.

Look over each year's taxed earnings carefully. If you find any mistakes, it's up to you to report it. You can print your Social Security statement and call the number on the page to clear up any discrepancy. You'll want to have your tax form for that year handy, as proof of what you paid.

>> **Confirm your receipt of benefits.** Another section of the My Social Security page shows if you're currently receiving benefits.

>> **Order a replacement Social Security card.** If you can't find your Social Security card, I forgive you. After all, your parents probably stuffed it in a shoebox when you were born. Some employers require you to produce a Social Security card before you start a job. You can order a replacement here. Just be careful; you can request only 10 replacement cards during your lifetime.

>> **Update personal information.** You use your email address to verify your identity when you return to the site. If you get a new email address, update it here.

By default, the main My Social Security screen shows your monthly retirement benefit amount at full retirement. Are you curious about what your payout would be if you retired earlier or later? And what about disability or survivor benefits? No problem. Click the View Estimated Benefits link to the right of the monthly account (refer to Figure 10-3).

The screen shown in Figure 10-4 appears, breaking down all your estimated benefits. You can see how much you'd receive monthly if you retire early or late. The page also shows your estimated payout for disability and survivor benefits (including for your child, your spouse, and total family benefits). If you're 65 years old, you can also see your estimated Medicare benefits.

Understanding your history of Social Security credits

Why is it so important to track your past earnings? That's ancient history, right? Nope. The number of years you work determines if you're eligible for Social Security. And the amount of money you earned each year determines how much you'll get when you retire or become disabled.

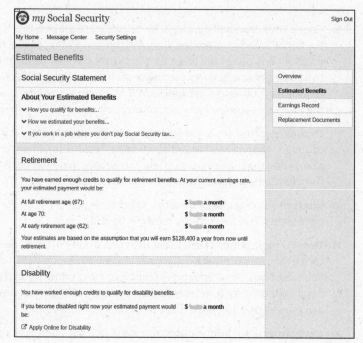

FIGURE 10-4:
You can drill down into your Social Security and see how much you'd get if you retired early (or late).

Becoming eligible for Social Security

When it comes to Social Security, the number $1,360 is important. Any time you earn $1,360 in wages or self-employed income, you get one credit with Social Security. A *credit* is a point notched in your Social Security work history belt. You can earn up to four Social Security credits a year.

Why do these credits matter? You need 40 credits to become eligible for Social Security. For instance, as soon as you've earned at least $5,440 a year for 10 years, you're in the Social Security club. Congrats!

TIP

If you have kids who take on paid summer jobs or internships, they can earn credits to speed up their eligibility for Social Security.

Measuring the amount of Social Security benefits

Determining the size of your monthly Social Security payment takes some ninja-like math skills. It's a good thing the Social Security Administration calculates our estimated benefit for us. Here's the Dummies-style summary of how it's done:

WARNING

>> **Your payment is based on your lifetime earnings:** Your entire working career is analyzed, not just the years closest to retirement.

>> **The 35 years you earned the most (during your entire career) are used for the calculation.** Social Security takes the average earnings in the years you made the greatest amounts. If you don't have 35 years of earnings, Social Security averages $0 for any missing years.

If you decide to retire early, your Social Security benefit will be reduced. Let's say you made $60,000 a year for 30 years. Social Security will take your average earnings of $60,000 a year for 30 years plus $0 a year for five years. That average is $51,429. Had you worked for 35 years at $60,000 a year, your average would have been $60,000. This reduction may not be enough to keep working, but it is enough to keep in mind.

>> **Mathematical indexing is applied to get your primary insurance amount.** Social Security applies a mathematical formula to your earnings history to see how much you'll get if you retire at your full retirement age. It's quite a calculation. If you'd like to see the math, go to www.ssa.gov/pubs/EN-05-10070.pdf.

>> **Cost-of-living adjustments are added.** Your Social Security payments are adjusted higher periodically to keep up with inflation.

>> **Adjustments are made for government pensions.** If you get, or will get, a government pension on which Social Security wasn't paid, a Windfall Elimination Provision (WEP) kicks in. If you're in this situation, go to www.socialsecurity.gov/gpo-wep to see how your benefit will be affected.

Planning for Social Security in Retirement

While you're working, Social Security punches a big hole in your paycheck. It's yet another tax added to all the other deductions. But your perception of Social Security will change when you retire. Rather than paying Social Security taxes, you'll get a Social Security check. And who said there's no upside to getting older?

But how do you know when you should apply for Social Security? If you apply for benefits early, before reaching full benefit age, you take a big hit in what you receive. Online tools can help you make this important decision. And after you decide what you plan to do, you need to know how to apply to receive your benefits. Read this section for more.

WILL SOCIAL SECURITY BE AROUND FOR YOU?

No conversation about Social Security would be complete without a discussion about whether the program will even be around when you retire. The younger you are, the more skeptical you might be about the program's viability — and for good reason. Social Security's 2019 annual report (www.ssa.gov/oact/TRSUM/index.html) shows that, at the current pace, the system will deplete its reserves by 2035.

People are living longer and the number of young people paying into the system aren't keeping up with the amount needed for older people pulling out benefits. That imbalance is putting a strain on the cash cushion in the Social Security reserves. Over the system's inception in the 1930s, it has paid out $19 trillion and collected $21.9 trillion. That excess amount, $2.9 trillion at the end of 2018, will shrink over time.

Will Social Security vanish? No, says AARP. But changes are likely. According to the AARP, if no reforms are made, Social Security will be able to pay only 80 percent of the benefits that retired and disabled workers are entitled to.

Following are some possible changes to the system:

- Require higher earners to pay more into the system or reduce their benefits.

- Raise the full retirement age.

- Change the benefit calculation to reduce monthly Social Security payouts.

- Reduce the cost-of-living adjustment.

- Raise the employee portion of the Social Security tax from 6.2 percent to 6.45 percent.

- Apply Social Security taxes to other benefit plans. Employees pay Social Security taxes on 401(k) contributions but not on other plans such as Flexible Spending Accounts, which allow workers to hold aside pre-tax dollars to pay for qualifying medical costs.

None of these proposals has gone far in Congress. But it's important to know that Social Security in the future could be different than it is today. Benefits could be cut or pushed out. When planning for your retirement, always look at scenarios that leave out Social Security, too. Then you won't be disappointed (or unprepared).

Claiming your Social Security benefit

When Social Security started, it was assumed that most people would retire at age 65. That was the *full retirement age,* or the age at which you're eligible for your entire Social Security monthly benefit. But in the early 1980s, Congress approved a law that increased the full retirement age, over time, to 67.

Your full retirement age is based on your birthdate. You can get your full retirement age from Social Security at `www.ssa.gov/planners/retire/ageincrease.html`. Kiplinger's, a personal finance site, also has a helpful calculator for figuring out your full retirement age. Go to `www.kiplinger.com/tool/retirement/T051-S001-social-security-full-retirement-age-calculator/index.php`. Just enter your birthdate, and you'll see your full retirement age.

The full retirement age is a guide; you don't have to follow it. If you've retired early or need the income before your full retirement age, you can file for Social Security retirement benefits early. However, you'll receive a smaller payment. Similarly, if you delay taking your Social Security payment until after your full retirement age, you'll get more.

How much will taking benefits earlier or later than your full retirement age affect your payment? Table 10-2 shows how different situations affect a person whose full retirement age is 67 (anyone born in 1960 or later).

TABLE 10-2

Benefits with Full Retirement Age of 67

Age You Claim Social Security	Effect on Your Benefit
62	Reduced by 30%
63	Reduced by 25%
64	Reduced by 20%
65	Reduced by 13.3%
66	Reduced by 6.7%
68	Increased by 8%
69	Increased by 16%
70	Increased by 24%

www.kiplinger.com/tool/retirement/T051-S001-social-security-full-retirement-age-calculator/index.php

Suppose your monthly Social Security benefit at age 67 is $2,000 a month. If you take the benefit at 62, you'll get 30 percent ($600) less, for a total monthly payment of $1,400. If you wait until you're 70, you'll get 24 percent ($480) more, or $2,480 a month.

TIP

After you hit 70, there's no longer any reason to wait to claim your Social Security benefit. The benefit isn't increased after that point, so you might as well take it.

Why would you decide to take your Social Security benefit early or late? Factors that determine the optimal time to take Social Security include the following:

>> **Income needs:** If you are not working anymore and are having trouble making ends meet, you might need to take Social Security early. The reduction in benefit might be worthwhile if it means you can avoid taking on debt. Conversely, if you don't need the income, wait.

>> **Life expectancy:** If you think you're not going to live much longer than full retirement age, it's wise to take Social Security as soon as you can. But if you think you'll live longer than average, waiting will pay more money to you over time. Delaying Social Security also gives you an increased stream of income to help you avoid running out of money.

>> **Employment status:** If you're working and take Social Security benefits early, your benefits are reduced temporarily. The reduction goes away after you hit your full retirement age.

>> **Tax bracket:** Social Security can be taxable depending on your circumstances. If your modified gross income jumps over the limit, up to 85 percent of your Social Security benefit may be taxable. Modified gross income is your adjusted gross income plus interest from non-taxable sources (such as municipal bonds) and half your Social Security benefit. You can read more about this rule at www.ssa.gov/pubs/EN-05-10069.pdf. If you're in this situation, consider talking to a tax professional.

>> **Spouse's Social Security situation:** If your spouse is eligible for Social Security, you have additional strategies regarding when to start taking the benefit. A common suggestion from financial planners is for the lower-earning spouse to take benefits early at 62 and the higher-earning one to take benefits later at 70. Charles Schwab steps you through this strategy at www.schwab.com/resource-center/insights/content/when-should-you-take-social-security.

To determine the best time for you (and your spouse) to take your benefits, you could run through all the scenarios, or meet with a financial planner. Another approach it to use a specialized online calculator. You enter all the variables, and the calculator uses sophisticated algorithms to maximize your benefit. AARP's Social Security Resource Center at `www.aarp.org/work/social-security/` `social-security-benefits-calculator.html` is the gold standard for determining when you should claim your Social Security benefit. The AARP tool will help you make the call on when to claim your Social Security benefit.

REMEMBER

Unless you know exactly when you'll die, you can't know for sure the best time to take Social Security benefits. The Social Security *break-even analysis* is a helpful calculation to guide your decision. The calculation figures out the age at which your lower benefit (if you take Social Security early) equals the higher benefit (if you take it at your full retirement age or later). For instructions on performing the break-even calculation, to `www.dummies.com/personal-finance/retirement-` `options/how-to-perform-a-break-even-analysis-for-your-social-` `security-benefits/`.

Don't read too much into the break-even analysis. It's just one way to look at this personal decision.

Applying for benefits

Deciding when to take your Social Security benefit is the tough part. The easy part is filing for it. You can do it online in just a few minutes:

1. **Head to Social Security's application section at** `www.ssa.gov/benefits/` `forms`.

This site allows you to apply not only for retirement benefits but also spousal benefits, Medicare, and survivors benefits.

2. **Choose the benefit you're applying for.**

If you apply for retirement benefits, you'll see the screen shown in Figure 10-5.

3. **Click the Start a New Application button and respond to the screens that appear.**

You step through all the information you must enter to apply. Keep in mind that you'll need your My Social Security username and password.

4. **Wait, for weeks or months.**

You must wait for the approval process before getting your benefits. It's the government, after all!

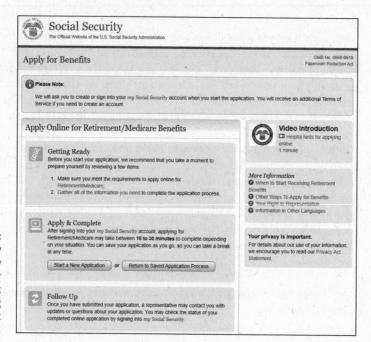

Social Security
The Official Website of the U.S. Social Security Administration

Apply for Benefits

OMB No. 0960-0618
Paperwork Reduction Act

ⓘ Please Note:

We will ask you to create or sign into your *my* Social Security account when you start the application. You will receive an additional Terms of Service if you need to create an account.

Apply Online for Retirement/Medicare Benefits

Getting Ready

Before you start your application, we recommend that you take a moment to prepare yourself by reviewing a few items:

1. Make sure you meet the requirements to apply online for Retirement/Medicare;
2. Gather all of the information you need to complete the application process.

Apply & Complete

After signing into your *my* Social Security account, applying for Retirement/Medicare may take between **10 to 30 minutes** to complete depending on your situation. You can save your application as you go, so you can take a break at any time.

[Start a New Application] or [Return to Saved Application Process]

Follow Up

Once you have submitted your application, a representative may contact you with updates or questions about your application. You may check the status of your completed online application by signing into *my* Social Security.

Video Introduction

📷 Helpful hints for applying online
1 minute

More Information
- When to Start Receiving Retirement Benefits
- Other Ways To Apply for Benefits
- Your Right to Representation
- Information in Other Languages

Your privacy is important.
For details about our use of your information, we encourage you to read our Privacy Act Statement.

FIGURE 10-5: Social Security makes it easy to apply for retirement benefits, as long as you're at least 62.

TIP

What if you decide to take your Social Security benefit early, say at age 62, but then change your mind and decide you'd like to take your benefit later? You have up to 12 months from filing to change your decision. You must fill out Form SSA-521 to initiate the do-over, or application withdrawal, and repay all the benefits you received. The Social Security Administration explains the rules and offers the forms at www.ssa.gov/planners/retire/withdrawal.html. Note that you get one do-over in your lifetime.

3

Maximizing Your Retirement Knowledge

Find ways to build a retirement plan that works in concert with your other financial goals.

Tune your portfolio asset plan to improve your retirement success.

Use online tools to make sure your retirement plan is on track.

Manage your retirement plan after you step away from your day job.

Know the fundamentals of pension plans.

Make sure you're fully protected.

Chapter **11**

Balancing Retirement Savings with Other Needs

I f all you had to do was save for retirement, you'd hardly feel it. How hard is it to put away 15 percent of your salary if you could spend the rest on whatever you'd like?

But life is more complicated than that. IRAs and 401(k)s are just two parts of your financial life that demand your cash. Competing uses of money need attention, too. You might also have debt, from a credit card, car loan, or college loans. Perhaps you want to save to buy a home.

And whether you have children or plan to, if you start saving for college early, you can amass much more money than your children could on their own. A little bit of saving now, when your children are young, can help them avoid loading up on student loans.

You might want to enjoy life by taking vacations or going out to eat.

Welcome to life. It's a world of balancing wants and needs. Your retirement is the biggest financial demand, but it's not the only one. Retirement might seem so far off that you're tempted to put off saving for it. But as you now know, putting off retirement planning is one of the worst financial decisions you can make.

But what you can do is enhance your retirement planning by optimizing your other plans for saving. So, although this is *Retirement Planning For Dummies*, I hope you'll appreciate that you can put your retirement plan on more solid footing by planning for some of your other big financial goals.

Cleaning Up Your Personal Balance Sheet

When companies want to prove to investors that they're moving in the right financial direction, they'll often say they're "cleaning up their balance sheet." This means they're using cash to reduce debt and other obligations that might hurt their performance or financial health in the future. When times are good, paying interest on loans isn't a big deal. But when money gets tight, debt payments can be crushing.

You can — and should — clean up your balance sheet too. If you're loaded down with debt and have low cash reserves and few assets, it's going to be difficult to meaningfully save for retirement. A lost job, a medical crisis, or skyrocketing rent — and suddenly the money you saved for retirement is needed just to make ends meet.

It's easy to see how a money hiccup can snowball into a catastrophe. As shown in Table 11-1, more than 750,000 Americans filed for nonbusiness bankruptcies in 2016 and 2017. The number of people filing for bankruptcy spikes in the year following a recession as they exhaust all their financial resources.

TABLE 11-1 **Total Nonbusiness Bankruptcies**

Year	Number of Bankruptcies
2008	1,004,171
2009	1,344,095
2010	1,538,033
2011	1,417,326
2012	1,219,132
2013	1,072,807

Year	Number of Bankruptcies
2014	935,420
2015	835,197
2016	781,123
2017	767,721

www.uscourts.gov/news/2018/03/07/just-facts-consumer-bankruptcy-filings-2006-2017

This doesn't have to happen to you.

TIP The New York Federal Reserve puts out reams of data on the type and amount of debt that people have. You can read all about what Americans owe in the Fed's quarterly Household Debt and Credit report at www.newyorkfed.org/medialibrary/interactives/householdcredit/data/pdf/HHDC_2019Q2.pdf.

Building an emergency fund

Although it pains me to say this, one financial milestone is so important that you'll want to prioritize it over going full bore on retirement planning. Building an emergency fund is your number-one savings job. A rainy day cash fund can help you stem potential financial problems before they become major.

Understanding why you need an emergency fund

If you don't have a cash cushion and life throws you a curveball, at best you may stop making retirement account contributions until you get back on your financial feet. At worst, you might be forced into debt to pay off the unexpected expense. Falling into the debt quicksand trap is one way you can set your retirement plan back by years — or longer.

Emergencies that might require you to dip into your fund include the following:

>> **An unexpected medical event:** A broken leg or a more serious medical setback can deal a major financial blow. Even if you have medical insurance, you have to pay deductibles. More challenging is lost income while you're recovering from your illness, if it's serious enough. Hospital admissions cause 5 percent of bankruptcies, as found in a 2018 study published in the American Economic Review (https://pubs.aeaweb.org/doi/pdfplus/10.1257/aer.20161038).

>> **Damage to home or car:** A leaky roof can cost tens of thousands of dollars. And while you might be prudent and avoid car payments by keeping your car

a long time, alternators and brakes wear out. Fixing those parts requires money outside your normal budget.

>> **Unemployment:** Unemployment has been low — and jobs plentiful — for so long that you might not think you'll have to look for your next gig. Finding one could take longer than expected, though. Randstad, a placement firm, reports that it takes an average of five months to find a new position (www. randstadusa.com/jobs/career-resources/career-advice/the-art-of-the-job-hunt/631/).

WARNING

In its Financial Security Index survey, Bankrate found that just 39 percent of people have enough cash to cover a $1,000 financial hit. This statistic shows how a relatively minor financial blow can put many people in a bad place. Why? Because if you're not one of the 39 percent who can't pay the cost from savings, you'll have to borrow.

And that's exactly what happens. Nearly 40 percent of people would have to borrow money if they had to handle a $1,000 expense. Some would even hit up family or friends for cash, as you can see in Table 11-2. Awkward!

TABLE 11-2

Covering an Unexpected $1,000 Cost

Solution	Response
Pay from savings	39%
Put on credit card	19%
Cut spending on other things	13%
Borrow from family or friends	12%
Take personal loan	5%
Other (don't know)	12%

www.bankrate.com/banking/savings/financial-security-0118/

Calculating the size of your emergency fund

In general, everyone needs to have a minimum of $1,000 in the bank at the ready. You don't want to be that person who needs to hit up friends for money to hire exterminators to get rats out of the attic.

After you build a $1,000 fund, you can be a bit more strategic. Most financial planners recommend that you have at least three to six months of living expenses in cash in your emergency fund.

REMEMBER

You should know your run rate, which tells you how much money you spend in a year. To calculate your run rate, see Chapter 2.

PNC Bank offers an Emergency Fund Calculator, shown in Figure 11-1, to help you figure out how much you should have in your cash pile. To access the calculator, go to www.pnc.com/en/calculators/investments-and-retirement/emergency-fund-calculator.html.

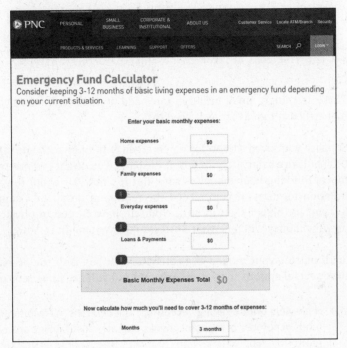

FIGURE 11-1:
PNC's Emergency
Fund Calculator
shows you
how big your
emergency
fund should be.

Deciding where to put your emergency fund

Much of this book has to do with investing for the long term. And for long-term investments, an IRA holding stocks and bonds is tough to beat. But a different strategy is in order for emergency cash. You primary goal for your cash is making sure you have immediate access to it at any time.

You might think that you should keep your cash in a box in your house, but that's not a winning strategy. Each year, inflation eats away at the purchasing power of your cash, as shown in Table 11-3.

TABLE 11-3 **U.S. Inflation Rate**

Year	Inflation Rate
2019	1.8%
2018	1.9%
2017	2.1%
2016	2.1%
2015	0.7%
2014	0.8%

www.usinflationcalculator.com/inflation/current-inflation-rates/

These seemingly small inflation rates add up fast. And before you know it, your money doesn't go as far as it used to.

Suppose you saved $1,000 for an emergency fund in 2014 and stuff all ten of the $100 bills in a safety deposit box at the bank. You might feel pretty good about this move, thinking your money is safe. But it's not. It's about to get chewed up by inflation termites. If you needed the money in 2019, for example, prices were 8.4 percent higher than in 2014. You still have $1,000 in physical currency, but now the money will buy what $916 would have bought in 2014.

So, if putting your money in a safety deposit box isn't the answer, what is? You have several options to keep money safe and still get some return:

>> **High-yield online savings accounts:** This choice is my favorite for emergency funds. A number of reputable banks operate mostly online and can offer higher returns by skipping fancy bank branches. These banks let you easily move cash between different accounts by using their mobile apps or website. Some of the leading banks in this category are Ally (www.ally.com), Discover Bank (www.discover.com/online-banking/), and Capital One (www.capitalone.com/bank/savings-accounts/). Need to deposit a check? No problem. Just take a photo of it using the app (Ally Bank's app is shown in Figure 11-2). And if you need to use an ATM to get cash, most online banks will reimburse you any fees you're charged by other banks.

>> **High-yield sweep accounts at brokerage firms:** If you're already investing, some brokerage firms offer cash management options. Fidelity, for instance, allows you to request that any uninvested cash in your brokerage account be swept into a high-yield account. Robo-advisors offer high-yield cash vehicles for parking cash, too. For instance, Wealthfront provides a Wealthfront Cash Account, which offers rates competitive with online banks.

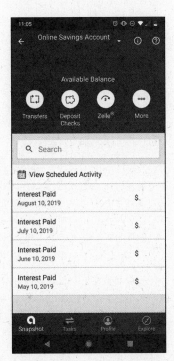

FIGURE 11-2:
Ally Bank's mobile app makes it easy to deposit or transfer money.

WARNING

Don't assume that your cash held at a brokerage is automatically being moved into a high-yield account. Even some large online brokerages sweep your cash into accounts that pay practically 0 percent. Also, make sure the cash accounts provide FDIC insurance to protect you in case the bank runs into financial difficulty. You can find out why FDIC insurance is so important in the "What Is FDIC Insurance?" sidebar.

» **Your local bank:** You won't get a good interest rate at your neighborhood bank, but you will get convenience. If you're not comfortable using your phone to bank, there's something to be said for walking into a bank branch where people know you. However, most local banks pay next to no interest.

WARNING

Some local banks will tempt you with higher interest rates available from certificates of deposits (CDs). And it's true, CDs offer interest rates similar to what you might get from a high-yield online bank. The longer they lock up your money, the higher the interest rate you get. But CDs are a bad idea for your emergency fund because most lock up your money for three months to five years and charge large penalties if you take the cash out early. Banks bury the disclosures of the fees they charge so you might not see them. If you take money out of a Bank of America one-year CD early, for example the bank will charge you the amount of interest you received over 90 days.

You may need access to your emergency fund at a moment's notice. CDs don't make sense for this purpose.

WHAT IS FDIC INSURANCE?

Most banks will tout that they offer Federal Deposit Insurance Corporation (FDIC) protection on deposits. Look for this important guarantee when you're opening a savings account. The FDIC is a U.S. government agency that makes sure a bank doesn't run off with your money. If anything happens to your cash held in an FDIC-insured bank, the agency will give it back to you.

The rules, though, are strict and have important limits. Simply stated, every depositor gets $250,000 of coverage in each insured bank. Let's say you put $250,000 in an FDIC-insured bank. You're protected up to $250,000 in that bank. But if you put $500,000 in the bank, you're still protected only up to $250,000. So if you have a half million bucks, put $250,000 in one bank and $250,000 in a different bank. That way you get $500,000 of total coverage — $250,000 in each bank.

The bank must be a member of FDIC. Go to the FDIC's BankFind tool at https://research.fdic.gov/bankfind/ to see whether a particular bank is a member.

Lastly, you must put your money in an account that's FDIC insured. That includes checking accounts, savings account, money-market accounts, and CDs. If you buy a mutual fund from a bank, it's not covered by the FDIC. Rather, your securities are covered by another entity, the Securities Investor Protection Corporation, or SIPC. The SIPC covers brokerage accounts; if a firm is a member, up to $500,000 (but only up to $250,000 in cash in the account) is covered. To see which financial assets the FDIC protects, go to www.sipc.org/for-investors/what-sipc-protects.

If you're not sure how much FDIC insurance you have, enter your account and balance information in the FDIC's Electronic Deposit Insurance Estimator at https://edie.fdic.gov/.

Finding the best interest rates

FDIC insurance, convenience, and a good mobile app are all important aspects of choosing a place to put your emergency cash. But the interest rate on your money is important, too. Depending on how much money is in your emergency fund, the interest rate you're paid can make a big difference.

Let's say you spend $40,000 a year, and your goal is to save six months of living expenses, or $20,000. Assuming there's no emergency and you don't take any money out of the account for five years, Table 11-4 shows how a higher interest rate will benefit you.

TABLE 11-4

Interest Rates Influence an Emergency Fund

Interest Rate	Value of $20,000 Emergency Fund in 5 Years
0.1%	$20,100
0.5%	$20,505
1.5%	$21,546
2.0%	$22,082
2.5%	$22,628
3.0%	$23,185

www.bankrate.com/calculators/retirement/roi-calculator.aspx

Clearly, a higher interest rate is preferable. But with tens of thousands of banks to choose from, how do you find the ones with the highest rates? That's where Bankrate comes in. This online service sorts through all the interest rates being offered so you can find the best bank for you. Just do the following:

1. Go to Bankrate at www.bankrate.com.

2. Choose the Savings/MMA option.

This is where you research interest rates for savings accounts.

3. Enter your savings details on the left side of the page, including how much you'll be saving and your zip code.

A list of banks offering the highest interest rates appears, as shown in Figure 11-3.

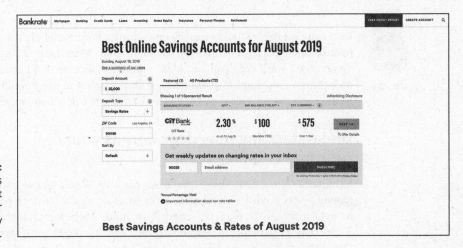

FIGURE 11-3: Bankrate helps you find the best place for your emergency money.

Cutting the debt anchor loose

Sadly, crushing debt is all too common. Americans carried $13.96 trillion in debt as of the second quarter of 2019, according to the Federal Reserve Bank of New York (www.newyorkfed.org/microeconomics/databank.html). With about 78 percent of the U.S. population (325 million) over the age of 18, that means roughly 253 million people are carrying nearly $14 trillion in debt. That works out to more than $55,000 in debt per person!

Discovering the types of debt that people have

Debt comes in several primary forms. Table 11-5 shows you where most Americans hold their $13.9 trillion in debt.

TABLE 11-5

Forms of Debt

Type of Debt	Value of Debt in Trillions	Percent of Total Debt
Mortgage	$9.41	67.9%
Home equity	$0.4	2.9%
Auto loans	$1.3	9.4%
Credit card	$0.87	6.3%
Student loans	$1.48	10.7%
Other	$0.41	3.0%
Total	$13.86	100%

www.newyorkfed.org/microeconomics/databank.html

WARNING

Debt can be a useful tool to unlock opportunity but financially ruinous if misused. An affordable mortgage can be an excellent long-term financial move. But loading up on credit-card debt is a bad idea, especially because most credit card companies charge exorbitant interest rates. If you're going to use a credit card, pay it off in full each month. Get your cashback rewards, but don't pay any interest.

Understanding how debt derails your retirement savings plan

Eliminating your debt should be a top priority. When you're carrying debt, the money you're paying to lenders as interest could be put to much better use adding to your retirement plan or emergency fund. Money-management firm TIAA found that 73 percent of people with student loans are putting off maximizing their retirement savings (https://tiaa.new-media-release.com/mit-agelab/).

Among people who aren't saving for retirement at all, 26 percent blame their student loan debt.

TIP

You likely can't save enough for retirement until you get the debt beast off your back. After you save at least $1,000 for your emergency fund and contribute at least enough in your 401(k) to maximize any company match, it's time to get serious about wiping out debt.

Seeing the cost of credit card debt

If you have debt, you need to wipe it out — and fast. Credit card debt is especially damaging because it's typical for credit cards to charge *annual percentage rates*, or APRs, of 20 percent or more. The APR is the rate of interest the lender charges to lend you money.

Just think for a minute how ridiculous this is. That level of interest is twice the average annual 10 percent return on large U.S. stocks. The way credit card interest is calculated makes it even more troubling. Interest you pay is compounded daily, not annually!

To see how much a $10,000 credit card balance would costing you, Bankrate comes to the rescue again with its Credit Card Calculator at www.bankrate.com/ calculators/managing-debt/minimum-payment-calculator.aspx. Let's say you're borrowing $10,000, the APR is 20 percent, and your minimum monthly balance is $266.67, or interest plus 1 percent of your balance. But more importantly, as shown in Figure 11-4, if you pay only the minimum monthly payment, you'll wind up paying $16,057 to borrow $10,000. The Bankrate calculator shows you how difficult it is to save for anything else if you're carrying credit card debt.

FIGURE 11-4:
Bankrate helps you see how much you're paying for your credit card bill.

Coming up with a debt-busting plan

If you're buried in a pile of debt, it might seem impossible to wipe it out. I won't lie — it's going to take some sacrifice — but you'll feel liberated. You'll also have more money left over to contribute to your retirement rather than to someone else's profits.

An investment banker friend of mine told me his definition of the American Dream: Not a better life, whatever that means, but being financially independent, which means being debt-free.

Here's a game plan that can help banish debt:

>> **Fix your budget.** You can't save money if you're wasting it. Everyone has needless spending, but you can't afford to squander any cash when you're in debt. Even $100 a month applied to your credit card bill could ultimately save you thousands.

Go through your budget and pinpoint areas where you could stop wasting money. Is it your daily latte? I have no idea. Only you can decide what you can live without. Maybe coffee is more important to you than TV, which sounds reasonable to me.

If you don't know where your money is going, review Chapter 2, which describes online tools that can help you figure out your run rate.

>> **Seek and destroy your worst debts.** It's hard to tackle your debt until you understand what you owe and to whom. Take inventory of all your debts. You want to know how much you owe and the interest rate you're paying.

It might seem old school, but start by making a list of your debts using Excel, or paper and pencil. You should end up with a grid like the following:

Institution	Type of Debt	Amount Borrowed	Interest Rate
Bank 1	Credit card	$10,000	20%
Store 1	Store card	$500	25%
Mortgage	Mortgage	$150,000	4.475%

When you're paying down debt, try to get some quick victories. I've seen people have great success targeting accounts with low balances but high interest rates, such as the store credit card in the table, which has a high interest rate and a balance of only $500. You should be able to wipe it out fairly quickly. When you have fewer bills coming in, you'll feel like you're getting somewhere, which may encourage you to keep going.

TIP

>> **Use balance transfers.** Credit card companies want your business. Easy credit is a trap that snares many people, but you can turn the tables on the credit card companies and use their aggressiveness against them. Many card companies will let you consolidate your debt with them and also offer introductory 0 percent interest. Bankrate keeps a list of credit card offers of 0 percent rates, many stretching for nearly two years, at www.bankrate.com/credit-cards/zero-interest/.

Transfer larger balances to a card with a 0 percent rate and pay it down as fast as you can. You'll be amazed at how quickly the balance will fade when you're not paying 20 percent interest. Is your balance too big to pay in 21 months? No problem. When the 0 percent rate expires, transfer to another card with 0 percent. Keep doing this until you pay off the balance.

>> **Sell stuff.** Your home or apartment is filled with items you put on your credit card. It's time to go through your belongings and sell things that have value but you no longer want or need. For inspiration on paring down, check out Japanese tidiness guru Marie Kondo's site at https://konmari.com/.

An explosion of online venues will help you sell your unneeded items to ready buyers. Craigslist and eBay are great options. If you have designer apparel, RealReal (www.therealreal.com/) may fetch you a higher price. In addition, check out Poshmark (https://poshmark.com/) and Depop (www.depop.com/) if you're selling fashionable apparel items. Anything with a good brand will likely sell. For example if you have used LEGO sets, go to Bricklink (www.bricklink.com/v2/main.page). And if you're crafty, sell items on Etsy (www.etsy.com). To deal with people in your area, so you don't have to package and ship items, check out Facebook Marketplace (www.facebook.com/marketplace).

You'll be surprised by how much money you can raise — and debt you can wipe out — by selling items in your home that you're not using or you've handcrafted.

TIP

Ever notice how your bill at the grocery adds up, as seemingly low-cost items accumulate? Well, I'm happy to say that the same thing happens in reverse. Sell a $10 item here and a $20 item there, and you'll have an extra $100 before you know it.

Opening a taxable brokerage account

If you're paying down debt and saving for retirement, every extra penny is likely spoken for. But if you're in the fortunate position of having money left over, a regular taxable brokerage account can be a great idea.

A regular taxable brokerage account sounds like what it is. Unlike with a traditional IRA or 401(k) account, which gives you tax breaks when you put money in, you put after-tax dollars in a taxable brokerage account. Most of the brokerages you evaluated for your IRA dollars in Chapter 6 will also open a traditional account for you Robo-advisors such as Wealthfront and Betterment also offer taxable accounts. You can buy individual stocks or bonds, mutual funds, or target-date funds in a taxable account.

Taxable brokerage accounts can be great for you, if you

>> **Can save more than you can put in retirement account:** Keep in mind that you can't put unlimited money into retirement accounts. The limit (without a catch-up contribution) for 401(k)s in 2019 was $19,000. The contribution limit for IRAs in 2019 was even lower, at $6,000. There's no limit to how much you can put into a taxable account.

>> **Want to retire super-early:** If you want to quit your day job before you're 50, even maxing out your 401(k) likely isn't going to cut it. You'll need to invest more than $19,000 a year to pull off your goal. And putting your money in a high-yield savings account won't give you the return you need.

>> **Need access to the money:** Although you can borrow from your 401(k), major strings are attached. For instance, if you leave the company, you need to repay what you borrowed. But money put in a regular brokerage account is yours. You can take it out whenever you please, although taxes might be due on gains if you sell.

>> **Want some fun money to choose individual stocks:** Let's face it, mutual funds and ETFs are prudent ways to plan for your retirement, but they're for the long term. You might want to research and find companies with new and exciting prospects that can make you more money. If you're interested in taking more control of choosing stocks and bonds, check out my *Online Investing For Dummies* (Wiley).

TIP

Don't assume that a taxable brokerage account is worse, tax-wise, than your IRA or 401(k). You'll want to take advantage of tax traits of taxable accounts, in what's called *asset location*.

For instance, taxable brokerage accounts qualify for lower tax rates on dividends and long-term capital gains. Any dime that comes out of a retirement account, on the other hand, is taxed at your ordinary income tax rate. This distinction offers unique tax-planning opportunities.

Let's say you own a $10,000 stock that yields 2 percent a year, or roughly $1,000 in income after five years. If you put that stock in a retirement account, the $1,000 is taxed at your ordinary income tax rate when you take it out, which can be up to 37 percent. A 37 percent tax rate applied to a $1,000 dividend would be $370. However, dividends in a taxable brokerage account may qualify for the lower rate of 0 percent, 15 percent, or 20 percent, depending on your income and the type of dividend paid. Most dividends paid by U.S. corporations qualify for lower tax rates.

REMEMBER

Bonds, on the other hand, are different. The interest they pay is taxed at your ordinary income tax rate in both a retirement account and a taxable account. You might stuff all your bonds in retirement accounts because you'll pay the same tax rate and put off paying the tax bill until you take the money out.

Saving for a Home

Home buying and retirement planning often intersect. Both are long-term, involve large financials goals, and require careful consideration. In addition, retirement plan provisions can help you reach home ownership.

REMEMBER

Although it's a good idea to use your retirement savings only for retirement, a case can be made for tapping it, if you must, to buy a home. Owning a home can be an excellent long-term investment. Depending on where you live, a home's price can appreciate as much, or more, than stocks and definitely bonds. This situation is especially true for people who live in fast-growing cities with low inventories of homes. (I'm looking at you, San Francisco.)

But in most parts of the country, home prices rise much more slowly. The S&P/ Case-Shiller U.S. National Home Price Index, at `https://fred.stlouisfed.org/ series/CSUSHPINSA`, is a widely followed gauge of home values. Between the 10 years from May 1, 2009 and May 1, 2019, U.S. home prices rose 3.5 percent per year. That's nowhere near the more than 10 percent average annual return of the Standard & Poor's 500 during that time. But remember, too, that you can't live in your mutual fund.

Seeing how a retirement plan can help

Various retirement accounts have clauses designed to give you a break when buying a home. Most conventional loans require you to come up with at least 20 percent of the home price in cash as a down payment. It's always best to save this much if you can. And it's better if you save it in a savings account or in a taxable brokerage account.

But let's face it, it can be tough to save enough to make a 20 percent down payment. The IRS provides ways to pull money from retirement accounts without the 10 percent early withdrawal penalty for first-time home buyers. The IRS defines a *first-time home buyer* as someone who hasn't owned a primary residence in the past two years.

Different options for using retirement accounts to help you buy a house are available based on the type of account:

REMEMBER

>> **Traditional IRA:** Both you and your spouse may pull up to $10,000 out of a traditional IRA to apply to a home purchase. You won't pay the 10 percent penalty for pulling the money out. You will, however, owe ordinary income tax on the amount you withdraw.

The $10,000 per IRA account exemption for buying a home is a once-in-a-lifetime event. If you buy another home, you can't do this again.

>> **Roth IRAs:** You can always withdraw an amount equal to what you contributed to a Roth. If you need to pull out more than you contributed, you can withdraw up to $10,000 for a first-time home purchase. If you've had the Roth IRA for less than five years, you'll need to pay taxes on the earnings on your contributions.

>> **401(k):** If you live in a major city, the $10,000 limit on IRA withdrawals won't get you very far. Again, I want to stress that saving and investing money outside your retirement account to buy a house is always the best route. But if owning a house will be an important investment for you, it's possible to take a loan from your 401(k). Most 401(k) plans allow you to borrow up to half your balance, to a maximum of $50,000, without tax or penalties. If you're borrowing for a home, 401(k) plans will usually let you repay the loan over 15 years.

WARNING

If you leave your job for any reason, you must repay the 401(k) loan within 60 to 90 days.

Knowing how much you can afford

When you go shopping for a home, the first question you'll need to answer is how much you can afford. Notice I said *afford*. When you buy a house, you need to make sure the purchase fits your budget.

WARNING

Some new home buyers confuse what they can *afford* with how much they can *borrow*. They are not the same thing. A bank will often extend you a larger loan than you can comfortably handle. The bank knows full well that if you miss your payments, that's a bummer for you but the bank will get the house. In fact, lenders who lent more than borrowers could handle led, in part, to the 2008 financial crisis.

If you're like many people, you'll go to a bank's website and use the home afford-ability calculator. If you do this, you'll likely be surprised at how much you can borrow. Again, don't take this number as your home-buying budget until you do your own due diligence.

Here are a few approaches for calculating how much you can afford:

>> **Rule of thumb:** The ultimate rule when it comes to home affordability is that your mortgage should be 28 percent or less than your gross income. If you make $60,000 a year, or $5,000 a month, your mortgage payment should be no more than $1,400 a month. If you don't have any other debt, you might be able to bump the amount up a little higher. In general, your total debt (including student loans and car payments) should be less than 36 percent of your gross income.

>> **A before-and-after budget:** If you know your run rate, which you should in the course of planning for retirement, most of the work is completed. You know how much income you have and how much you're spending. Then, before buying a house, experiment with modifying your current run rate. I did this home-buying modeling exercise by building a spreadsheet using a template in *Home Buying Kit For Dummies* (Wiley).

Create a spreadsheet in which one column shows your current expenses. In the row for housing cost, you would enter rent. Then, in the second column, you would enter your mortgage. Bankrate's Mortgage Calculator at `www.bankrate.com/calculators/mortgages/mortgage-calculator.aspx` shows you what your mortgage payment would be.

>> **A "how much home you can afford" calculator (not from a lender):** If building a spreadsheet sounds like too much work, let online calculators do it for you. Zillow.com, a home-buying site, offers a powerful home affordability calculator at `www.zillow.com/mortgage-calculator/house-affordability/`. The Zillow calculator does the math and all the estimating for you, as you can see in Figure 11-5.

In addition, Bankrate offers a handy worksheet at `www.bankrate.com/calculators/mortgages/new-house-calculator.aspx` that walks you through the calculations on how much home you can afford. This helpful guide also pulls in up-to-date interest rates.

Budgeting for homeownership

Buying a home is like most investments you'll make. By sacrificing now and for-going spending in the moment, you'll benefit later. Why? Mortgages typically last no more than 30 years. After paying your mortgage down, you suddenly have a free place to live. Rent, on the other hand, is forever.

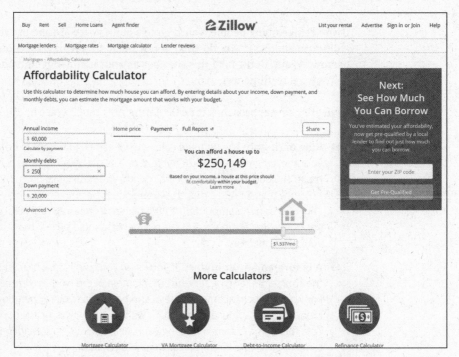

FIGURE 11-5:
Zillow's Affordability Calculator does the math to help you see how much home you can handle.

Also keep in mind that your mortgage, if it's a conventional loan, stays the same or might even fall over time. If interest rates decline, you can *refinance* your loan, or reborrow at the lower rate. After refinancing, you will pay off the loan in the same time but face a lower payment. When you pay off your mortgage, I hope in your 50s or 60s, you can redirect to your retirement account the money you were paying for the mortgage each month.

TIP

Homeownership can dovetail with retirement nicely. If you're able to pay off your loan by the time you're 50 — a lofty goal, I know — a giant savings opportunity opens up to you. After you turn 50, you can boost savings to 401(k) plans and IRAs in catch-up contributions.

How do you model all this money coming in and going out for rent or mortgage payments? I recommend that you use a detailed income statement. Just like a company's chief financial officer, you should know what your income and expenses are if you own a home or not.

For instance, what happens if your rent is replaced with a monthly mortgage payment? You can use the following tools to play what-if scenarios:

>> **A spreadsheet:** If you just want to model your home budget, it's hard to beat Excel. You probably already have access to it, so there's no cost to get started.

After firing up Excel, click the New tab and then type *budget* in the search field, as shown in Figure 11-6. You'll see a variety of free budget-planning tools. The Personal Monthly Budget template is especially powerful. And you can save your budget on your computer or on your OneDrive and refer to it later when budget amounts change.

>> **An online template:** If you don't have Excel or would like more structure, check out some of the many online budget-planning tools. Kiplinger offers a powerful online worksheet at www.kiplinger.com/tool/spending/T007-S001-budgeting-worksheet-a-household-budget-for-today-a/index.php that lets you model your expenses and estimate how changes might affect your cash flow.

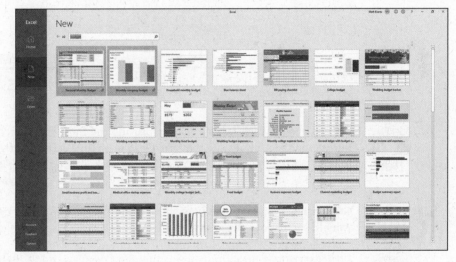

FIGURE 11-6: Excel has a variety of templates to help you see how a mortgage will affect your budget.

Saving for College

Here's where this chapter becomes a little circular. If you recall from Table 11-5, student loan debt is a financial obligation that sinks many lives. A college education is a great investment for you or your children. But when the loan gets so much larger than the income generated from the career, the debt becomes difficult to repay.

The statistics on student debt are eye-opening. In 2018, 69 percent of college students borrowed to go to school, says Student Loan Hero (https://studentloanhero.com/student-loan-debt-statistics). And these students graduated with $29,800 in debt upon graduation. On average, monthly student loan payments are $393 a month. No wonder 11.5 percent of student loans are 90 days late or worse.

It's tough to enter the work force so far behind financially. Given the rising cost of college, as shown in Table 11-6, it's not surprising that so many students get into money trouble.

TABLE 11-6 ## Increasing College Costs

Tuition, Fees, Room, and Board	Public Four-Year In-State	Public Four-Year Out-of-State	Private Four-Year
2018–2019	$21,370	$37,430	$48,510
2017–2018	$20,790	$36,480	$46,990
$ Change	$580	$950	$1,520
% Change	2.8%	2.6%	3.2%

https://trends.collegeboard.org/college-pricing/figures-tables/average-published-undergraduate-charges-sector-2018-19

TIP

Curious about which college majors provide the most income? The U.S. Census Bureau runs a Pathways site that provides the lifetime earnings of people according to their college majors. For this fascinating look at what most people earn, go to www.census.gov/library/visualizations/2012/comm/pathways-series.html.

Guess what? You can help your child avoid this student-loan debt mess if you work in saving for college as a goal, along with retirement savings.

WARNING

Do not sacrifice your retirement planning to save for a child's higher education. If necessary, you can easily borrow money for college. No, it's not ideal, but it's an option. But you can't borrow for retirement. Saving for college is only for people who have their retirement plan on track — or better — and are looking for ways to further optimize their money.

Understanding why your help matters

If you're able or willing to help save for college for you or your children, the benefits are enormous. College-savings accounts, just like retirement accounts, offer tax benefits to make saving easier.

College-savings plans allow you to make contributions with money taxed at the federal level. But when you take the money out, you pay no tax on any of the withdrawals as long as you use them for legitimate and approved college costs. You read that right. No tax on capital gains and dividends. Talk about a sweet deal!

You already know how costly it can be to borrow money for college. But how much difference does it make if you save in a college account versus a taxable brokerage account? A huge difference. If you start early, the amount you save on taxes in a college-savings account can be almost like getting a free year of tuition.

REMEMBER

In a taxable account, money you save for retirement generates dividends and income annually. You pay taxes annually on any dividends paid, even if you plan to use the money to pay for college. If you put the money in a college-savings plan, you don't pay taxes on income or on the gains on selling the investments.

Choosing a college-savings account

Just as you can choose different retirement accounts, you have choices when it comes to where you put your college-savings funds. Each type of account comes with advantages and disadvantages.

The 529

The 529 plan is the granddaddy of college-savings plans and is most likely the route you should go. Various 529 plans, sponsored by each of the 50 states, allow you to put aside college money to grow tax free. You can also take the money out and pay college tuition or up to $10,000 for private elementary or secondary education and not owe a dime of tax. The 529 plan is tough to beat for the following reasons:

>> **You're in control of the money.** Money in a 529 is yours, and you can designate a beneficiary. That means your kids can't cash in the 529 accounts when they turn 18. (Other accounts allow the kids to take control of the money.) You can change the beneficiary anytime you want, including to yourself if you'd like to use the money for college!

>> **Additional tax breaks are available.** More than 30 states allow you to deduct your contributions to 529 plans, says www.savingforcollege.com. That makes a sweet deal even sweeter.

>> **The plan has high income and contribution limits.** Anyone can put money in a 529 because there are no income limits. In addition, the plans offer generous contribution limits of up to $520,000. And you can also put in up to $15,000 a year or up to $75,000 every five years.

Coverdell Education Savings Account

The Coverdell Education Savings Account has long been in the 529's shadow. You can use the money in a Coverdell for a variety of education costs, such as private high school tuition. The contribution limits are low, though: up to $2,000 a year per beneficiary. Also, you can't contribute at all if you make more than $110,000 annually for a single taxpayer or $220,000 or more for a married couple.

Coverdell accounts work in some specialized situations, but for most people, the 529 is the way to go.

Roth IRA

You might think about tapping a Roth IRA to pay for college. And yes, the government will waive the 10 percent early withdrawal tax if you take money out before turning 59½ to pay qualified higher education costs. However, the contribution limits are much lower with a Roth IRA than with a 529. You find all the details on Roth IRA contribution limits in Chapter 4.

Choosing a 529 provider

If you've decided to go with the 529, as you likely should, it's time to figure out where to open the account. Each state offers its own 529 plan. However, you don't have to use your state's plan and you don't have to send your child to a college in the state of the plan you choose. (So yes, an Ohioan couple could use Utah's 529 plan and send their daughter to college in California.)

With so many options, how do you decide on a provider? Start with your state plan because some states allow residents to deduct contributions to their own state's 529 plan. It's hard to beat this deal. How do you know if your state offers this tax benefit? Savingforcollege.com's Browse 529 Plans by State tool at www. savingforcollege.com/529-plan-details shows you how a state's plan measures up. Click your state and you'll get a full rundown of all its attributes, including whether you get a state tax benefit on contributions. For example, California's 529 plan doesn't offer a state tax deduction benefit, as you can see in Figure 11-7.

If your state doesn't offer a contribution benefit, feel free to look around. Savingforcollege.com offers a Best 529 plans list at www.savingforcollege.com/intro-to-529s/which-is-the-best-529-plan-available. You can look through the list of 529 plans and see which make the most sense for you.

FIGURE 11-7: Savingforcollege.com is a valuable tool to use to see if a state's 529 plan offers unique benefits.

TIP

After you settle on a 529 plan, you'll have several options. Target-date funds are available not only for retirement plans but also for college-savings plans. Target-date options are a good way to go. Determine the year that your child will go to college and buy the target-date fund for that year. The target-date fund will adjust the mix of asset classes as your child grows up and approaches the time for college enrollment.

Figuring out how much you should save

You have your 529 plan set up. Congratulations. Now it's time to put money in the plan. But how much should you contribute?

REMEMBER

Knowing how much money to put into your 529 plan is relevant to your retirement plan. Why? It's a balancing act. Your first objective is preparing for retirement. If you have extra money, you can help set up your kids for success with a college-savings plan.

A number companies offer excellent online calculators to help you figure out how much money to put into your 529:

>> **Vanguard:** The college-savings calculator at Vanguard looks simple, as you can see in Figure 11-8, but it's deceivingly powerful. Enter the basics, such as your child's age and desired school, and Vanguard will show you how much money you need to save. It will even get the school's tuition and room and board costs for you. You can also download a full report showing you all the calculations.

>> **Savingforcollege.com:** Our friends at Savingforcollege.com, not surprisingly, offer a college-savings calculator too at `www.savingforcollege.com/calculators/college-savings-calculator`. This calculator takes an interview approach, asking you a number of questions that determine how much you should save. After telling you where you stand with savings, the calculator will explain why a 529 can help you.

>> **Bankrate:** Bankrate's college-savings calculator is set up as a number of on-screen sliders you can adjust up or down. This slider approach is handy because it gives you a range to work with. For instance, the calculator defaults to a 4.8 percent annual inflation rate for college costs. Simply slide the control higher, for example, to see how faster-rising tuition costs would affect your plans.

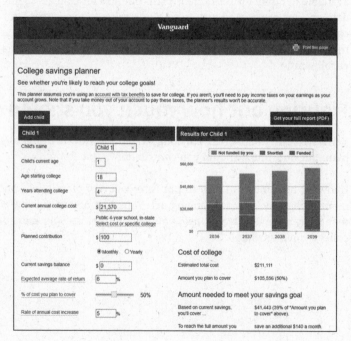

FIGURE 11-8:
Vanguard's planner helps you set a college-savings plan.

Chapter **12**

Fine-Tuning Your Asset Allocation

Opening a retirement account, vowing to regularly put ample money in, and choosing a target-date fund with a reputable provider are as much effort most people want to expend when making a retirement plan.

However, other people want to do more. Some retirees are interested in personal finance and would like to boost their knowledge and play a more active role in building a perfect and unique retirement plan. Others think they can build a better portfolio than an off-the-shelf target-date fund. And some people are in a situation that calls for a more customized portfolio. If any of these people sound like you, you've come to the right chapter.

In this chapter, you discover some of the limitations of target-date funds and what they might leave out in the name of simplicity. You know stocks and bonds are the primary asset classes used to build portfolios, but these are broad catch-all categories. Here, you find out about several types of stocks and bonds with unique traits.

Thematic investing for retirement is also gaining popularity, especially with younger workers. *ESG (environmental, social and governance) investing,* also called sustainable or impact investing, involves investing in companies that treat employees and customers well, respect the environment, and balance the needs of all parties that rely on the company.

REMEMBER

This chapter is for those building a more advanced retirement plan. As mentioned throughout the book, a target–date fund is the best option for most investors. But if you want to learn more or determine whether you'll benefit from a customized retirement plan, read on.

Exploring Stock Strategies

One–size–fits all target–date funds and robo–advisor recommendations work for most people. However, you might be a candidate for a customized portfolio if you

WARNING

>> **Have unusual goals for your age:** Target-date funds use your age as a primary variable to determine your portfolio's asset allocation. For most people, that's fine. But if you envision a different future than others your age, a target-date solution might not be best for you. For instance, if you're planning to retire when you're 40, your portfolio should look different than someone who is planning to retire at 70.

You might point out that target-date funds are selected not by age but by expected date of retirement. That's true, but your age is assumed in the choice of the year. If you're 40 years old in the year 2020 and expect to retire in five years, you'll get the same portfolio as a 60-year old planning to retire at 65. But because you'll retire in the same year, you'd have the same target-date fund and therefore the same portfolio.

>> **Like some investments better than others:** When you buy a target-date fund, you don't have any say in the funds you own. If you choose a large, well-known provider of target-date funds, the underlying funds are likely well thought out. But you may prefer one large-cap mutual fund over another. With a target-date fund, you can't make any substitutions. You might also prefer a fund that costs less than the ones in the target-date fund.

>> **Don't want to be tied to a single provider:** If your retirement plan is offered by a company that owns mutual funds, you can be pretty sure the target-date funds will be comprised of their mutual funds (or ETFs). If you like one fund company's bond funds and another fund company's stock funds, a target-date fund may not be the best choice.

If your 401(k) is with a third-party provider, the target-date fund will likely have funds from multiple providers. Check the providers of the underlying funds.

>> **Prefer a certain style:** If you like actively managed mutual funds, or funds run by money managers who pick individual stocks, a target-date fund that chooses an index fund might not be appropriate.

>> **Aim to hone your asset location:** You might want to keep your bond funds primarily in your retirement accounts (so you don't get hit annually with taxes on interest income) and your stock funds primarily in your taxable brokerage accounts. This way, you can take advantage of preferential tax rates. If that's the case, a target-date fund is too much of a blunt instrument because it likely owns both stocks and bonds and you won't be able to separate the two.

Understanding small versus large companies

Target-date funds and robo-advisors often look at stocks like an amorphous blob. If you examine the portfolio allocation recommended for you, you'll likely see that a set percentage of your money is in stocks or bonds.

But to say your portfolio has stocks in it is akin to saying your bookshelf has books in it. Many categories of stocks exist, each with its own characteristics.

For those who want to customize their portfolios, perhaps the most important distinction of stocks is size: small versus mid-sized and large. Size is determined by a company's value, or *market capitalization,* which is calculated by multiplying all the shares of a company that are available by the share price. The amount to qualify for a particular category has changed over the years.

Microsoft is an example of a very large company. In mid-2019, the software giant had 7.6 billion shares outstanding. Let's say the stock price was $130 apiece. To calculate Microsoft's market value, you multiply the 7.6 billion shares by the $130 share price and arrive at $988 billion.

Now, how do you know where that puts Microsoft in the large-to-small continuum? Table 12-1 from S&P Dow Jones Indices shows how the measurement is made and how it has changed over the years. You'll see that Microsoft is easily considered a large company.

TABLE 12-1   **Defining Company Size**

Effective Date	Large Market Cap (in Billions)	Mid-Sized Market Cap (in Billions)	Small Market Cap (in Billions)
2/20/2019	At least $8.2	$2.4 to $8.2	$0.6 to $2.4
3/10/2017	At least $6.1	$1.6 to $6.8	$0.45 to $2.1
7/16/2014	At least $5.3	$1.4 to $5.9	$0.4 to $1.8
6/19/2013	At least $4.6	$1.2 to $5.1	$0.35 to $1.6
2/16/2011	At least $4.0	$1.0 to $4.4	$0.3 to $1.4

S&P Dow Jones Indices

When you're customizing your portfolio, the retirement plan provider will ask you to decide the mix of assets you'd like in small company stock versus large. As a group, smaller companies are less proven, so they're riskier than large companies. But with the extra risk comes a shot at a higher return. If you'd like to see how the risk and reward of small and large companies compare, flip to Chapter 8.

A company's size is an important factor when choosing investments for your plan. Let's say you want to use popular iShares ETFs as a key part of your retirement plan. As you can see in Figure 12-1, when you're looking at the menu of iShares ETFs, the main sub-asset classes are differentiated by size.

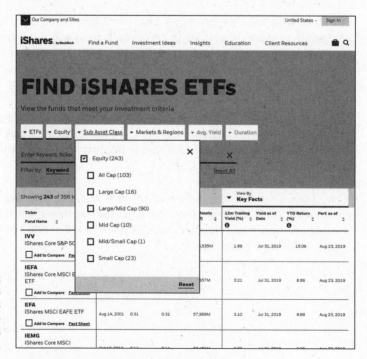

FIGURE 12-1: iShares categorizes its stock-exchange-traded funds by size.

WHICH COMPANY IS WORTH THE MOST?

A company's market value, which measures how much investors think it's worth, rises and falls every second of the trading day. Watching which companies are worth the most tells you where investors are placing their bets on the future. However, if you buy a large-company mutual fund or ETF, it will own not just the largest company's stock but also shares of all the giants.

If you're curious about which U.S. companies are the largest, you can look at the top holdings in the iShares Core S&P 500 ETF at www.ishares.com/us/products/239726/ishares-core-sp-500-etf. Following is a list of how the giants ranked in mid-2019, according to S&P Global Market Intelligence:

- Microsoft: $1,026.5 billion

- Amazon.com: $932.3 billion

- Apple: $910.6 billion

- Alphabet: $751.1 billion

- Facebook: $550.9 billion

Knowing where your money is: international, global, and emerging markets

Size matters when building a portfolio allocation — but country of domicile does too. The global economy is a complex web of trade and commerce, and the unique traits of nations create opportunities for investors.

When you're building the stock portion of your portfolio, you'll most likely want to include mutual funds or ETFs that own shares of companies based outside the Unites States. These investments come in three primary varieties:

>> **International funds:** These funds own pieces of companies in developed countries outside the United States. Most international funds own all or some of the companies in the MSCI EAFE index, which owns big companies in Europe, Asia, and the Far East. International funds are appealing because they tend to have similar risk and return characteristics as large U.S. stocks. But international stocks are not completely correlated with the Standard & Poor's 500. That means when Europe is struggling, like it did in 2019, stocks in the U.S. aren't necessarily hurt, too.

>> **Emerging markets:** Emerging markets are the Wild Wild West of investing. Owning companies based in developing nations such as China, Brazil, and India can add some excitement to your portfolio. Companies in these nations can generate impressive growth because the markets are so young. Emerging markets stocks are even less correlated to the S&P 500, making them a good way to diversify, too. Emerging markets funds usually track the MSCI Emerging Markets index, which owns giant companies in emerging parts of the world.

As you know, with more reward comes more risk. However, over time, emerging markets pay investors back with ample extra returns to justify their higher risk.

>> **Global funds:** These funds own stocks all over the world, including the U.S., non-U.S. developed nations, and emerging markets. These funds usually track the MSCI ACWI (All Country World) index.

TIP

How to you know if an asset class such as emerging markets is worth its risk? A risk-return grid, such as the one from IFA.com in Figure 12-2, can help. To access the grid online, go to www.ifa.com/charts/35h/.

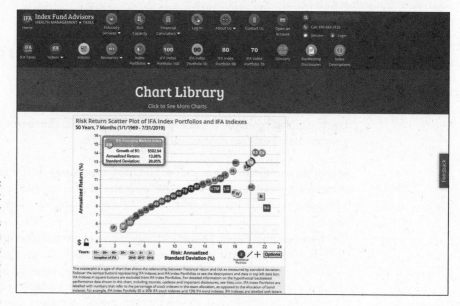

FIGURE 12-2:
IFA.com's Risk Return scatter plot shows you which asset classes deliver returns commensurate with their risk.

The graph shows all the major asset classes on a grid. Risk, or standard deviation, is the X-axis. The farther to the right on the grid, the higher the asset class's risk. As you can see in the figure, emerging markets are very risky, lying far to the right.

But there's more to this emerging story. The Y-axis is the annualized return of the asset class. The higher on the grid, the greater the return. And as shown in the figure, emerging markets deliver enough of a higher return to justify the risk.

If you're serious about customizing your retirement portfolio, you'll need to know Figure 12-2 well. The dots moving up at a 45-degree angle with the number labels are called the *efficient frontier*. You never want to own an investment below the efficient frontier. If an asset class falls below the efficient frontier line, you're not getting enough return for the risk you're taking.

The EM dot represents emerging markets. The dot lies right on the efficient frontier line, which is why it's an asset class worth owning.

Even if you're highly risk-adverse, putting just 1 percent of your portfolio in emerging markets can help diversify your holdings.

The SG square indicates small-growth stocks. These are small companies with high valuations. The square is all the way to the right, indicating that it's one of the most volatile asset classes you can buy. But also look how far below the efficient frontier line small-growth stocks are. You're simply not getting paid for the risk you're taking when you own small-cap growth stocks long-term.

Trusting real estate investment trusts

Most people think of stock as ownership in giant companies such as Microsoft and General Electric. But you can also add real-estate exposure in your stock portfolios, which is recommended.

I'm not talking about buying a house or an apartment and putting it in your IRA. You can't do that with traditional IRAs, anyway. I'm talking about owning real estate investment trusts (or REITs).

REITs are unique financial structures that allow a company to own income-producing property in a wrapper that trades like a regular stock. For instance, American Tower is a Boston-based company that owns 171,000 communications properties, including cell towers. You can buy the REIT itself. American Tower is a stock. You can also buy a real-estate investment trust mutual fund or ETF that own a number of REITs, including American Tower.

For instance, Vanguard offers a Vanguard Real Estate ETF, which owns shares in 188 REITs, including American Tower. Why bother with REITs? You might want to add REITs to your asset allocations due to the following features:

>> **Excellent income generation:** REITs own rental property, so they're constantly collecting rent from tenants. And it doesn't take long before that rent money becomes yours, as an investor. Due to tax rules, REITs are required to return at least 90 percent of their income to investors in the form of dividends. These dividends let you enjoy the cash flow of owning commercial real estate without the headaches of being a direct landlord. That means you won't get a call at 3 in the morning about a leaky faucet.

TIP

Most of the dividends paid by REITs are taxed at your ordinary income-tax rate, not the usually lower long-term dividend tax rate applied to dividends paid by typical corporations. As a result, if you own REITs, they are excellent holdings for your traditional IRA or 401(k). Money withdrawn from these accounts is taxed at your ordinary income tax rate anyway.

>> **More real-estate exposure than the Standard & Poor's 500 index:** Back in 2016, S&P Dow Jones Indices created a new sector in its popular S&P 500 index for real estate. That means if you own an S&P 500 index fund, which belongs in just about any portfolio, you own REITs but not very much. The popular Vanguard S&P 500 ETF put just 3.1 percent of its assets in real-estate stocks as of July 31, 2019. You can find updated statistics at https://investor.vanguard.com/etf/profile/VOO.

You might want more REIT exposure than you get from your S&P 500 index fund. Even if you have a traditional portfolio that's 60 percent stock and 40 percent bonds, about 6 percent exposure to REITs is considered prudent to maintain diversification.

>> **Strong long-term track record:** Why go to all the trouble of adding REITs to your customized retirement plan? The asset class has delivered outstanding long-term returns. As you can see in Table 12-2, although REITS are riskier than many asset classes, their long-term returns make up for the extra volatility.

TABLE 12-2

REITs: More Risk but More Gain

Asset Class	Annualized Return	Annualized Standard Deviation (Risk)
Large U.S. stocks	9.86%	18.74%
Real-estate securities	10.77%	23.93%

IFA.com, annualized returns from 1928

Diving for Income

The stock portion of portfolios gets most of the attention — and for good reason. When you're planning for retirement, a majority of your portfolio will be in stocks. Additionally, stocks historically are more volatile than bonds, so they tend to command more of your attention.

But it would be a mistake to gloss over the types of bonds available to put into your portfolio. Keep in mind that bonds are simply IOUs. When you buy a bond, you're allowing a government, a company, or another entity to borrow money from you. The returns you get from bonds come from two primary sources: capital appreciation and interest.

Interest is what people associate with bonds. When you buy a bond, you receive a set amount of interest over the life of the bond until it matures. For instance, suppose you buy a bond with a face value of $1,000 that pays 3 percent interest annually. You'll receive $30 a year in interest payments.

REMEMBER

You don't have to keep your bond forever. You're free to sell it to another investor at the market price. What makes the price of a bond rise or fall? Interest rates on competing bonds. Let's say the government you lent money to decides to sell bonds that pay 2 percent in interest. Now your 3 percent bond is looking much better. As a result, if you sold your 3 percent bond, you'd get more for it than you paid. That's a capital gain. Similarly, though, if the bond issuer borrowed new money at 4 percent interest, your bond's value would take a hit. No one would be willing to pay the $1,000 you paid when they could buy a new bond yielding more. The price of your bond would therefore fall, and you'd have a capital loss.

Two factors drive how much yield you get from a bond:

>> **Quality of the bond:** The higher the financial strength of the entity borrowing the money, the lower the interest rate. If you're lending money to the U.S. government or Microsoft, you can be confident that you'll get your money back. Companies with the highest credit ratings, or measures of credit quality, are called *investment grade.* They pay the lowest interest rates. Bonds sold by issuers with low credit ratings are called *high-yield,* or *junk,* bonds. They pay the highest rates, but you're taking a greater risk of not getting your money back.

>> **Duration of the bond:** *Duration* is a measurement of how many years it will take for you to get back the money you lent. Keep in mind that duration is a factor in the periodic interest payments you receive. The higher the duration of a bond, the longer it takes for you to get your money back and the riskier the bond.

Getting to know bonds better

Given what you now know about bonds, you can see that there's more to building a bond portfolio than simply buying bonds. If you're fine-tuning your portfolio, you need to consider who you're buying bonds from and when you'll get your money back.

Bonds sold by governments make up an enormous slice of the market. Using the Bloomberg Barclays Aggregate U.S. Bond Index as a guide, roughly 40 percent of the overall bond market consists of bonds sold by the U.S. government, not includ-ing the nearly 4 percent of the market sold by government agencies. Mortgages are the second-largest source of bonds at nearly 27 percent of the market.

When buying mainstream bond funds and ETFs, you'll want to keep the following factors in mind:

>> **Time frame:** When you're buying U.S. government bonds, you're not con-cerned about the government not paying you back. But you are interested in how long it will take for you to get your money back. During normal economic times, you'll get a lower interest rate from Treasuries that mature sooner, say one year. If you lend money for a longer period of time, investors usually demand a higher interest rate. When interest rates on short-term U.S. government bonds surpass those on long-term bonds, it's called a *yield curve inversion*. And when the yield curve inverts, it's a sign that investors expect the economy to weaken.

When you buy a bond fund, you should know the credit makeup of the bonds it holds. How much of the fund is made up of U.S. government bonds and how much from junk bonds? If you just buy the fund with the highest yield, it might be riskier than you realize.

>> **Issuing nation:** The U.S. isn't the only nation that borrows money. Countries around the world sell bonds to investors. Some investors like to buy these global bonds, with the idea that they're spreading their risk and might get a higher return.

Remember the golden rule of investing: Risk and return are connected. Table 12-3 shows you how, over the long run, you get the lowest returns and the lowest risk from short-term U.S. bonds (which mature in less than a year). If you buy bonds with longer maturities issued by global governments, you get a higher interest rate but also more risk.

UPSIDE-DOWN: WHAT'S AN INVERTED YIELD CURVE?

Yelling "inverted yield curve!" is the financial equivalent of shouting "fire" in a crowded theater. When the yield curve inverts, it's considered a harbinger of bad economic events on the horizon. Recessions sometimes occur after the yield curve inverts; the yield curve inverted before the last two recessions in 2008 and 2001.

During normal economic times, investors know they'll get a lower rate of interest when they lend money for a shorter period of time. But when the yield curve inverts, this thinking is turned on its head. Investors are willing to lock up their money in a long-term loan for a low rate because they think that economic growth will barely grow so inflation won't be a problem.

How do you know if the yield curve inverts? The Federal Reserve Bank of St. Louis plots the yield curve at https://fred.stlouisfed.org/series/T10Y2Y. When the line dips below 0, you're looking at an inverted yield curve. Check out the figure to see the ups and downs of the yield curve.

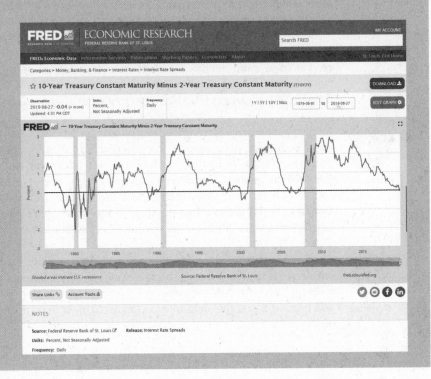

TABLE 12-3

Know Your Bonds

Asset Class	Annualized Return	Annualized Standard Deviation (Risk)
One-Year Fixed Income index	3.77%	1.48%
Short-Term Government index	4.64%	3.50%
Two-Year Global Fixed Income index	4.40%	2.91%
Five-Year Global Fixed Income index	4.76%	3.53%

IFA.com, annualized returns from 1928

Going to town with municipal bonds

Next time you drive across a bridge or attend a game in a stadium, think about where the money came from to pay for such projects. Usually, these city projects are so massive and long term that paying for them out of a local budget is difficult. The city or state borrows the money by selling *municipal,* or *muni, bonds.*

Muni bonds are unique in that they aren't as safe from default as the U.S. government's bonds, but they're still rock solid. It's unusual for a muni bond to default.

Why would you buy a municipal bond as opposed to a Treasury? The interest you receive from muni bonds is exempt from federal income tax and, many times, from state tax. Given that bond yields have been tiny in the late 2010s, any extra tax benefit you can get translates into money in your pocket.

WARNING

Municipal bonds are often included in bond mutual funds. But generally speaking, muni bonds are poor choices for tax-advantaged retirement accounts such as 401(k)s and IRAs. Remember, with 401(k)s and traditional IRAs, you pay tax when you take out money. If you own a muni bond in one of these accounts, you've converted a tax-free investment into a taxable one. Not good. And withdrawals from a Roth IRA are tax-free anyway, so you're not getting any benefit and possibly a lower yield. Muni bonds are much better choices for taxable accounts.

TECHNICAL STUFF

Given the huge tax advantage of municipal bonds, you can't simply compare them with regular bonds. If a muni bond is yielding only 2 percent while a Treasury is yielding 3 percent, don't assume that the Treasury is better due to its higher yield. You need to adjust the yield to a tax-adjusted yield to compare it with a Treasury yield.

To calculate the tax-equivalent yield on a muni bond, follow these steps:

1. **Subtract your tax rate (as a decimal) from 1.**

   If your tax rate is 34 percent and your state tax rate is 10 percent, subtract 0.34 from 1 to arrive at 0.66.

2. **Divide the municipal bond's yield from your answer in Step 1.**

   If the municipal bond yield is 3 percent, divide 3 by 0.66 to arrive at 5.55 percent.

3. **Compare the tax-adjusted municipal yield to the equivalent Treasury yield.**

   This comparison will tell you if the muni bond is worthwhile on an after-tax basis.

Does calculating the tax-equivalent require too much math? Not a problem. Bankrate offers an online calculator that will crunch the numbers at www. bankrate.com/calculators/retirement/tax-equivalent-yield-calculator-tool.aspx.

Using Morningstar to study bonds

The bond market is one of the largest and most active in the world. You'll encounter all sorts of bonds as you customize your retirement plan, including corporate bonds sold by companies. Yes, you can buy individual bonds. If you'd like to learn how to do this, pick up my *Online Investing For Dummies* (Wiley).

But when planning for retirement, you'll usually add bonds to your portfolio by using mutual funds or exchange-traded funds. You'll need to check with your 401(k) or IRA provider to see which funds are available to you. Then use Morningstar to study the bond fund, as follows:

1. **Head to Morningstar.com at** www.morningstar.com.

2. **Click the Search Quotes and Site link in the upper left.**

3. **Enter the name or symbol of the bond fund.**

4. **Under the bond fund's name, click the Portfolio option.**

5. **Examine the portfolio details page, shown in Figure 12-3.**

   Find the details that reveal the key elements of a bond: the quality of the issuers and the duration.

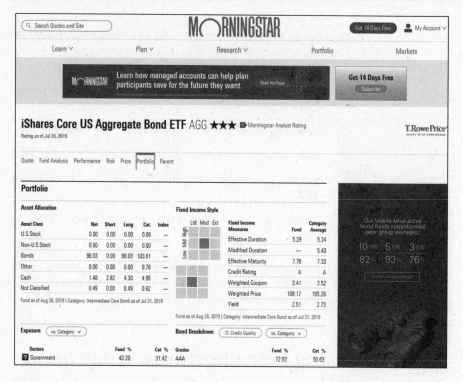

FIGURE 12-3:
Morningstar's Portfolio page highlights the key aspects of bond funds.

TIP

What should you look for on the portfolio page of the bond fund? Bond investors differ on the traits they look for; I pay the most attention to the following:

>> **Effective duration:** On average, how long it takes to get your money back from the individual bonds owned by the fund. The longer the duration, the longer it will take for you to get your money back, hence the riskier the portfolio.

>> **Credit rating:** The quality of the bonds in the portfolio. The higher on the rating scale, the more likely you'll be repaid in full and on time. Table 12-4 shows you the credit rating scale, so you can see where your bonds fall.

>> **Weighted coupon:** The average amount of interest paid by the bonds in the portfolio relative to the initial amount borrowed.

>> **Yield:** The amount of interest paid to investors who buy the fund at the previous day's price.

>> **Exposure:** How much of the portfolio is in different types of bonds, such as government, muni, and corporate bonds.

>> **Bond breakdown:** The percentage of the portfolio that falls into each ratings category. Morningstar breaks the credit rating down further for you.

TABLE 12-4

Standard & Poor's Credit Ratings

Credit Rating	Grade
AAA	Prime
AA	High
A	Upper medium
BBB	Lower medium
BB	Non-investment speculative
B	Highly speculative
CCC	Significant risk
CC	Extreme risk
C	Near default

Standard & Poor's

TIP

Morningstar's Quote page also contains important information. The expense ratio tells you the fee you're paying each year that you own the fund. The Total Assets field tells you the size of the fund. Smaller funds, with $100 million in assets or less, are more likely to end operations. When funds end operations, or close, they return all the money investors put into the fund. You'll want to stick with larger funds.

It's Easy Being Green: The Rise of ESG

If you're the type of person who drives a Toyota Prius and carefully separates your recyclables from landfill trash, you might be surprised at what's in your portfolio.

Oil companies and coal-fired power producers are likely in most mainstream large U.S. funds. For most people, that's fine. But a rising number of investors — usually younger ones — want portfolios that reflect their social beliefs. One in five Americans marched or participated in street protests or political rallies between 2016 and April 2018, says a Washington Post-Kaiser Family Foundation poll (www. kff.org/other/press-release/new-washington-post-kff-survey-examines-activism-in-the-trump-era). In addition, more than 60 percent of Millennial investors, 54 percent of Gen X investors, and 42 percent of Baby Boomer investors claim that their beliefs on social, political, and environmental issues will likely affect their investment decisions, according to an August 2019 poll by Allianz Life (www.allianzlife.com/about/newsroom/2019-press-releases/socially-responsible-investing-and-esg).

Deciding whether to include ESG in your retirement plan

Given investors' interest in doing good with their portfolio providers, the entire financial system is coming forward with new products and services. These new offerings factor in how companies address environmental, social, and governance, or ESG, issues. The rise of ESG is one of the more high-profile shifts in investing philosophy in some time. ESG is such a buzzword, it already has synonyms, such as *impact investing* and *socially conscious investing*.

You might find ESG offerings in your IRA or 401(k). Fidelity, for instance, offers five mutual funds that target specific social causes (www.fidelity.com/mutual-funds/investing-ideas/socially-responsible-investing). Three Fidelity funds own stock and bonds issued by companies prioritizing sustainability (by, for example, using solar power in factories to reduce carbon emissions). Another Fidelity fund invests in companies directly building products in alternative and renewable energy. And yet another fund targets the governance part of ESG by investing in companies led by women.

Fidelity is far from alone in offering ESG products. Vanguard (https://investor.vanguard.com/investing/esg/), Blackrock (www.ishares.com/us/strategies/sustainable-investing), and State Street (www.ssga.com/our-insights/viewpoints/esg-investing.html) all offer ESG funds that you can add to your retirement plan.

REMEMBER

You can have strong personal views on environmental or social issues separately from your retirement plan. In fact, most people do. Only 17 percent of Millennials, 7 percent Gen Xers, and 3 percent of Boomers use ESG principles directly in investing, the Allianz Life study found. Rather than allowing your political views to bleed into your portfolio, you can donate to causes you believe in or volunteer. You might have a much larger effect that way.

Also, keep in mind that some ESG products cost more. The money you're paying in higher fees go to the asset manager. You could have donated the money directly to the cause instead.

Let's say you invested $50,000 in the iShares ESG MSCI USA ETF (www.ishares.com/us/products/286007/ishares-esg-msci-usa-etf-fund) as your core U.S. stock exposure. The fund charges 0.15 percent annually, or $75 a year. You could have used the mainstream iShares Core S&P 500 ETF (www.ishares.com/us/products/239726/ishares-core-sp-500-etf) instead, which charges just 0.04 percent a year, or $20, and then donated $55 to the cause.

Understanding ESG investments

Given all the interest in socially aware investing, an abundance of information is available. Many financial sites are adding ESG filters to their pages so you can see whether an investment you're interested in passes muster.

Not surprisingly, Morningstar provides in-depth information on ESG. Want to know how a fund in your 401(k) or IRA measures up with ESG? Follow these steps:

1. **Go to Morningstar.com at** www.morningstar.com.

2. **In the search field, enter the fund's name or symbol.**

   I typed VFINX, the symbol for the uber-popular Vanguard 500 Index Fund.

3. **Click the Portfolio tab.**

4. **Scroll down and you'll find the sustainability section, as shown in Figure 12-4.**

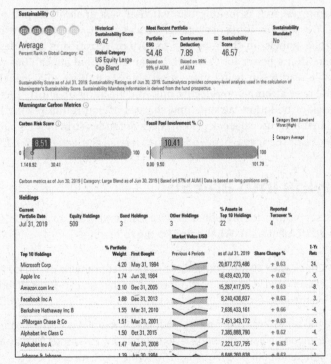

FIGURE 12-4: Morningstar's Portfolio feature offers an in-depth sustainability analysis.

Following are a few sustainability measures to pay close attention to in the Morningstar data:

>> **Sustainability score:** Want the bottom line? The Sustainability score gives it to you plain and simple. A fund with five globe icons holds mostly sustainable companies. The Vanguard S&P 500 index fund scores an average three-globe rating. This score is average, not high or low, because the fund owns all large U.S. stocks.

>> **Sustainability mandate:** If the fund includes sustainability in its purpose, it's noted here. The Vanguard S&P 500 fund does not include sustainability in its investment selection criteria.

>> **Morningstar carbon metrics:** Two carbon metrics are available. The Carbon Risk score tells you how much the companies owned in the portfolio are working to reduce carbon. The lower the metric, the more green they are. The Fossil Fuel Involvement percentage shows you how many companies in the portfolio are exposed to fossil fuels.

REMEMBER

Growing research is looking into whether sustainability is just plain good business. We typically think of sustainability as a cost, whether the expense of installing solar panels on the roof of a factory or retrofitting factories to release less carbon. Doing better for the earth has an emotional appeal, but could being sustainable also mean being more profitable? Installing solar panels, for instance, could lower a company's electric bill. And cleaning up a dirty factory could lower the risk of pollution lawsuits and charges. If you're interesting in learning how sustainability affects stock prices, check out index firm MSCI's published research at www.msci.com/www/blog-posts/has-esg-affected-stock/0794561659.

Buying into an ESG

Let's say you're totally onboard with ESG and want to include sustainability in your retirement plan. What now? Do the following:

>> **Check your 401(k):** Some 401(k) plans offer premade portfolios that keep ESG in mind. If an ESG portfolio isn't available, an ESG-focused fund might be on the menu.

>> **Add an ESG mutual fund to your IRA:** If your IRA is with a major mutual fund company, you no doubt have access to many ESG funds. Fidelity and Vanguard both offer a suite of ESG funds, as do most others.

>> **Put an ESG ETF in your IRA or taxable account held at an online broker-age firm:** Going this route opens a massive array of choices because you can mix and match ESG funds from a host of providers. Table 12-5 shows you some ESG ETFs. According to ETF.com (www.etf.com/channels/socially-responsible) nearly 90 socially responsible ETFs were available in mid-2019, and that number is likely to grow.

TABLE 12-5

ESG Exchange-Traded Funds Are Plentiful

Sustainable ETF	Symbol	Assets Under Management (in Millions)
iShares ESG MSCI USA Leaders	SUSL	$1,390
Xtrackers MSCI U.S.A. ESG Leaders Equity	USSG	$1,280
Vanguard ESG U.S. Stock ETF	ESGV	$568.4
iShares MSCI ACWI Low Carbon Target ETF	CRBN	$450.5
SPDR S&P 500 Fossil Fuel Reserves Free ETF	SPYX	$363.9

ETF.com

Chapter **13**

Keeping Your Retirement on Track

You've set up — and perhaps even customized — a retirement plan. You're contributing to the plan regularly. You're done, right? Isn't it time to dream about retiring happily ever after? Not exactly.

Life doesn't always go the way we think. Our goals change. For example, maybe retiring young was your vision when you were 30, but now that you're 40 and like your job, you have no intention of hanging it up. Or maybe you now want a second child or to buy a vacation home. Changing what you want is natural and expected. You just need to update your plan.

Likewise, portfolios don't always do what we expect. Asset classes can behave abnormally in the short term. Stocks can put up exponential gains during powerful bull markets. Markets can crash during nasty bear markets.

This chapter is your financial checkup: Making sure your financial plan is still appropriate for you and your goals as you age. Financial plans are heavily based on estimates and educated guesses. As time passes, you'll have a more realistic idea of what your expenses will be and the kinds of returns you might expect. This new information could mean that you need to step up your savings goals — or that you're saving more than you need and can start enjoying some of the things you gave up to build your retirement.

Tracking Your Portfolio's Health

When you build your retirement portfolio, you make many educated guesses, largely based on history. But although history often repeats itself, surprises and disappointments are likely, too. Stock and bond markets are infamous for making unexpected moves in the short term — sometimes at inopportune times.

Following are a number of ways your best-laid plans may not turn out how you expected:

» **Market returns:** Long-term models tell us how different asset classes tend to perform. You can get a good idea of the risk and return you might expect from a type of stock or bond in your portfolio. But asset classes commonly misbehave in the short term.

For example, large U.S. company stocks tend to return 10 percent a year on average, but there's no guarantee they'll do that in a given year. Large U.S. stocks haven't returned exactly 10 percent in any year in the 20-year span from 1999 to 2018, according to IFA.com.

For a fascinating chart that reveals just how unpredictable markets can be, look at IFA.com's Style Drifters chart at www.ifa.com/charts/83h. The chart, shown in Figure 13-1, shows you how the returns of even the major asset classes bounce around from year to year. For instance, large U.S. stocks, shown in the chart as LC, fell by 4 percent in 2018, well below the asset classes' long-term 10 percent return. But in 2017, the opposite happened, and large U.S. stocks returned 22 percent, or twice their average.

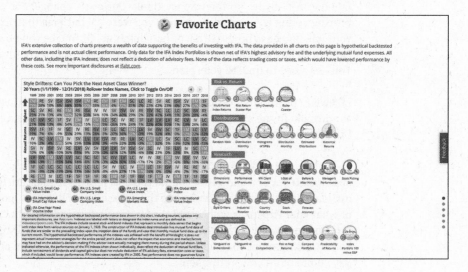

FIGURE 13-1:
IFA.com's Style Drifters chart illustrates how different assets perform from year to year.

>> **Legislative rules:** Retirement plan decisions made to minimize your tax bill can be fouled up when the government modifies the rules. When you build a retirement plan, you do it based on the best information you have at the time. But you should remember that taxation rules can change.

For example, lawmakers drafted the Setting Every Community Up for Retirement Enhancement (SECURE) Act. The rule, approved in June 2019 by the House of Representatives (but still not law at press time), targets sweeping changes to how retirement accounts are taxed. The rule would change the ages at which retirees must take money out of accounts. It would also cut the capability to extend the tax-free status of Roth IRA funds when given to non-spouses.

Measuring returns and asset allocation

Your 401(k) or IRA provider's website should provide information on how your portfolio has performed during different time frames. If it doesn't, you can figure it out using a separate online service or using Quicken personal finance software.

In this section, you explore all three options. In addition, if you need more detail than what these options provide, it's time to fire up a spreadsheet. I show you how to make the needed calculations later, in the "Seeing if you're still in balance" section.

Using your retirement plan provider's site

Retirement plan providers understand that their role is more than giving you a place to hold your assets. Workers building retirement plans are increasingly looking to their online broker or IRA and 401(k) firm to provide online tools to help them manage and track their retirement progress.

TIP

Your retirement plan provider's website should be your first stop in determining how your portfolio is doing. If you're not satisfied with the tools you find, it might be time to move your account elsewhere.

Following are a few examples of the online tools that retirement account providers offer to investors:

>> **Vanguard:** The mutual fund giant is aggressively enhancing retirement tools for investors, but the site is designed to keep information simple. When you log in to your retirement account, you see a dashboard like the one shown in Figure 13-2.

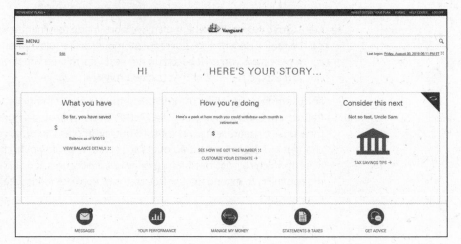

FIGURE 13-2:
Vanguard provides a central information hub to help you on your way to retirement.

A few tools worth pointing out are Your Performance, How You Are Doing, and Consider This Next. The Your Performance function tells you how much money you've contributed to your retirement account. You then see how your portfolio has performed in the past year, past three years, and since you opened the account. You can also define a custom time frame.

The How You Are Doing function makes the calculations more practical. Here, the Vanguard tool looks at your portfolio and measures your likely returns. Using this information, Vanguard's tool calculates your estimated savings at retirement, how much income you can draw from the account, and how long it will last.

The Consider This Next function is a massive library of articles and videos to help you stay on track.

» **Charles Schwab:** This online broker's site aims to give you more detail on how your individual asset classes are performing. Advisor-level tools not only show you how well you're doing but also check up on individual funds you own. For instance, you can find out whether the large U.S. funds you own are keeping up with or beating the market.

On the Portfolio Performance tab, the Rate of Return feature tells you how your portfolio is doing in various time periods, from three months to five years. Schwab also shows you how, say, your small company stocks are doing relative to the average of all other small-company stocks. If your mutual funds are lagging the market, it might be time to think about other options.

TIP

Don't miss Schwab's Portfolio Checkup, shown in Figure 13-3. This tool looks at what your asset allocation is supposed to be — and how your portfolio differs. When your portfolio significantly diverges from your target asset allocation, it's time to rebalance. *Rebalancing* is the process of realigning your asset classes to the appropriate weighting in your portfolio.

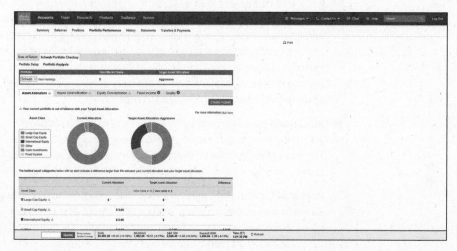

FIGURE 13-3:
The Schwab Portfolio Checkup gives you a detailed look at where you stand and how you might make changes.

Suppose your portfolio was worth $100,000 and was 60 percent stock ($60,000) and 40 percent bonds ($40,000). But the portfolio has grown to $150,000; the value of your stocks is now $105,000 and the value of your bonds is $45,000. That's the good news.

However, stocks are now 70 percent of your portfolio and bonds are just 30 percent. To restore your percent stock and 40 percent bond allocation, you need to sell a portion of your stock portfolio to reduce it to $90,000 and buy bonds to increase your position to $60,000.

When thinking about rebalancing your retirement accounts, note the following:

>> **Sell winners in your retirement account:** If you're selling stock positions for a gain, you'll want to try to sell stocks in a retirement account. Doing so will avoid the sale triggering a taxable event.

>> **Think about your willingness to rebalance at least annually:** Does all this rebalancing seem like too much effort? Then you're a perfect candidate for a target-date fund or a robo-advisor because rebalancing is handled for you.

Using an online service

You can use a third-party online service to help you study your performance and balances. Following are a few free services to consider:

>> **Morningstar:** Not surprisingly, Morningstar offers a swath of tools to help you keep your retirement plan on track. The Instant X-Ray (www.morningstar.com/instant-x-ray) gives you a point-in-time assessment of your portfolio and its weaknesses, if any. If you're planning on using Morningstar regularly to track your retirement progress, you might want to spring for Morningstar Premium to get access to Portfolio Manager (www.morningstar.com/portfolio-manager). This tool keeps tabs on your portfolio and alerts you to underperformance or the need to rebalance.

>> **Macroaxis** (www.macroaxis.com/invest/portfolioThemeOptimizer): If you really want to put your portfolio through the paces, Macroaxis is for you. The site helps you measure exactly how much risk you're taking and offers suggestions for improving your portfolio. If you want detail, you'll find it here.

>> **Personal Capital** (www.personalcapital.com): Good old Personal Capital is a powerful tool in monitoring how your retirement account is doing. You'll see your performance statistics whether your portfolio is drifting from your ideal asset allocation. Personal Capital gives you some guidance on rebalancing, too.

Using Quicken

Quicken, in many ways, is a throwback. It's a piece of software that you download and install on your computer. Remember those days? However, the software has survived because of its power and the control it gives its users.

Even if you don't want to use Quicken, it's worth understanding what it does so that you'll know what to look for on a retirement plan provider's site or a third-party website or app.

Following are a few Quicken features worth exploring:

>> **The Morningstar Portfolio X-Ray:** Yes, you're reading this right. The powerful Morningstar Portfolio X-Ray is embedded in the Premier version of Quicken. If you click Quicken's Investing tab, you'll get this high-quality examination of your portfolio.

>> **The Allocations tab:** Click the Allocations tab and Quicken will analyze your portfolio and see if it's time to rebalance, as shown in Figure 13-4. You'll see if your allocation in large U.S. stocks, for instance, is higher than it should be.

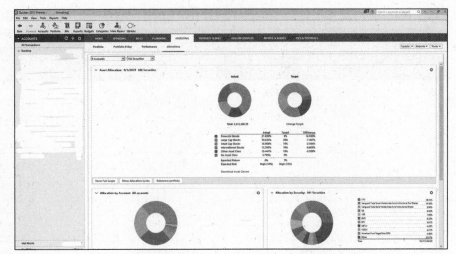

FIGURE 13-4:
Quicken examines your entire financial picture to see if your asset allocation is on target.

>> **The Performance tab:** The Performance tab tells you how your portfolio is doing relative to how much you've invested (your cost basis) over time. You can also see if your portfolio is rising or falling compared with major market indices, such as Standard & Poor's 500 index.

Staying on a balanced portfolio path

No matter which website or software you use to analyze your portfolio, you'll want to make sure that your asset allocation is on target.

TIP

In general, if your portfolio's asset class weightings deviate more than 5 percentage points from your target, it's time to bring them back into balance.

TIP

Again, if you use target-date funds or a robo-advisor, modifying your target allocation over time is done for you. With a target-date fund, as you get closer to retirement, the fund makes your allocation more conservative. Most target-date funds and robo-advisors call this modification to your plan over time a *glide path*. The idea is that over time your portfolio's risk should gradually decline as you get closer to needing the money you've invested.

A look at Vanguard's Target Date Fund for a person retiring in 2065 shows you how the glide path adjusts over time. The glide path, shown in Table 13-1, shows how stock exposure should fall to lower your risk as you near retirement. Bonds aren't as volatile as stocks, and they don't rise as much in the long term either.

TABLE 13-1   **A Sample Glide Path for Someone Retiring in 2065**

Years Until Retirement	U.S. Stocks	International Stocks	U.S. Bonds	International Bonds	Treasury Inflation-Protected Bonds (TIPS)
45	54%	36%	7%	3%	0%
35	54%	36%	7%	3%	0%
25	54%	36%	7%	3%	0%
15	44.55%	29.7%	18.0%	7.7%	0%
10	40.95%	27.3%	22.23%	9.5%	0%
5	35.45%	24.3%	27.48%	11.78%	0.8%
At retirement	30.6%	20.4%	29.26%	12.54%	7.2%
5 years into retirement	20.57%	13.71%	35.56%	15.24%	14.91%

Vanguard

TIP

Inflation-adjusted bonds, often called *TIPs*, are government debt securities that help safeguard your portfolio from rising prices. The value of TIPs are adjusted to make sure your purchasing power is maintained, even if there's inflation. These bonds, despite usually paying lower interest rates, can be useful to add to an asset allocation as retirement nears.

Modifying your plan

As you can see, while you have a retirement plan, changes over time might require you to adjust your percentage of holdings in the various asset classes. Any of the tools discussed in this chapter can help modify your retirement portfolio; in this section I show you an example using Quicken because it's a bit easier to follow.

REMEMBER

As mentioned, if you're using a target-date fund or a robo-advisor, rebalancing is done for you. However, you are paying a premium for this service and you lose some control. For instance, in the example I'm about to show you, the asset allocation includes emerging markets and real-estate stock, which are not included in many plain-vanilla target-date funds.

The following steps show you how to use Quicken to see where your portfolio needs an adjustment:

1. Download your current asset allocation.

You can download your holdings and their weights from your retirement plan or third-party analysis provider. Or, if you're using Quicken, go to the Investing tab and choose Investment Asset Allocation under the Tools option. You see a report similar to Figure 13-5.

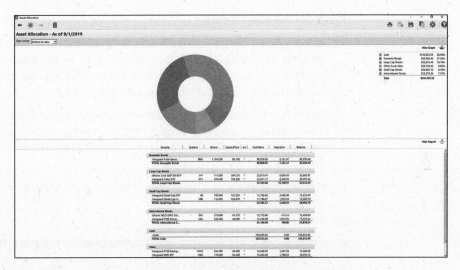

FIGURE 13-5:
Quicken picks apart your plan to show your asset allocation.

2. Get your asset allocation (and the associated percentages) into a spreadsheet.

Quicken and other asset allocation tools, such as Personal Capital, offer a Copy to Spreadsheet option. If yours doesn't, you'll need to enter how much in each asset class you own. The asset classes follow:

- Bonds

- Large U.S. stocks

- Large value U.S. stocks

- Small U.S. stocks

- Small value U.S. stocks

- International stocks

- International value stocks

- Emerging markets stocks

- Real-estate investment trusts (REITs)

3. Compare your actual allocation percentages with the target allocations.

Let's say your portfolio should be 40 percent bonds but currently is only 27.3 percent bonds. That means you need to add a 12.7 percent allocation to bonds. Multiply 12.7 percent (or 0.127) by your portfolio's total value to see how much, in dollars, you need to add to that asset class to get back into balance.

4. Make the adjustments.

Let's look at an example using the spreadsheet shown in Figure 13-6. The portfolio is worth $344,707.20. Of that, $93,950.40, or 27.3 percent of the portfolio, is invested in domestic bonds. The target is 40 percent. Adding 12.7 percent to the allocation means adding $43,932.

This person is investing in bonds using the Vanguard Total Bond Market ETF. The bond ETF on this day is selling for $85.10 a share. So the investor will need to buy 516 shares of the bond ETF ($43,932 divided by $85.10) to get the bond portfolio back into balance.

You would enter the purchase order or allocation change with your IRA or 401(k) provider.

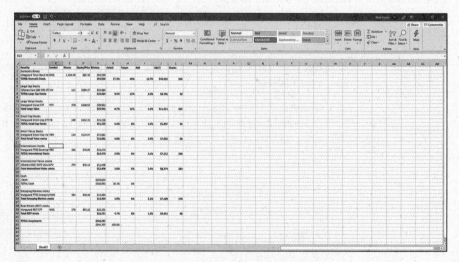

FIGURE 13-6: Excel can help you keep your asset allocation on track — to the dollar.

Tracking and Updating Your Goals

Your retirement plan should be flexible enough to make room for change. Every year, reexamine your current retirement plan to make sure it's putting you on the path to achieve what's important to you now.

Assessing your goals

The market isn't the only thing that might change your plans. Life itself has a funny way of not always following the script. Perhaps you have new priorities, either alternative paths you chose or changes you didn't see coming.

Following are a few examples of how your goals might change over time:

>> **Changing your expected retirement age:** When you created your retirement plan, you might have assumed you'd work until 67 but have since changed your mind. Changing when you plan to retire is one of the most sensitive factors in your financial plan.

   Moving your expected retirement age up or down affects how you invest. For instance, a 60-year-old planning to work 10 more years can have a more aggressive portfolio than a 60-year-old planning to hang it up at 61.

>> **Making more money:** Making more income than expected can dramatically change the math for your plan. You could save more, and then either spend more during retirement or retire earlier. Either way, more income changes the math of retirement.

>> **Saving more money:** Making a goal to boost your savings is a powerful way to put your retirement on the fast track. Saving more money becomes an option especially after hitting age 50, when you can automatically put more money into your 401(k) or IRA as part of a catch-up contribution.

   Don't discount the power of catch-up contributions. Sure, we're talking about contributing only $6,000 more a year to your 401(k) and $1,000 more a year to your IRA, but these seemingly small amounts make a big difference. Charles Schwab found that a 50-year-old with $100,000 in retirement savings could end up with $987,013 at age 65 by maxing out a 401(k), including the catch-up contribution. Without the catch-up contribution, the person would end up with $807,549. You can see the full findings of the study at www.schwab.com/resource-center/insights/content/power-catch-up-contributions.

>> **Adjusting to a major life event:** Marriage. Death. Children. All these events are life-changing and will alter the trajectory of our savings, goals, and income.

TIP

   When you experience a major life event, there's an easy step you should take immediately. Go through all your accounts and see if you need to change your beneficiary designation. Your *account beneficiary* is the person or entity who will receive the assets in an account if anything happens to you. If you pass away, the financial institution holding your account will transfer the assets to whomever you chose as the beneficiary.

WARNING

If you have a large or complicated estate, consult with an estate planner on the best way to set up beneficiaries. You might be a good candidate for one of many types of trusts. *Trusts* are legal entities that can hold assets while you're living or dead and follow your prearranged instructions. Properly setting up a beneficiary, or a trust, can allow you to dictate what happens to your assets. It can also keep your financial affairs out of probate court, where assets that are not properly addressed in life are put into the hands of the legal system. Yes, if you don't set up a beneficiary, the judge will do it for you. And probate fees can easily cost between 3 percent and 7 percent of the estate — nearly $18,000 in court fees on a $250,000 retirement account!

Seeing if your goals change your plans

Shifting goals and life changes will almost always affect your retirement plan. The question is how much your plan will change and what the change will mean for you.

TIP

The AARP retirement calculator is handy for seeing how life changes might affect your plan. The calculator uses a series of sliders that allow you to tweak settings and determine the effect at www.aarp.org/work/retirement-planning/retirement_nest_egg_calculator.

In this section, we use the AARP calculator to estimate how twists and turns in life will affect a retirement plan. I use the example of Sarah, who

>> Is 45 years old

>> Plans to retire at 67

>> Earns $50,000 a year and expects that to rise by 2 percent a year

>> Has $250,000 saved for retirement

>> Needs at least 90 percent of her current income in retirement, or $45,000

>> Plans to live until age 100 (she has good genes)

>> Expects to earn 7 percent investment returns while working, 4 percent returns while retired, and experience 2.9 percent inflation

>> Plans to collect Social Security

Now that you know where Sarah started, let's see how the math changes. Read this section using this example first. After you get the hang of how to do the calculations, go through the section again using your own numbers.

Changing your retirement age

Deciding to work longer or retire sooner can have an enormous effect on your retirement plan. Calculating the effect is mostly a mathematical exercise. Using Sarah, our investor described in the preceding section, we'll plug various retirement ages into a calculator, as shown in Figure 13-7.

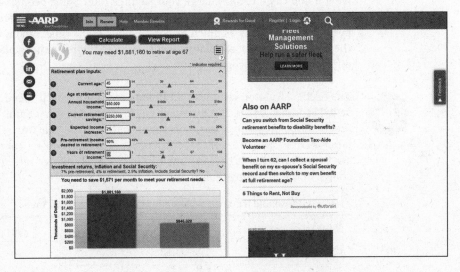

FIGURE 13-7:
The AARP retirement plan calculator helps you play what-if with your retirement age.

When you make the adjustments, keep in mind that you change not only the age at retirement but also the years in retirement. For instance, if Sarah retires at 67 and lives until 100, she'll spend 33 years in retirement. If she retires at 60, she'll spend 40 years in retirement. The following table from AARP shows how retiring later dramatically reduces the amount of money that must be saved each month:

Age at Retirement	Amount Needed to Retire	Monthly Savings Required
60	$1,907,383	$4,666
65	$1,895,470	$2,210
67	$1,881,160	$1,571
70	$1,847,727	$830

TIP

Money isn't the only factor in deciding to retire early, although it's a big one. Even if you can afford to say goodbye to the 9-to-5 early, pay close attention to some of the non-financial considerations. Humans crave meaningful activity, purpose, and connections with like-minded people. A job can provide all these things, in addition to money. If you're planning on retiring early, you need to think about replacing not only your income but also your purpose.

Making and saving more money

Working longer clearly makes a massive difference in your retirement plan. But what if you could turbo-charge your savings rate? Some people who retired early worked in high-paying finance or technology jobs that they hated, with the purpose of socking away as much as possible in a short time. Again, with the help of the AARP retirement calculator, we'll see how the retirement plan changes with different levels of income.

REMEMBER

The AARP calculator assumes that if you earn more, you'll spend more. And that, sadly, is probably true. But for our exercise, we assume that Sarah's income needs are the same: $45,000 a year. This time, you'll use the CalcXML retirement calculator at www.calcxml.com/calculators/retirement-calculator?skn=#top to see by how much a higher income can lower your savings rate. The findings are shown in the following table:

Annual Household Income	Percent of Annual Income to Save
$50,000	37.3%
$75,000	24.9%
$100,000	18.7%
$125,000	16.5%

As you can see, when you earn more, the financial sacrifice to save for retirement becomes that much easier.

TIP

If your income rises, you get another opportunity. No, you can't stuff more than the maximum allowed in your 401(k) or IRA. But rather than blowing all the extra money, you can open a taxable account. Opening a standard brokerage account gives you another place to invest your extra cash. Although you don't get an immediate tax break, taxable accounts get other perks. Most dividends paid by U.S. corporations qualify for reduced tax rates. And if you own index mutual funds or exchange-traded funds, they rarely generate taxable capital gains. If you put index funds in your taxable account, you'll find you get many retirement-account-like benefits.

Becoming a parent

Being a parent can bring enormous joy, but it isn't cheap. The U.S. Department of Agriculture estimates that it costs $233,610 to raise a child from birth to age 18 (www.usda.gov/media/blog/2017/01/13/cost-raising-child). The cost jumps to $284,570 if you factor in expected inflation. That amount does not include the cost of college, which can easily add upward of $115,000, according to www.savingforcollege.com/calculators/college-savings-calculator.

I'm not trying to discourage you from having a child. Just make sure you're factoring in all the costs. Think of it as an investment!

Making and saving less money

Getting bonuses and raises are expected when you're in your 20s and 30s. Let's face it, a 3 percent raise doesn't cost a company much when you're talking about an entry-level salary. But after you hit your mid-40s, employers need to dig deeper for a 3 percent raise and you might have fewer raises and less job security.

If your income falls, you'll need to adjust your spending and look for new forms of income. But you knew that already. What you might not realize is that changing jobs, especially to a lower-paid one, might open up another opportunity for you to save money, without even feeling it. If you're in your 50s or 60s and are using a target-date fund or robo-advisor in an employer plan, you can roll it over to an IRA. And if you find yourself with more time, you can save money by building your own portfolio by selecting funds and asset classes.

Suppose that you are 55, you have $500,000 saved in a retirement account, and your money is in a target-date fund. The typical target-date fund charged an annual expense ratio of 0.82 percent in 2018, according to The Investment Company Institute (www.ici.org/pdf/2019_factbook.pdf). That was fine when you were working crazy hours. But at 0.82 percent, you're paying $4,100 a year. Even if you use a robo-advisor, you're likely paying 0.25 percent for an advisory fee plus underlying fund fees of up to 0.11 percent, which means you're paying up to 0.36 percent, or $1,800 a year.

Following are two ways you can save money:

>> **Keep it simple.** If you roll your money over to an IRA, you could buy your own mix of low-cost mutual funds or exchange-traded funds. If you want to keep things really simple, you could put 60 percent of your money in a low-cost stock index fund such as the oldest and largest ETF, the SPDR S&P 500 ETF. The fund exposes you to the large-cap market for just 0.095 percent. Then mix the remaining 40 percent in a bond ETF such as Vanguard Total Bond Market, which charges just 0.035 percent. That means your total cost is just 0.071 percent. The annual cost is $355, for a savings of $1,445 a year with the robo-advisor or $3,745 a year with the target-date fund.

>> **Build a more advanced portfolio.** In addition to the U.S. large-cap ETF, you might add small-cap value stocks, REITs and emerging markets. All in, you'll have a diversified portfolio and save some money. A sample complex portfolio is shown in Table 13-2.

TABLE 13-2

A Prudent Portfolio

Asset Class	Percent of Portfolio
Large U.S. stock	12%
Large value U.S. stock	12%
Small U.S. stock	12%
Real-estate stocks	6%
International stocks	6%
International value stocks	6%
Emerging markets stocks	6%
Bonds	40%

IFA.com

Tracking retirement progress and milestones

Psychologists say comparing what you have against what others have is a recipe for unhappiness. That may be true. But benchmarking your retirement savings balance against people your age might be a way for you to know if your plan isn't working.

Typically, people worry that they're not saving enough — and they're usually right. But some people are so worried about running out of money that they save too much. What's the problem with saving more than you need? You might not be enjoying life now as much as you could.

Table 13-3 shows you typical amounts saved at different ages. This method of analyzing your retirement plan won't tell you if you're saving enough, but it will tell you how you're doing compared to the average.

TABLE 13-3

Are You Above Average?

Age	Average Retirement Savings
Under 25	$4,773
25-34	$24,728
35-44	$68,935
45-54	$129,051
55-65	$190,505
65+	$209,984

https://investor.vanguard.com/retirement/savings/how-much-to-save

WARNING

Remember that these are averages to give you an idea of where you stand relative to others. You should always rely on multiple retirement calculators for a more accurate estimate of how much money you need to retire and where you should be if you plan on hitting that number.

TIP

If you're running behind where you think you should be with your savings, try to save at least 12 percent and preferably closer to 15 percent of your pay. If you can't swing that much now, try inching up your contributions by 1 or 2 percent a year until you get where you want to be.

Chapter 14

Gearing Up for Retirement

Retirement is such a long-term goal, it might seem like it will never arrive. So when you finally are retired, the situation might feel surreal. How will you spend your days when every day "feels like Saturday?"

This chapter is your guide to putting your retirement dreams into action and starting to think about how you'll pay for the wonderful life you have in mind. You've likely planned and saved for your retirement for decades, and now it's time to enjoy the fruits of your labor. Financially, the key to a successful retirement is income.

The first change you'll need to appreciate is how your budget will morph. Some expenses will rise and others will fall. Understanding healthcare costs in retirement will be critical to balancing your retirement budget.

After you retire, another important shift occurs. You go from building and investing money to withdrawing money. This chapter will explore some of the nuances that go into the draw-down phase of your life.

One of the biggest adjustments newly retired people face is the first payday that they don't get a paycheck. If you don't like the idea of not getting a regular paycheck, look into an annuity, an often-misunderstood financial tool that can help you create a regular income stream. An annuity is helpful also for people who think they might outlive their financial resources.

Lastly, for many people, their home is their most valuable asset. Even if they didn't save much in their 401(k)s, their monthly mortgage payments forced them to invest in real estate. Best of all, unlike stocks and bonds, which can be easily sold in a panic, most people hold onto their home, which is now an asset that can be tapped if needed. A reverse mortgage is complicated and has many drawbacks, but it can also be a powerful tool.

Creating a Retirement Budget

Let's face it. Life as a retiree has different challenges and perks than those faced by working stiffs. Your immediate financial and work time commitments are gone, but so is your paycheck. Much of the financial modeling you did while you were working no longer applies. However, the same tools you used to measure your run rate while you were working can help you figure out your post-retirement budget.

Test-driving your budget

It's best to have a good idea of what your spending will look like in retirement before you begin retirement. Review the section on measuring your spending in Chapter 2. The tools discussed in that chapter will help you see how much you're spending. Many people fixate on their "number," or the total dollar amount they need to retire. But your run rate, or spending needs, truly determines how much you need.

TIP

After you use the tools described in Chapter 2 to determine how much income you need, follow that budget for a year or so before you retire. Try as best as you can to live the way you plan to in retirement — before you leave your job. You want to be certain that your forecasts for your retirement income needs are accurate.

Also, make sure you factor in changes to your budget in retirement. For instance, if you work downtown, you won't need to pay for the expensive monthly parking pass anymore. On the other hand, your budget for travel might increase. Typically, spending falls as we age. Research by the Society of Actuaries (www.soa.org/globalassets/assets/files/resources/research-report/2019/2019-spending-asset-management-report.pdf) found that people simply spend less in most categories, other than health, as shown in Table 14-1.

TABLE 14-1

Average Spending Falls As We Age

Category	Age 65-74	Age 75-84	Age 85+
Home	$18,720	$14,732	$13,111
Food	$4,526	$3,994	$2,520
Health	$4,383	$4,624	$6,603
Transportation	$5,169	$3,666	$1,971
Clothing	$1,311	$950	$888
Entertainment	$4,300	$3,277	$1,609
Other	$3,583	$3,565	$3,188
Total	$42,805	$35,315	$30,610

Figure 2 from EBRI Notes, Sept. 2014 – How Does Household Expenditure Change with Age for Older Americans?

In addition to updating your post-retirement budget, you'll want to do the following:

>> **Review your pension, if you have one.** A pension can be an important source of income. Pensions are covered in detail in Chapter 15.

>> **Consider how retirement will affect your Social Security.** Make sure you know how your Social Security benefit is calculated. And check your records with the Social Security Administration to verify that your work and income history are appropriately recorded. For help with these tasks, flip to Chapter 10, which shows you how to navigate your Social Security benefits and the website.

>> **Be mindful of insurance costs.** You might not realize how much insurance coverage you're employer provides, including disability, dental, and eyecare. For more on this important topic, see Chapter 16.

>> **Think about your income and the 4 percent rule.** Studies have shown that the safe amount to withdraw from your retirement savings is 4 percent, increased annually by inflation. So if you retire with $1 million, in the year you retire you can take out $40,000. Then, in your second year of retirement, you can increase that amount by the rate of inflation. Following the 4 percent rule most likely will leave you with plenty of money for 30 years.

However, financial advisor Michael Kitces thinks the 4 percent rule might be too safe. He found that in most scenarios, following the 4 percent rule leaves the retiree with more than double their beginning wealth (www.kitces.com/blog/the-ratcheting-safe-withdrawal-rate-a-more-dominant-version-of-the-4-rule). As a result, Kitces suggests modifying, or *ratcheting*, the 4 percent plan a little. He says after the portfolio rises 50 percent from its initial value, boost spending by 10 percent. So using this logic, if your $1 million retirement portfolio hits $1.5 million, each year you can take out $44,000 adjusted for inflation rather than $40,000.

Keeping your stock exposure

One of the key aspects of the 4 percent rule, as well as Kitces's modification to it, is that you maintain at least 60 percent of your portfolio in stocks. If you use a target-date fund, you'll want to make sure the fund doesn't move you too heavily into bonds too soon.

REMEMBER

Bonds tend to be less volatile than stocks, which is why shifting to more bonds as you age can be a good idea. But going overboard and loading up with too many bonds can starve your portfolio of the growth it needs to keep generating money. Some recent retirees cut stock allocations to just 30 percent or lower, thinking it's prudent action. But cutting stock allocation by this much is overly conservative and subjects you to greater risk.

The asset allocations from major asset management companies can act as a guide. Vanguard, for instance offers the allocation shown in Table 14-2 for someone entering retirement. Vanguard suggests close to 50 percent stock, not 60 percent.

TABLE 14-2

Suggested Stock Allocation at Retirement

Asset Class	Allocation
Stock	51.4%
Bonds	48.59%
Short-term reserves	0.01%

Vanguard

WARNING

You should still maintain a cash reserve — money not invested— to hold you over for at least six months, if not longer.

Waiting until 70 to collect Social Security

One of the ways to bolster your financial standing is getting the most out of Social Security. And for most people, the prudent Social Security strategy is waiting as long as you can before you start collecting it. Although you can collect Social Security when you're as young as 62, doing so will reduce your benefit by about a third.

You get an 8 percent boost to your benefit for each year after your full retirement age that you wait. The Stanford Center on Longevity finds that nearly all retirees will be better off waiting before taking Social Security (http://longevity.stanford.edu/retiring-too-early).

How do you know if you can afford to delay your Social Security benefit? Fidelity Investments says you should plan to have saved eight times your salary when you're 60 and ten times when you're 67 (www.fidelity.com/viewpoints/retirement/how-much-do-i-need-to-retire). And T. Rowe Price (www.troweprice.com/financial-intermediary/us/en/insights/articles/2018/q2/are-my-retirement-savings-on-track.html) says when you're 65, you should have banked at least eleven times your income; the benchmarks for various ages are shown in Table 14-3.

TABLE 14-3

Retirement Benchmarks

Age	Income Savings Multiple
30	1/2
35	1
40	2
45	3
50	5
55	7
60	9
65	11

T. Rowe Price

Having a healthcare plan

You need a strategy to deal with the growing cost of medical care in retirement (refer to Table 14-1). If you're 65 or older, you have Medicare, although you may need additional insurance to cover dental, long-term care, and other costs (see Chapter 16).

If you retire before turning 65, make sure you have coverage either through your former employer or your state's healthcare insurance exchange.

REMEMBER

You might want to load up on your health savings account before you retire. These HSA accounts, typically attached to a high-deductible insurance plan, will be your best friend when you retire. You can contribute tax-free money up to $3,500 individually or $7,000 for a family in 2019. While you're working, stuff as much money into your HSA as possible. Just know that as soon as you sign up for Medicare, you can no longer contribute to an HSA.

Your employer might offer an HSA, or you can open one yourself. Investor's Business Daily tracks the best HSA plans at `www.investors.com/best-hsa-accounts/`.

Knowing the bucket strategy

One thing's for certain: There will be recessions and bear markets during a recession. When you're retired, you want to ensure that your portfolio won't get hit too badly.

Your number-one defense against a recession is your asset allocation. When you're retired, make sure you're adequately exposed to bonds, which tend to hold up better than stocks in bad markets. Christine Benz, director of personal finance at Morningstar (`www.capitalgroup.com/ria/practice-excellence-center/wealth-perspectives/morning-stars-benz-consider-these-3-buckets.html`), suggests that you put your money into the following three buckets:

>> **Bucket #1, near term:** Money you'll need in two years or less. This money is not invested. Instead, it should be held in cash, such as in a high-yield savings account. When the market tanks, you can rely on this money.

>> **Bucket #2, intermediate term:** Money you'll need in two to ten years. Bonds with high credit ratings and Treasuries make sense here. When the markets recover, you can refill bucket #1 with money from this bucket.

>> **Bucket #3, long term:** Money not needed for ten years or longer. Your stock positions make sense in bucket #3, as do some high-yield and emerging markets bonds. It's likely that investments you make in this bucket will rise in value. When the prices of your long-term assets rise, as you'd expect, you can sell them and move the proceeds to your near-term or intermediate-term buckets to help cover more immediate financial costs as needed.

Working longer

Yes, this chapter is about entering a new chapter of your life: retirement. And for many, hanging it up at work is a long-term goal. I'm not trying to discourage you from retiring, but it's important to think through additional considerations, such as the following:

>> **What are you going to do with your time?** You might be happy for a week or two sitting on the beach, but people need goals and a purpose. A good friend of mine was considering taking an early retirement package. He planned to fill his days with activities he couldn't get to while he was working. But he couldn't think of more than two activities that could give him purpose and occupy his time, so he turned down the buyout offer and kept working. The decision wasn't about the money but about having structure to his life, deadlines to meet, and a sense of contributing to a worthwhile project.

WARNING

Retiring without a plan of what you'll do is a recipe for emotional disaster. Hate your job? Maybe it's time to not retire but retool. Find a job you enjoy more, even if it pays less. Some companies will take on older workers as interns, in programs called *returnships*, with the idea that they'll train you and perhaps hire you if it works out. Searching for *senior intern* at job sites such as Indeed (`www.indeed.com`) can alert you to leads. If you're interested in doing a different type of work, check out tips on the I Relaunch blog (`www.irelaunch.com/`).

>> **How will you maintain social connections?** We're hardwired to spend time with each other. We support each other. We tell each other stories. Or we just sip coffee and read next to each other. Many people get this human interaction in their workplace. If you retire, you need a way to replace this sense of belonging and connection.

>> **Could you gain financial peace of mind by working longer?** If you're not quite confident about your retirement plan, working four more years could pad your plan by more than $440,000, according to the Investor's Business Daily analysis at `www.investors.com/etfs-and-funds/retirement/retirement-savings-boost-delay-social-security-benefits/`.

TIP

You might worry that working longer might hurt your Social Security payouts. The opposite is the case. The longer you work, the more likely you are to hold out on collecting Social Security until you turn 70. That's a win. Additionally, there's no effect on your Social Security payments when you work if you don't take benefits until after reaching your full retirement age.

The only time working affects your Social Security payouts is when you take benefits before hitting your full retirement age. Here, depending on how much you earn, your benefits will be reduced until you reach your full retirement age. The adjustments, which are complicated, are explained at `www.ssa.gov/planners/retire/whileworking.html` and `www.ssa.gov/pubs/EN-05-10069.pdf`.

Thinking about Annuities

What's the number-one shock many new retirees experience? The first payday when they don't get their paycheck deposited into their account. When it comes to retirement, monthly cash flow or income is the name of the game. It's up to you to build your own paycheck by cobbling together forms of income. Fidelity Investments finds that most people need to replace between 55 percent and 80 percent of how much they earned pretax before retiring (www.fidelity.com/viewpoints/retirement/retirement-income-sources).

Income might be composed of any of the following:

>> **Social Security:** The lower your income, the more important Social Security will be to your total income. Table 14-4 shows you the significance of your Social Security income, relative to your own savings and investments, in replacing the income you'll need in retirement.

>> **Income from investments:** Dividend payments from your stocks and interest payments from your bonds and savings will provide cash flow.

>> **Withdrawals from portfolios:** If you don't get enough income from Social Security and investment income, you'll likely need to take out money from your investments.

>> **Pensions:** With a pension, a former employer agrees to pay you a set amount of money every month. Pensions are covered in Chapter 15.

>> **Annuities:** Annuities are almost like insurance policies in reverse. You hand over a big chunk of money to an insurance company, and they send you a monthly allowance of an agreed-upon sum. Annuities have a bad reputation with many retirees, and for good reason. Some poorly designed annuity products are loaded with fees. But if you're careful in your choice of annuities, they can be a useful way to create your own paycheck.

TABLE 14-4 **Sources of Retirement Income**

Retirement Income	Savings	Social Security	Total Income Replaced
$50,000	45%	35%	80%
$100,000	45%	27%	72%
$200,000	45%	16%	61%
$300,000	44%	11%	55%

Fidelity Investments, Based on Consumer Expenditure Survey (BLS), Statistics of Income Tax Stat, IRS tax brackets and Social Security Benefit Calculators; local and state taxes not included; retirement age 67 for base case

Understanding the types of annuities

Annuities come in many forms. An annuity that's appropriate for your financial situation can offer you a steady stream of income and peace of mind. But a bad annuity can suck your retirement plan of valuable cash and sock you with fees.

Deferred annuities

Did your grandmother or grandfather live until they were 110? Then you might consider *deferred annuities,* in which you hand over a pile of money (or make payments) to the annuity provider, usually an insurance company, and get a promise in exchange. The insurance company vows to pay you a set amount of money after you hit a specific age.

Deferred annuities pay off big time if you live a long time. Let's say you're Jiroemon Kimura of Japan and, when you were 60 years old, you bought a deferred annuity to kick in when you hit 80. Your money sat in the deferred annuity, tax free.

When you reached 80 and your portfolio was getting a bit light, you started getting much-needed annuity payments. Kimura, who died in 2013, lived until the age of 116. That means he would have collected annuity payments for 36 years, or as long as a standard retirement.

WARNING

Kimura is an unusual case, which is why deferred annuities aren't for most people. Depending on the deferred annuity's structure, if you die early, you surrender the amount you put in the annuity, which won't thrill your heirs.

Fixed annuities

With *fixed annuities,* you also hand over a chunk of money in exchange for payments in the future. However, the insurance company tells you ahead of time what rate of return you'll get and for how long. You can elect to take regular payments, and some plans allow for larger annual withdrawals.

WARNING

The fees on these annuities can be large. And if interest rates rise, the fixed rate you agreed on might not look so good.

Variable annuities

Variable annuities — surprise — are variable. Unlike with a fixed annuity, with a *variable annuity* you're taking the returns the market delivers. Returns on variable annuities can rise and fall with no warning. Variable annuities come in different forms, but typically the insurance company takes your money and tries to get a better return. There's no guarantee, though, and payouts might be disappointing.

WARNING

Variable annuities are an exotic financial product and a poor choice for most people. Fees can also be very high and getting money out can be difficult (even in the case of emergencies). In many ways, variable annuities fail to fulfill the promise of a steady paycheck. Why not just build a low-cost portfolio yourself or use a robo-advisor?

Immediate annuities

Immediate annuities are the best choice for most people looking at annuities. They're straightforward. You hand over a pile of money and the insurance company agrees to pay you a set amount of money for a set period of time (usually your entire lifetime). You can also buy immediate annuity policies that keep paying your spouse after you pass away.

Following are the advantages of immediate annuities:

>> **You get payments right away.**

>> **The rate of return you receive is usually higher than what a savings account or certificate of deposit would pay.**

>> **Payments are locked in.** You get the pre-agreed upon amount of money. If you purchase the appropriate annuity contract and forecast your income needs, you don't have to worry about running out of money.

TIP

Immediate annuities are perfect for covering your basic expenses. Figure out how much you spend on housing and food, and if your annuity pays this amount, you know that at least your basic needs will be covered.

Following are the disadvantages of immediate annuities:

>> **After you hand over your money, it belongs to the insurance company.** If you get hit with a big or costly emergency, such as a leaky roof, you'll need another source of income to come up with the cash.

>> **Inflation can eat away at the buying power of your annuity income.** Your pre-agreed monthly payout might look good in 2020. But by 2030, inflation could eat away at your purchasing power. Some immediate annuities offer riders that adjust for inflation, but your monthly payment will go down. (*Riders* are special policy add-ons that give the policy new features.)

>> **Fees can be high.** As with all annuities, fees are deducted from your payments. Some fees can be high, so make sure you know what you're paying.

>> **Low interest rates can reduce your annuity payments.** The size of your immediate annuity payment is mainly a function of your age and interest

rates at the time you sign up. The older you are when you sign up, the larger the payment. But when interest rates are low, as they were in 2019, you're locking in a low return. Also, the returns you get from immediate annuities are usually lower than what you'd get from a deferred annuity.

>> **Returns are lower than if you invested the money yourself.** You could likely build a portfolio that returns more than an annuity would. You're taking a lower return in exchange for transferring to the annuity provider the risk and responsibility of managing the portfolio.

Finding an immediate annuity

When you're looking for an immediate annuity, it's easy to get bogged down with all the variables that go into how your payment is calculated. But as you know, websites will help you calculate just about any financial problem, and annuities are no exception.

Pricing your annuity payment

Curious what your pile of money is worth as an immediate annuity payment? Just do the following:

1. **Head over to** www.immediateannuities.com/.

2. **In the Amount to Invest field, shown in Figure 14-1, enter the amount of cash you expect to plunk down into the annuity.**

   For the example, I used $250,000.

3. **Enter when you want to start getting money.**

   This is an immediate annuity, so the answer is most likely today!

4. **Enter your personal details.**

   Age, gender, and state are all the basics that the site needs. For the example, I used a 65-year-old male living in California.

5. **Decide if you want someone else to receive payments after you pass away.**

6. **Click the Get My Quote button.**

You see some initial quotes on how much of a monthly payment you might expect. But you're not finished yet.

FIGURE 14-1:
Calculating an annuity payment.

Tweaking your immediate annuity

Immediate annuities are contracts between you and the insurance company. You can make a number of adjustments, which affect how much you'll receive as a monthly payment.

Some of the adjustments you can make include defining terms such as the following:

>> **Life:** This annuity will pay you the set amount for your lifespan.

>> **Life and 10 years certain:** The annuity will pay you your entire life, with a twist. If you pass away in less than ten years, your beneficiaries will receive payments up until the time the policy is ten years old.

>> **Life with cash refund:** Here you get paid for your lifetime, but again with a twist. If you die before receiving at least the amount you put in, your beneficiaries get the difference. Because this structure reduces your risk of loss, it usually provides the lowest payment of any annuity option.

>> **Five-year period certain:** With this immediate annuity, you don't get paid for life. You get paid for five years. A ten-year period certain option is usually available too.

Figure 14-2 shows how some of these different options affect your annuity payments.

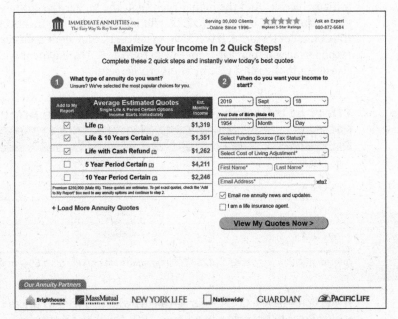

Running sample annuity numbers

Enough immediate annuity theory. It's time for some real numbers. With ImmediateAnnuities, you can see how additional changes might affect your monthly payments.

Paying up for inflation protection

One of the biggest problems with immediate annuities is inflation. Let's say our 65-year-old Californian male plunks down $250,000 and signs up for the life policy. He'll get a $1,319 payment a month (refer to Figure 14-2). And in 2019, that payment is likely enough to cover his food costs.

But if food costs rise just 2 percent a year, the same monthly grocery bill in 2019 would be $1,608 in just ten years. All of a sudden, his annuity payment is $289 a month less than what he needs for food.

To address this concern, you can add an inflation rider to your immediate annuity. With an inflation rider, your annuity payment will rise to keep up with inflation. You choose the *COLA*, or *cost of living adjustment*, which is the percentage amount your annuity payment increases annually.

Yes, an inflation rider is comforting because you know you'll get money to keep up with rising prices. But as you can see in Table 14-5 (which uses our example of a $250,000 annuity bought by a 65-year old male), COLAs reduce the amount you initially receive. And the higher the COLA, the bigger the cut to your initial payment. Over time, however, a COLA will increase your payments by the amount of the COLA. For instance, if you have a 1 percent COLA, your monthly payment in the second year will increase from $1,186 to $1,198. The payment with a COLA would rise again in the third year by another 1 percent.

TABLE 14-5

Effect of Inflation Riders on an Immediate Annuity

$250,000 Annuity	Monthly Payment
No COLA	$1,319
1% COLA	$1,186
2% COLA	$1,068
3% COLA	$960

ImmediateAnnuities; based on $250,000 immediate life annuity for a 65-year-old male

If you don't have a COLA, your payments will be frozen. If prices rise, your seemingly higher initial payment without a COLA will lose purchasing power over time. A payment of $1,319 a month might look great now, but if a Big Mac costs $10 in 30 years (instead of $4 now), you won't be feeling as rich.

As you can see in Table 14-5, a 3 percent COLA comes at a steep price. Yes, you're protected from inflation, but your monthly payment drops by more than a quarter from $1,319 to $960. You need to make sure you're willing to pay that price. Inflation, typically, doesn't run at 3 percent. In most years, inflation is closer to 2 percent, as shown in Table 14-6.

TABLE 14-6

Recent Inflation Has Been Tame

Year	Average Annual Inflation
2018	2.4%
2017	2.1%
2016	1.3%
2015	0.1%
2014	1.6%

www.usinflationcalculator.com/inflation/historical-inflation-rates/

Climbing annuity ladders

The economic climate in which you buy your annuity is important. If you buy your annuity when interest rates are low, as they were in 2019, you're locking in a life-time of lower payments.

What if you want to start getting guaranteed income but are afraid interest rates will rise? After all, if you plunk down $250,000 when rates are 3 percent, you'll be mightily disappointed if rates jump to 6 percent and your monthly payment could have roughly doubled.

TIP

An easy answer to this dilemma is the annuity version of spreading your bets, or *diversification.* Don't buy the annuity all at one time, especially when interest rates are low. Instead, space out your annuity purchase over time, a process called an *annuity ladder.* You might buy a $50,000 immediate annuity, wait a year or two, and then buy another $50,000 immediate annuity. Repeat this process several times over three to six years and you're spreading your risk.

WARNING

The downside to annuity laddering is if interest rates fall. Then you'll wish you bought the $250,000 annuity at one time when rates were higher. That's why you need to be mindful of interest rates. Unfortunately, there's no way to know where interest rates will go, so deciding whether or not you're better off with an annuity ladder is a crapshoot.

Unlocking a Goldmine: Reverse Mortgage

You might have a 401(k) and IRA. But if you're like many retirees, you're literally sitting on a gold mine. Homeowners aged 62 and older own homes valued at $7.14 trillion, as of the first quarter of 2019, according to the National Reverse Mortgage Lenders Association (www.nrmlaonline.org/2019/06/25/senior-housing-wealth-reaches-record-7-14-trillion).

To put that massive number into perspective, the value of older people's homes is just shy of the $8.8 trillion held in IRAs and $7.5 trillion in defined contribution retirement plans, such as 401(k)s, as of December 2018, says the Investment Company Institute (www.icifactbook.org/ch8/19_fb_ch8).

But you can take money out of an IRA or 401(k) to pay your bills or pay for a vacation. Your equity in your home is locked up, right? Wrong. If you're at least 62, you can tap the ownership in your home by using a reverse mortgage. It's a way to gain liquidity when all your other retirement accounts are emptied out.

As with any major financial instrument, though, reverse mortgages have advantages and disadvantages. Reverse mortgages are popular tools for scammers looking to take advantage of older people who need a cash flow.

Understanding reverse mortgages

A *reverse mortgage*, simply stated, is a home loan. But instead of the homeowner making payments to ultimately own the home debt-free, the opposite happens. The homeowner receives payments and over time builds up a loan balance. The home is used as the collateral for the debt the homeowner racks up.

Many types of reverse mortgages are available, but the most popular type is the home equity conversion mortgage, or HECM. With an *HECM*, no payments on the loan are due from homeowners or their estates until they sell the home, die, or move. And if the value of the home falls below the size of the reverse mortgage, the homeowner (or their estate) never owes more than the value of the home.

Suppose you take out a reverse mortgage on a home that the bank values at $250,000. And over many years, you receive loan payments of $240,000. If you sell the home for $200,000, you need to pay back only $200,000. The remaining $40,000 is paid for by the Federal Housing Administration (FHA).

REMEMBER

Even if you have a reverse mortgage, it's still the homeowner's responsibility to keep paying property taxes and homeowner's insurance.

Because the FHA is providing financial support for home-equity conversion mortgages, the government agency has strict rules about who can receive one. To qualify for an HECM, you must

>> **Be at least 62 years old.**

>> **Have money left over from the reverse mortgage payment.** If every dime is used to pay your monthly expenses, the FHA gets nervous.

>> **Have good credit.** You need a solid track record of paying your debts on time.

>> **Own a primary residence.** You can't get an HECM on your vacation home. Also, if you have any mortgage left on the property, most of it must be paid off. (The lender determines the allowed mortgage size.)

Understanding the drawbacks of reverse mortgages

Reverse mortgages are great options for some retirees, but they come with some potential major drawbacks. It's important to understand the downsides of these complicated financial tools before you sign up:

>> **High fees:** When you take out a reverse mortgage, a litany of costs are incurred, and some are hard to find. You must pay a mortgage insurance premium, which starts at 2 percent of the value of the loan. You're then charged 0.5 percent of the mortgage balance annually. Then add third-party costs, such as an appraisal, a title search, and an inspection. And include the loan origination fee, which is 2 percent of your home's value plus 1 percent over any amount over $200,000. (The origination fee is capped at $2,500.) The FHA spells out all these fees at www.hud.gov/program_offices/housing/sfh/hecm/hecmabou.

>> **Complications and ripe for scams:** The terms of reverse mortgages can be confusing, with all sorts of limits and rules. Furthermore, people don't usually consider reverse mortgages if they have other options. The combination of need, confusing rules, and lots of money up for grabs make reverse mortgages an attractive mix for scammers.

>> **Estate-planning issues:** If any borrower moves out of the home for 12 months, dies, or sells the home, the loan comes due. In the case of a death, the heirs must pay off the loan. This might come as a big surprise to children who were expecting a financial windfall instead of a massive bill.

Using a reverse mortgage

A reverse mortgage can give you access to cash, making it easier on the wallet than some other options.

For instance, you can tap the money locked up in your home in other ways, such as a home equity line of credit. But if you take out a home equity line of credit, you need to make payments while you're still alive. Additionally, if the economy gets rocky, the bank can pull back on the line of credit, so you can't count on it.

If you're looking for a reverse mortgage, the National Reverse Mortgage Lenders Association maintains a list of vendors it works with at www.nrmlaonline.org/vendors. You can also get bids on reverse mortgages at LendingTree (www.lendingtree.com/) by selecting Home Loans and then Reverse Mortgage, as shown in Figure 14-3) Lastly, the FHA provides a list of reverse mortgage lenders at www.hud.gov/program_offices/housing/sfh/lender/lenderlist.

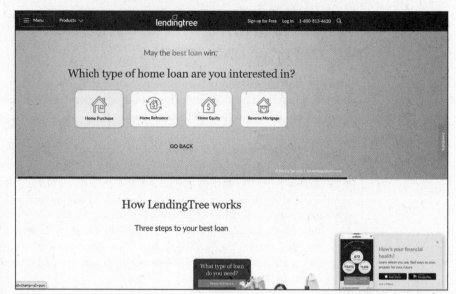

FIGURE 14-3:
LendingTree's reverse mortgage search tool helps you find the most compelling offers.

WARNING

Be careful when dealing with anyone pitching a reverse mortgage. It might not be the best option. Fees can be very high on reverse mortgages and you might be able to borrow money at a much lower cost.

TIP

Are you taking out the reverse mortgage to make repairs to your home or to pay property taxes? If so, government programs for this purpose are more cost effective than reverse mortgages.

You need to make sure a reverse mortgage is truly your best option before signing up for one. How do you find out the pros and cons of a reverse mortgage? The Federal Trade Commission, at www.consumer.ftc.gov/articles/0192-reverse-mortgages#shopping, spells out the risks and dangers of reverse mortgages and what to do if you get swindled.

TIP

If you agree to a reverse mortgage but realize you made a big mistake, you have three business days to stop the process. Most reverse mortgages give you the right to cancel if you notify the lender in writing. Keep all your documentation. The lender has 20 days to return any money you put up for the deal.

» Grasping the different types of pensions

» Tracking and rolling over your pension

» Getting the most from your pension in retirement

Chapter **15**

Understanding Pensions

Pensions formed the core of retirement plans in the 1950s and 1960s. You'd get a job with a big company or governmental body in what was practically a lifelong bond. You gave 30 or more of your most productive years, and in exchange, the company or government would promise to provide for you — and perhaps your spouse — for the rest of your life.

More than 85 percent of state and local government workers are offered pensions and 77 percent of workers participate in these plans, says the Bureau of Labor Statistics (www.bls.gov/ncs/ebs/benefits/2018/ownership/govt/table02a.htm). But if you work for a private employer, only 17 percent of workers are offered a pension and just 13 percent participate in them.

If you're lucky enough to get one, a pension can be a large and important part of your retirement plan. A pension is a *defined benefit plan,* which means you know what you're going to get paid. With a *defined contribution plan,* such as a 401(k), the benefit is up to you — and you don't know how much your plan will be worth in the future.

Managing a pension is different than looking after your IRA or 401(k). Usually, pensions are managed by a separate division of the company or public entity that offered it to you. Other times, pensions are managed by a third party, usually an insurance company. And surprisingly for such a long-term financial asset, it's common for pensions to change. They're frozen, transferred, or sweetened to talk you into retiring early. In some cases, you can also rollover a pension to an IRA to give you more control. And in some rare cases, pensions can be cut.

What are the different types of pensions? What choices do you need to make when signing up for one? How do you keep track of your pension and make sure you're optimizing the benefit? These questions are all answered by the time you finish reading this chapter.

Checking a Private Pension's Funding

If your company offers a pension plan, you should receive an annual mailing telling you how *funded* it is. The closer to 100 percent funded the plan is, the lower the odds that the company will need to dig into its pockets and make an additional contribution.

Because pension obligations are so large, any company offering a pension must tell regulators and investors how fully funded the pension is. If you work for a publicly traded company, you can find out how well-funded your company's plan is by following these steps:

1. **Go to the Securities and Exchange Commission's website at** www.sec.gov/.

2. **Click the Company Filings link in the upper-right corner.**

3. **Enter the name of the company you work for or its trading symbol.**

   To follow along with the example, enter GE for General Electric.

4. **In the list of regulatory filings, find the entry for 10-K and click its link.**

   All types of documents are available on the SEC website, but you're looking for the annual report, which is commonly known as the 10-K.

5. **Scan the 10-K for pension information.**

   A simple word search will turn up the sections you're looking for. In the pension section, you'll find vital statistics about the company's pension. For instance, you'll find the expected rate of return, which is how much the company thinks it will earn on the money invested in the pension. In GE's case, in 2018 it expected a 6.75 percent annual return.

   You also see how much money is in the pension and the estimated amount to be paid out when workers retire. Most importantly, you'll see how funded the plan is. That tells you how much of the expected payouts are stored in the account. GE, as shown in Figure 15-1, says its pension plan is 91 percent funded. Not bad.

FIGURE 15-1: General Electric discloses key facts about its pension plan in its 10-K filing with the SEC.

WARNING

Two warning signs to look for in pension plans are overly aggressive expectations for returns (10 percent or higher) and largely underfunded plans. Overly high returns expectations allow a company to put less money in the pension plan. You also want your plan to be at least 85 percent funded — and preferably much higher. The Employee Retirement Income Security Act (ERISA), places requirements on funding levels. The company's 10-K should include a mention of its compliance with ERISA. For more on ERISA, go to www.dol.gov/general/topic/retirement/erisa.

TIP

To check the health of your public pension, you need to rely on another watchdog because public pensions don't fall under the watchful eye of the SEC. PEW Charitable Trusts does an in-depth analysis of many public pensions. The report, which is updated periodically, is available at www.pewtrusts.org/en/research-and-analysis/issue-briefs/2019/06/the-state-pension-funding-gap-2017.

Understanding the Problems with Public Pensions

One of the top bonuses of working for the government is the high probability that you'll be offered a pension. If you're a public teacher, firefighter, police officer or any public employee, chances are very good that you'll be offered a pension plan.

All 50 states offer a retirement system for employees — and many offer several. California, for example, offers both the California Public Employees' Retirement System, known as CalPERS, and the California State Teachers' Retirement System, or CalSTRS. Some of these state-run pensions are massive. CalPERS, for instance, holds more than $350 billion in assets. Various cities must pay money into CalPERS to fund the pension liability for their workers.

If you're a public employee with a pension, your private-industry buddies with their 401(k)s might look enviously at your government-backed monthly payments for life. And there's comfort in knowing that you can visit your state's pension site and see your monthly payments.

But don't get too smug, public employees. You should to be aware of the following issues:

>> **Pensions can reduce Social Security benefits:** If you earned money as a public employee in certain states, you might trigger the *windfall elimination provision*, or WEP. If WEP kicks in, your Social Security benefit might be reduced because you're getting a pension. WEP doesn't apply if you put in 30 or more years of working credits with Social Security.

Earnings aren't covered by Social Security in the following states: Alaska, California, Colorado, Connecticut, Georgia (in some locales), Illinois, Kentucky (in some locales), Louisiana, Maine, Massachusetts, Missouri, Nevada, Ohio, Rhode Island (in some locales), and Texas, as you can see at www.nea.org/home/16819.htm.

>> **Pensions can limit your ability to change careers:** Most public pensions are designed to pay out if employees spend their entire career on the job. But let's face it, some people burn out or want to do something else. Switching jobs can dramatically reduce pension payouts.

>> **Public pensions face financial insecurity:** A dirty little secret in the public pension world is that many states simply can't afford what they promised to workers. Through 2017, the latest data available, public pensions were short by more than $1 trillion from what they owe, according to PEW Charitable Trusts (www.pewtrusts.org/en/research-and-analysis/issue-briefs/2019/06/the-state-pension-funding-gap-2017).

States such as Illinois, Colorado, and Pennsylvania, are funded below 60 percent. Some states are adjusting by finding ways to pay out less. For instance, in September 2019, the Ohio Public Employees Retirement System froze the cost of living adjustment for two years.

>> **You need discipline to save more on your own:** If you'll be getting a public pension when you retire, you might be lulled into a false sense of financial security and blow your entire paycheck while you're working. But due to budgetary constraints, your pension-funded easy street might be less golden than you thought.

As a backup plan, it's a good idea to save on your own to complement your pension. Luckily, government workers get many options for tax-advantaged savings.

Teachers are offered *403(b) plans*, which allow them to put away tax-deferred dollars, as you would with a 401(k). However, 403(b) plans tend to be filled with higher-priced investments and fewer choices. You can read more about optimizing your 403(b) plan at https://403bwise.org/.

Additionally, if you're a state employee, you might be able to make tax-deferred contributions to a *457 plan* — in addition to accruing a pension. You can stuff up to $19,500 a year into your 457 (in 2020), plus a $6,000 catchup contribution after you turn 50. And with a 457 plan, you can take out money before turning 55 years old and not have to pay a 10 percent penalty. (You'll still owe taxes, though.)

If you're a public school teacher, you usually can contribute to a 457 in addition to a 403(b). Be sure to check with the school's human resources department. You could max out both if you want. In addition, if your employer also offers a 401(k), you can put money into that as well.

TIP

Pension options are even better for federal employees. In addition to a pension, you can likely contribute to the Thrift Savings Plan, or TSP. The *TSP* is a massive retirement savings plan widely lauded for its menu of low-cost index funds. More than 5 million people are part of the TSP, making it one of the largest retirement savings plans in the nation.

The TSP is set up to resemble the structure of a 401(k) plan, down to the $19,000 annual contribution limit for 2019. Civilian federal workers are automatically signed up to put 3 percent of their pay in the TSP.

The TSP offers the following five funds, each with low fees:

>> The G Fund owns U.S. Treasuries.

>> The F Fund is the fixed-income, or bond, offering. It uses a BlackRock U.S. Debt Index Fund, a low-cost index bond fund.

>> The C Fund is the common stock fund, BlackRock's Equity Index fund. This fund replicates the Standard & Poor's 500 index.

>> The S Fund is a small-company fund, which is BlackRock's Extended Market Index fund.

>> The I Fund owns international stocks in BlackRock's EAFE Index Fund.

Additionally, the TSP has retirement-date funds, which mix the aforementioned funds based on when you plan to retire. If you're a federal worker, you'll want to take advantage of the TSP.

Understanding Pensions Inside-Out

Three types of pensions are available, each with its own characteristics, advantages, and disadvantages. It's important to know what you own before trying to manage it:

>> **Traditional pensions:** These plans are what you normally associate with the term *pension*. With a traditional pension, you're entitled to a regular monthly payout. When you retire, you can activate your payment, which is typically linked to your earnings on your last day.

>> **Cash-balance pensions:** Each year you work, your employer puts a set amount of money in your plan. These plans usually come with a total dollar value that's not necessarily linked with how much you were earning when you retired.

>> **Frozen pensions:** Many companies, seeing the ballooning costs of traditional pensions, are eager to get out of the retirement business. They freeze the pension and no longer make contributions. When this happens, the company might sweeten the 401(k) match to ease the initial shock of the frozen pension.

WARNING

It's increasingly common for large companies to wiggle out of offering pensions. These companies not only freeze the pension but also convert it to a cash-balance plan. This might be okay if you're a younger worker and the company boosts its 401(k) plan because you'll have time to invest the money fairly aggressively. But if you're older, the transition could be a blow to your retirement plan. If you're in this situation and the documentation confuses you, a skilled financial advisor can help you adjust your financial plan and stay on track.

Choosing a lump sum versus ongoing payments

When it comes time to collect your pension, you'll have a number of important decisions to make. Perhaps the largest is whether to take the money as a giant *lump sum* payment or space it out in regular payments over the course of your life (or your spouse's, too).

Lump sum payment

If you take a lump sum, the pension provider calculates the present value of all the payments they would have likely paid and hands you the money. Getting this giant pile of cash feels great. And it can be a good option if you

» **Face large one-time costs:** For example, you might be dealing with a medical emergency.

» **Think you can invest the money more effectively and get a better return:** Many cash balance pensions will only give you annual cost of living adjustments, which are usually around 2 percent. That's an easy level to beat, without taking on much risk.

» **Worry about the company's financial strength:** A company might stop making contributions to the pension when the business isn't performing well, resulting in a seriously underfunded pension.

But taking a lump sum pension distribution has downsides, too, because you

» **Assume market risk:** By taking the lump sum, increasing and protecting the money is your responsibility. If the bond or stock market declines, the value of your lump sum will go down with it.

» **Give up lifelong payments:** There's something comforting about getting income for life, especially if it's coming from a company on solid financial footing. You'd need to buy an annuity to get the same benefit.

WARNING

Most large online brokerage firms offer annuities designed to give you pension-like income streams. But often the payments from an annuity are less than what you'd get from the pension because the fees for the annuity are higher.

Ongoing pension payments

If you're don't want to manage your own money, you might consider door #2: ongoing pension payments for life. Here, the pension company calculates your monthly payment and puts that amount in your account monthly.

The ongoing pension payment can be an excellent option if you

» **Think you'll live a long time:** If your parents and grandparents lived into their 90s, a pension payout can help you manage the risk of outliving your money. Just know that unless your plan gives you a cost-of-living adjustment, the purchasing power of the payments will fall over time.

>> **Don't want to manage your own money:** Do you panic during a market downturn? Do you have little interest in choosing stocks, bonds, and funds? Then it might be best to let the pension company take over.

>> **Think the pension plan is a good one:** How do you know whether the ongoing pension payment will be worth more than the lump sum? You can get the information you need by calling your pension provider or going to its website. See how much a lump sum would be worth if you bought an immediate annuity and compare that with the monthly payment. For details, see the "Calculating the value of a lump sum payment" section.

>> **Worked for a rock-solid company:** If your employer is financially strong and the pension is fully funded, you can feel more confident about choosing an ongoing payment.

>> **Aren't too concerned with your estate:** After you die (and your spouse passes away if you elected for survivor benefits), the payments end. That's it. No giant pile of money is available to hand down to your children or other beneficiaries.

But taking an ongoing pension payment has downsides, too, because you

>> **Put your trust in your employers' plan:** You're counting on your former employer to properly manage the pension liability for a long time.

>> **Limit your potential upside:** If you managed the money yourself, you could presumably get a higher return than you would from the pension. Also, when you retire, you might have other sources of income and be better off investing the funds in assets that will grow in value, not necessarily generate income.

WARNING

If you worked for a financially unstable company, seriously consider the risks of taking ongoing pension payouts. Although many pensions are guaranteed by the Pension Benefit Guarantee Corp., not all employers are members of the PBGC. Also, if you have a large pension, the PBGC will guarantee only a portion of your payments. Lastly, you must have faith in the financial strength of the PBGC, which faces challenges of its own. Parts of the PBGC's own business are underfunded, as detailed at www.pbgc.gov/news/press/releases/pr19-09. More on the PBGC in the "Who's Protecting Your Pension?" sidebar.

Choosing single life versus survivor

If you choose to take ongoing pension payments versus a lump sum, you must make one more decision. You must choose between a single-life payout or a survivor payout.

WHO'S PROTECTING YOUR PENSION?

With a pension, you're placing a great deal of trust in your pension provider. It's up to your employer to put money into the plan — and to make up for any shortfall if market returns are less than expected or retirees are living longer than expected.

Furthermore, you're counting on the company to be around to make the payments. The economy and technology can disrupt even entrenched companies. Giant companies such as Ford and General Motors, both large pension providers, have struggled since the financial crisis of 2008.

Sometimes, companies with pensions do more than struggle. Sears Holdings, the once-dominant department store, filed for bankruptcy protection in 2018. Investors, of course, lost most of their money. But what about the 90,000 Sears pension plan participants who thought the once-strong retailer would make payments to them for life?

That's when the PBGC stepped in. The PBGC is a corporation chartered by the U.S. government to insure pensions. When a company such as Sears is unable to put money into a pension plan, the PBGC takes over. And in the case of Sears, the pension plan was underfunded by $1.4 billion. Reading the PBGC's description of the situation at www.pbgc.gov/Questions-and-Answers-for-Sears-Participants is a good reminder of what happens when a company can no longer maintain its pension.

What happens when a company is no longer able to make good on its pension promises? The lifecycle of a pension starts when it's launched and the company is healthy. Companies with pensions pay an insurance premium to the PBGC long before any trouble starts. If you have a private company pension, check that the company is a member of the PBGC by using the PBGC's lookup tool at www.pbgc.gov/search-insured-plans.

The PBGC accumulates all the premiums paid by the pensions it insures to create a rescue fund. If a company runs into major difficulties, usually involving a trip to bankruptcy court, the pension becomes the PBGC's responsibility. All plan participants are notified that the pension is being taken over by the PBGC and are given an estimate of what they'll be paid.

And this is the key point: A vast majority of plans are insured by the PBGC, but they are not necessarily fully insured. The PBGC has limits of coverage that might be less than what you were promised. Specifically, a single-employer plan has much higher limits

(continued)

(continued)

than a multi-employer plan. The lookup tool will tell you how your plan is insured. In 2019, for a person retiring at 65, the annual payout limit was $67,295 for a straight annuity and $60,566 for a joint life pension with a 50 percent survivor annuity.

In addition to the limits on PBGC coverage, consider the health of the PBGC itself. In an August 2019 analysis, the PBGC described its multi-employer insurance program as "on the path to running out of money by the end of fiscal year 2025." Additionally, although the single-employer plan is improving, it operated with a deficit every year from 2001 through 2019. "The program remains vulnerable to an unexpected downturn in the economy," the report said. You can learn more about the health of the PBGC at www.pbgc.gov/news/press/releases/pr19-09.

With a single-life payment, you

>> **Get payments only during your lifetime:** When you die, the money stops coming in, which will be a problem if your spouse relies on the income.

>> **Get a larger check each month.**

>> **Must sign a waiver form with your spouse:** This form must be notarized.

TIP

The single-life pension option makes sense if you think you'll live longer than your spouse. It can also be a good option if your spouse has access to other income.

On the other hand, the survivor payout offers you

>> **Lifetime income for you or your spouse.**

>> **A lower monthly payment amount.**

>> **A menu of options:** The initial payments received in a survivor payout arrangement are based on the retired worker's benefits. As soon as the retiree or spouse passes away, the benefit is usually reduced. You decide when you sign up for the survivor payout how much the monthly amount is cut by, be it 50 percent, 25 percent, or less.

TIP

If your pension is the primary source of income for you and your spouse, the survivor payout makes sense. Predicting lifespans is difficult and you'd hate for your loved one to be financially strapped.

Managing Your Pension

Keeping track of your pension isn't as easy as logging onto your online brokerage. Most companies are eager to get out of the pension business, so they farm the entire thing out to firms that specialize in pensions, such as Willis Towers Watson.

If you need to call for pension help, you'll probably be talking to people who work for the firm your employer hired to handle the pension plan. However, the site operated by the pension firm will usually look like it's run by your employer.

Using online tools

Getting logged into your company's pension plan usually takes a bit of a work. You might need to call your employer's human resources department. Then, if your employer has outsourced their pension plan management, you'll probably be handed off to the company running the pension plan.

Most pension systems will allow you to look at the following information:

» **Pension estimate:** By entering your dates of employment, age, and beneficiary information, the site will tell you the payment you can expect when you retire, as shown in Figure 15-2. As you can see in this example, the single-life annuity results in the largest monthly payout of $641.39. When you add a 50 percent survivor annuity, you're looking at a monthly payment of $603.54. The survivor annuity payment is smaller than the single-life payment because the payments are likely to last for a longer period of time. Why? When the pensioner who worked at the company dies, a payout continues to the surviving spouse, who gets only half the payment, just $301.77.

» **Lump sum calculator:** The pension site should also show your lump sum payment if taken now versus later. This information will help you decide which choice to make.

» **Scenario analysis:** Pensions are complicated, with many variables affecting your payout amount. To help you understand the complexities, most pension sites offer scenario analyzers. You enter different retirement ages and whether or not your spouse will get benefits. The scenario analysis calculator then shows how these different choices affect your payout.

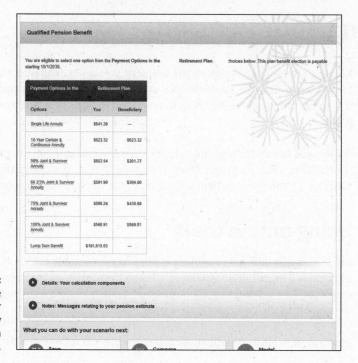

Qualified Pension Benefit

You are eligible to select one option from the Payment Options in the ___ Retirement Plan ___ choices below. This plan benefit election is payable starting 10/1/2036.

Payment Options in the	Retirement Plan	
Options	You	Beneficiary
Single Life Annuity	$641.39	---
10-Year Certain & Continuous Annuity	$623.32	$623.32
50% Joint & Survivor Annuity	$603.54	$301.77
66 2/3% Joint & Survivor Annuity	$591.90	$394.60
75% Joint & Survivor Annuity	$586.24	$439.68
100% Joint & Survivor Annuity	$569.91	$569.91
Lump Sum Benefit	$191,615.03	---

Details: Your calculation components

Notes: Messages relating to your pension estimate

What you can do with your scenario next:

Save   Compare   Model

FIGURE 15-2:
Your pension site calculates your expected monthly payment given various scenarios.

REMEMBER

You don't have to be retired to take money out of a pension. If you leave a company, you can activate monthly payments or take a lump sum. However, your payments will be reduced if you start taking them before reaching full retirement age. Also know that if you take a lump sum payout and don't roll it over into another retirement account, you might trigger a nasty tax surprise.

Calculating the value of a lump sum payment

One of the trickier decisions with pensions is whether you should take monthly payments or the lump sum. The pension's website can help you make this decision.

TIP

Although your decision is final, a workarounds exists. You can create your own pension, in a way, by using your lump sum payout to buy an annuity.

By using both your pension provider's site and an annuity pricing site, you can easily put some numbers around this complex decision. Here's how:

1. **Use the pension's online tool to get your lump sum payout.**

   Let's say a 48-year-old worker left a company and wants to take her pension with her. As shown in Figure 15-3, her lump sum payout is $70,897.10. The monthly payout amount is $338.46 for a single-life annuity and $337.62 for a ten-year certain and continuous annuity.

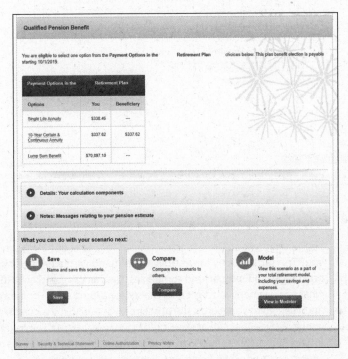

2. **Go to an annuity pricing site, such as** www.immediateannuities.com **and do the following:**

   a. *Enter the lump sum information.*

   b. *Enter your pension details and select the immediate payment option.* For the amount to invest, enter the lump sum payout from your pension site. I entered $70,897.10.

3. **Compare the monthly payouts.**

   As you can see in Figure 15-4, the monthly payout from the pension plan is higher than what our retiree can buy in the open annuity market. Using the lump sum amount, the payout from the privately bought annuity is $280 for a single life, which is 17 percent less than the pension payout. Similarly, the pension payout with the ten-year certain option is $675 a month. But with the annuity provider, it's 6 percent less, or $637 a month.

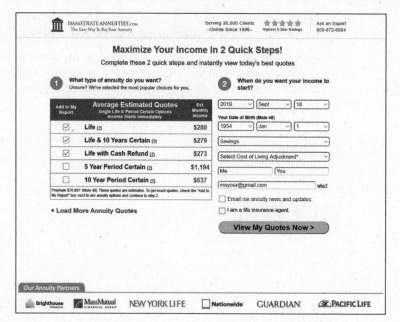

FIGURE 15-4:
An annuity
calculator helps
you measure
your lump sum
payouts.

4. **Get another estimate.**

   You wouldn't get only one medical opinion for a serious health condition, would you? The same is true for deciding what to do with a pension. Many online brokerages and mutual fund companies, such as Vanguard and Fidelity, tell you what size payment you'd get in exchange for a lump sum. For information on annuities, go to Vanguard's site at https://investor.vanguard.com/annuity/checkup, Fidelity's site at www.fidelity.com/annuities/overview, and Schwab's annuity site (see Figure 15-5) at www.schwab.com/public/schwab/investing/accounts_products/investment/annuities/income_annuity/fixed_income_annuity_calculator.

TIP

It's typical for the payouts from a pension plan to be higher than what you can buy on your own from an annuity. An annuity has fees whereas an employer-sponsored pension doesn't.

However, don't make your decision solely on the size of the lump sum. If you're young, you could easily invest the lump sum, and then, years later when you're looking to retire, buy an annuity with the now-larger amount of money.

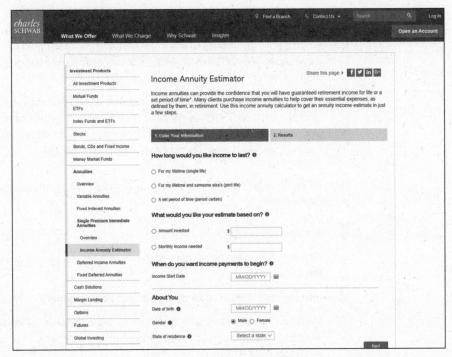

FIGURE 15-5:
Charles Schwab's Income Annuity Estimator helps you determine the income stream from a lump sum pension.

Rolling over a pension

Never assume you're trapped in a pension. And that's a good thing because many workers tend to not stay at the same job for more than five years. When you leave a job, you can take the pension with you by rolling it over.

WARNING

The rules around rolling over a pension are strict. Even a small mistake can make the lump sum you take from your pension a taxable event. You must rollover the pension into a qualified retirement plan, which for most people means a rollover IRA.

Depending on how long you worked at the company, a rollover is likely a good option. You might consider rolling over your pension if you

>> **Know the pension won't grow:** Check the pension's documentation. Many pensions provide only a modest cost-of-living annual adjustment, which is just the inflation rate. If you put the money into a diversified portfolio of stocks and bonds, your portfolio will likely grow much faster than inflation.

>> **Don't expect to retire in many years:** The longer the amount of time you have to put your money to work, the better. If you don't plan to retire in ten or more years, you still have time to put your portfolio into areas that are likely to grow faster.

>> **Have other forms of guaranteed income:** If you have other options for a steady cash flow, it makes sense to try to get a better return from your pension assets. If you don't have another form of guaranteed income, you can buy one, such as an annuity, by using other savings.

How do you conduct a rollover from your pension to a qualified plan? The steps are straightforward:

1. **Set up a rollover IRA.**

All the major online brokerages and mutual fund companies can help you with this task.

2. **Initiate your distribution with your pension provider.**

Most pension providers' sites allow you to begin the distribution process. You'll need to take the lump sum distribution method. The pension provider will mail you paperwork to fill out.

3. **Fill out the paperwork from the pension provider.**

Your spouse will need to sign a benefit waiver for you to get the lump sum.

4. **Make sure the check is made out to the company you're rolling into.**

This step is important. The pension lump sum amount must be made out to the financial firm where you have your rollover IRA. The check should not be made out to you.

WARNING

Depositing the lump sum and then immediately writing a check to the rollover IRA provider will not work. The Internal Revenue Service will think you took the money and want to tax it.

Chapter **16**

Getting Insurance

S aving money is job #1 of retirement planning. But another almost equally important part of retirement planning is hanging onto the money you have. And for this task, insurance plays a key role.

Healthcare costs, especially unexpected ones, can ruin even the most solid retirement plans. Most people nearing retirement or who are already retired "feel financially secure," according to a survey conducted by the Society of Actuaries (www.soa.org/globalassets/assets/files/resources/research-report/2018/risk-process-retirement.pdf). But the study also found that two-thirds of retirees expected to get by with less income in retirement, which leaves them exposed to unexpected financial shocks. Specifically, less than half of pre-retirees said they "felt prepared" to handle unexpected healthcare costs.

In this chapter, you'll find out how to be one of the people who feels prepared to deal with the unexpected. Putting together a healthcare insurance plan is the first place to start. If you're a full-time employee, the task is usually taken care of for you (as long as you selected all the right boxes on the forms). But if you are a freelancer or retired before you're eligible for Medicare, you'll need to know how to navigate the health insurance system.

Additionally, you'll want insurance to protect your assets from a variety of unforeseen events. Umbrella insurance, paired with homeowner's and auto insurance, puts a financial shield around your retirement plan. Nearly 60 percent of retired widows (and 52 percent of all retirees) feared that they might deplete their savings, the Society of Actuaries found. Life insurance safeguards you from this risk.

Building a Health Insurance Plan

If you're like most retired people, you and your partner will spend $285,000 for medical expenses in today's dollars over the course of your retirement, says Fidelity Investments (www.fidelity.com/viewpoints/personal-finance/plan-for-rising-health-care-costs). And that doesn't include the costs of long-term care, such as assisted living or a nursing home.

To best prepare for healthcare costs in the future, begin by taking certain steps while you're still working. For example, the Health Savings Account, or HSA, should be a critical part of your overall retirement plan.

And don't think all your medical costs will go away after you hit the magical age of 65 and qualify for Medicare. Fidelity found that 15 percent of retirees' annual budgets is consumed by healthcare costs, including your Medicare premiums and costs that aren't covered by Medicare. Most retirees also need to buy additional medical insurance.

TIP

The best way to make sure healthcare costs don't crush you is to prepare for them. The problem is that forecasting how much you'll spend on healthcare in the future isn't easy. Or is it? Fidelity offers a nifty online tool that will estimate your healthcare costs; visit https://communications.fidelity.com/wi/tools/retirement-health-care/. You'll step through a number of estimates, shown in Figure 16-1, to arrive at a reasonable guess of what you might expect to spend in retirement on medical care.

Unlocking the health savings account

One of the best ways to prepare for your medical costs in retirement involves taking smart steps while you're still working. You might not think much of medical costs as an employee because your employer is picking up much of the tab.

Annual healthcare premiums hit $20,576 in 2019 for a family, up 5 percent from 2018, says Kaiser (www.kff.org/health-costs/report/2019-employer-health-benefits-survey/). And of that amount, workers are generally responsible for paying $6,015. That's just the insurance premiums. You'll also incur out-of-pocket costs, such as deductibles, ranging from $800 to $5,000 a year (www.commonwealthfund.org/publications/issue-briefs/2019/may/how-much-us-households-employer-insurance-spend-premiums-out-of-pocket).

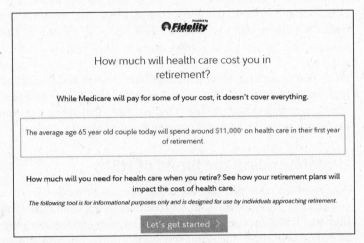

FIGURE 16-1:
Fidelity's online tool will help you get an idea of your future medical costs.

What's the solution? A fairly new innovation in medical savings that you can take advantage of while you're still working is the health savings account, or HSA. An *HSA* is a unique account into which you can put tax-free dollars, as long as you're in a high-deductible health plan. HSA are usually offered to you by your employer if you're eligible.

TIP

If you're looking to reduce taxes, you'll be hard-pressed to beat the HSA. You get triple-tax benefits at the federal level. You put in money tax-free, the money accumulates and grows tax-free, and then you can take the money out tax-free as long as you use it for medical costs. Most states extend tax breaks on contributions, growth, and withdrawals, too. But California and New York, for example, don't allow state tax-free HSA contributions. Also, state tax deductions don't exist in states that don't have income tax. Be sure to check your state's HSA tax rules. Even so, you won't find a better federal tax-shielded account that's so widely available.

Given the HSA's superior tax status, if you're still working and can swing it, you should put as much money in one as you can afford. If you can't max out both your 401(k) and your HSA, you might put in enough in your 401(k) to get the most from your employer match. And with any money left over, you can contribute to your HSA.

Seeing if you're eligible for HSA

If you want an HSA, you must be enrolled in a high-deductible health insurance plan, or *HDHP*. The definition of an HDHP changes periodically; for 2020, it's a plan with a deductible of at least $1,400 for an individual or $2,800 for a family. A *deductible* is the portion of medical costs that are your responsibility before insurance will pay. You can look up what defines an HDHP plan at www.healthcare.gov/glossary/high-deductible-health-plan/.

TIP

When you're signing up for a medical plan at work and would like to fund an HSA, look for a designation such as HSA eligible. And don't confuse the HSA with the *flexible spending account* (FSA). With an FSA, you must use up the money in a 12-month period; HSA funds can remain until you use them.

Understanding the limits of HSAs

Like most tax-shielded accounts, the Internal Revenue Service limits how much you can put into an HSA. The contribution limits change annually and are lower than you'll find for retirement accounts such as 401(k)s, but they're high enough to add up over time. The HSA contribution limits for 2019 and 2020 are shown in Table 16-1.

TABLE 16-1   **HSA Annual Contribution Limits**

Year	Individual	Family	Catch-Up (55 or older)
2019	$3,500	$7,000	$1,000
2020	$3,550	$7,100	$1,000

www.investors.com/etfs-and-funds/personal-finance/hsa-contribution-limits-hsa-rules/ and https://blog.healthequity.com/hsa-contribution-limits

Keep in mind, though, that after you enroll in Medicare, you can no longer put money in an HSA.

Using HSA money

The money you put in your HSA can be invested much like your funds in an IRA. The money grows tax-deferred, shielding you from tax hits from dividends generated by your investments or capital gains.

Investment options vary based on the HSA provider. A minimum HSA balance is usually required before you may invest in funds or stocks. When you do have enough money to invest, most HSA plans will offer you one of three choices (see Figure 16-2):

>> **Full robo-advisor:** Here you turn the management of the investments completely over to the HSA's algorithm. The plan will select your investments, usually low-cost index mutual funds, and buy them and rebalance them for you. Fees can be upwards of 1 percent a year.

>> **Robo guidance:** Some HSAs will tell you what they recommend, but you do the buying and selling. The HSA plan will typically recommend a mix of low-cost index funds. You'll save some money with this approach, with fees up to 0.7 percent a year. But you'll need to do the transactions and keep the account in balance.

>> **Self-guided brokerage:** With this option, you're on your own and decide which funds to buy. You'll save a bundle on fees by doing the work yourself and typically pay only the annual fees charged by the funds you choose. However, you can choose from only the funds and investments made available by the HSA provider.

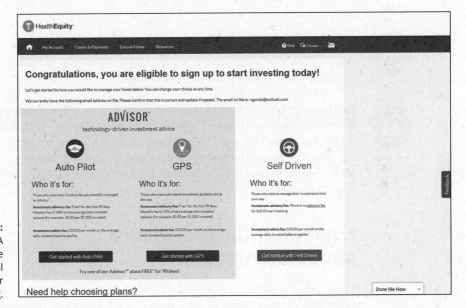

FIGURE 16-2: Most HSA providers give you several options for investing.

TIP

HSAs are flexible. You can take money out, tax-free, to pay for medical costs ranging from co-payments to eyeglasses, hearing aids, and other medical equipment. However, the money can't be used to pay for over-the-counter medication unless you get a prescription from a doctor.

While you're working, consider saving your HSA funds and paying for medical costs out of pocket instead. If you leave your HSA relatively untouched while you work, you can put the account's tax shield to maximum use over time. So rather than using the $200 to pay for the X-ray, the $200 stays invested and can grow so you'll have more money when you're retired.

Money taken out of an HSA for non-medical purposes before you turn 65 is socked with a 20 percent penalty. But wait until after you turn 65, and you pay only income tax on the withdrawal. If you think about it, that's not so bad. After all, it's no different from how money is treated when you take it out of a traditional IRA.

To read about more ways to maximize your HSA for preparing for retirement, check out the blog from HSA provider Health Equity at https://blog. healthequity.com/.

Opening an HSA

In nearly all instances, if you have a high-deductible plan with your employer, your employer will open your HSA. You can also open your own HSA. And if you had an HSA with a previous employer, you can transfer the money into another HSA account.

TIP If your employer offers an HSA, it's best to simply use that one. Doing so will make it easier for your employer to make contributions and for you to make tax-free contributions straight from your paycheck.

Keep an eye on any fees charged by an HSA plan. Many charge $2.50 a month unless you keep a minimum deposit of $5,000 or more. That doesn't sound like much, but given that you'll likely have your HSA a long time, the small fees add up. If you're being charged excessive fees, it might be time to choose your own HSA. Investor's Business Daily ranks the best ones at www.investors.com/etfs-and-funds/personal-finance/best-health-savings-account-providers/.

Understanding Medicare supplemental plans

Three months before turning 65, it's time to sign up for Medicare. You do this even if you're not ready to start receiving benefits. You can find all the details about signing up for Medicare benefits at www.ssa.gov/benefits/medicare/.

Many retirees think Medicare takes care of all their medical costs, but that's far from the truth. You have to pay for your deductibles and co-payments. Need glasses, dental care, and hearing aids? Those aren't covered. If these costs scare you, think about getting additional coverage. The drawback is the cost.

I am not saying Medicare is worthless. Medicare Part A, which covers trips to the hospital, costs nothing annually if you worked at least 10 years. Medicare Part B, which handles doctor visits, and Part D, which handles prescriptions, are based on your income. Most people pay $136 a month for Part B and $33 a month for Part D. (You pay more if you earn more.)

When you first enroll in Medicare, you can choose between the following:

>> **Original Medicare:** Here you get Medicare Part A and Part B coverage. You can also join a separate Part D plan for drug coverage.

>> **Medicare Advantage (also called Part C):** These plans include Part A, Part B, and Part D coverage and are offered by third-party insurers. You might pay less out of pocket with the Medicare Advantage plan than you would with Original Medicare if the limits are different. Some Medicare Advantage plans cost more if dental and eye coverage are included, too.

If you're worried about the out-of-pocket costs that Medicare might not cover, you can buy additional Medigap policies. *Medigap* covers items Medicare doesn't.

If you think that understanding Medigap could be an entire book, you're right! The government's free book on Medigap policies is the de facto and most accurate resource. You can download it for free at `www.medicare.gov/pubs/pdf/02110-LE-Medigap.pdf`.

What if you decide you'd like to buy a Medigap plan, also known as a Medicare Supplement or Medicare Supplement Insurance plan? The government can help you find a plan at `www.medicare.gov/medigap-supplemental-insurance-plans`. Simply enter your zip code, and you'll see all available Medigap plans. The screen details the plan type, coverage, and cost. You can drill down and get particulars by clicking the Plan Details button, as shown in Figure 16-3.

Exploring the exchanges

If you're not quite 65 and find yourself without employer-paid healthcare, you'll need to do some planning. After all, you'd hate to have unexpected medical costs eat away at money you've saved and invested as part of your retirement plan.

If you find yourself in this situation, you have a few options, including the following:

>> **COBRA:** COBRA is government-mandated coverage that your employer must offer to you if you leave. COBRA will keep you on the company healthcare plan for at least 18 months (longer in some states). The catch? The employer no longer must make their part of the premium payments. The entire premium payment is your responsibility, and it's not cheap.

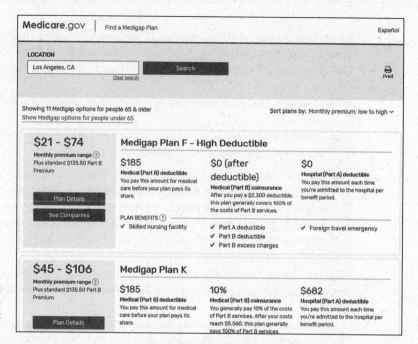

FIGURE 16-3:
Medicare's site helps you select a Medigap plan.

TIP

COBRA can be a good option if you leave a job in your early-to-mid 60s and are close to enrolling for Medicare. You'll have access to the same physician network and your coverage will stay the same. COBRA might make sense also if you're currently undergoing treatment and don't want any coverage changes.

>> **Health insurance through your spouse:** It's common for your spouse's employer to bar you from being on its health plan while you're working. But if you're not working, joining your spouse's plan is a great option.

REMEMBER

Losing your job is usually a qualifying event for you to join the plan. You don't need to wait until the end of the year's open enrollment period.

>> **Affordable Care Act Marketplace Exchange:** Major healthcare reforms in 2009 created an option for people who need health insurance. The system is surprisingly straightforward to use, given how long the idea was debated by Congress. First, go to www.healthcare.gov/ to see if you're eligible to enroll, as shown in Figure 16-4.

The site will take you to a directory of all major medical insurers who participate in your state's healthcare exchange (see Figure 16-5). You can also shop for vision and dental plans.

From your state's exchange site, you can look up what available plans cover and cost. Given the highly personalized nature of healthcare, examine how much you typically spend on medical expenses to help determine the best option.

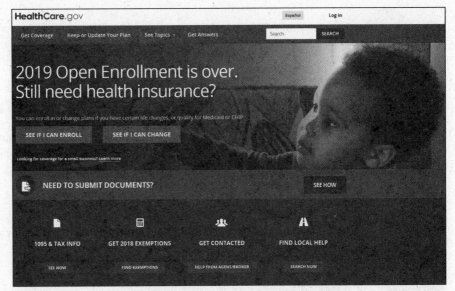

FIGURE 16-4:
HealthCare.gov will step you through the process of finding and signing up for healthcare insurance.

FIGURE 16-5:
Find a plan that balances the cost with your healthcare needs.

TIP

It pays to take a close look at your typical healthcare spending, so you can match your needs with your plan. Consider a high-deductible plan so you can also open a health savings plan.

Considering long-term care insurance

When you hit your 50s and 60s, you have another insurance decision to make: whether or not to buy long-term care insurance. As mentioned, Medicare does not pay for all your medical costs, and those uncovered costs include nursing homes and other skilled care.

Genworth, an insurance company, estimates that seven out of ten people will need long-term care during their lifetime. And the cost of long-term care is astronomical, as you can see in Table 16-2.

TABLE 16-2   **Cost of Long-Term Care**

Type of Care	Monthly Median National Cost (2018)
Homemaker services	$4,004
Home Health Aide	$4,195
Adult Day Health Care	$1,560
Assisted Living Facility	$4,000
Nursing Home (semi-private room)	$7,441
Nursing Home (private room)	$8,365

Genworth Financial

TIP

Genworth has a tool to help you calculate long-term care costs in your area. Simply go to `www.genworth.com/aging-and-you/finances/cost-of-care.html` and enter your zip code.

Given these sky-high costs, it's only natural that pre-retirees or retirees want to hedge their bets. Enter long-term care insurance. With a long-term care insurance plan, you pay a premium, usually in your 50s and 60s, and the insurance company agrees to pick up part of the cost of care if you need it.

WARNING

Long-term care plans sound reassuring, but they're not cheap. A single 55-year-old man looking for $200 in long-term coverage every day for up to five years would pay $3,094 a year in premiums. To look up how much a long-term care policy would cost, go to `www.genworth.com/products/care-funding/long-term-care-insurance/ltc-insurance-calculator.html`. In addition to deciding the number of years of long-term coverage and the amount of daily coverage, you decide whether you want an annual inflation adjustment. Long-term care costs are likely to only increase, so you might want at least a 2 percent annual inflation adjustment so your coverage can keep up somewhat.

You also need to carefully research the financial strength and reputation of the long-term care insurer. Nothing would be worse than to land in a nursing home only to find out that your insurer won't make the payments or find some reason to not cover your claim. Stick with reputable long-term care providers, such as members of the American Association for Long-Term Care Insurance (www. aaltci.org/)

Defending Your Money with Insurance

Protecting your retirement funds from disaster is a critical part of retirement planning. That's where insurance comes in. You want to make sure your plan can withstand an unexpected event. Typically, health scares are the culprits in disrupting a plan, but home and auto accidents can be major expenses, too.

TIP

Find your insurance declaration pages. These documents will tell you how much coverage you have, which you'll need to evaluate your plan and make certain you're protected.

Checking property and casualty coverages

If you're planning for retirement, it's important that you have in place the right amount of automobile and homeowner's (or renter's) insurance coverage, in addition to healthcare coverage:

>> **Automobile insurance:** Your car can be the source of enormous financial losses, not only to your vehicle but to someone else's vehicle and other personal property. Additionally, the financial hit from injuries can wipe out a financial plan overnight. If you're nearing retirement age, you likely have significant assets to protect. Simply accepting the minimum coverage required by your state is likely not enough.

>> **Homeowner's (or renter's) insurance:** If you own your home, it might be one of the pieces of bedrock in your financial plan. If you don't have rent or a mortgage, you're well ahead of those who spend 30 percent of their budget for housing. Protecting your home from a devastating fire or other catastrophe is important. Don't count on the insurance company to verify that you have enough coverage. Renters insurance can help safeguard your personal belongings.

TIP

Insurance needs remain fairly unchanged as you near retirement — you need to protect your home whether you're 34 or 64. But one factor that you might want to modify as you age is your deductible.

Your *deductible* is how much of a loss you're responsible for in an accident. Let's say your car sustains $1,500 in damage. If you're young, you might not have the financial resources to handle a large hit and so you opt for a lower $250 deductible. The lower deductible comes at a cost, in the form of a higher monthly payment.

As you age, however, you probably have a larger financial reserve. One easy way to save money on insurance is to push up your deductible to $1,000 and save on your monthly premiums.

Log into your insurance provider's site, as shown in Figure 16-6, to see whether a higher deductible is available. You'll also want to double-check that the limits are appropriate.

FIGURE 16-6:
Check your homeowner's and auto policy limits to see if you can boost your deductible to lower your premiums.

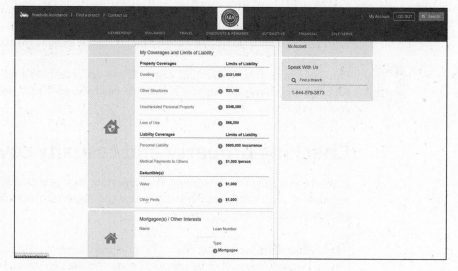

Getting ready for a rainy day: Umbrella insurance

Knowing your coverage limits on your automotive and homeowner's insurance policies unlocks the next phase of insurance. As you age and amass more money, you have more at risk from a big accident. Not only do you have more money to lose, you have less time to recover from a financial blow.

After looking at your limits on your homeowner's and automotive plans, you might see a disconnect. If your net worth exceeds your insurance limits, that's a red flag. If you've accumulated a big nest egg, you don't want to see it evaporate if you're caught in a massive car pileup on the freeway. Similarly, if someone gets seriously hurt on your property, lawsuit damages can be enormous.

How do you protect yourself other than never leaving the house or never inviting someone over to visit? Enter *umbrella insurance,* which unlocks millions of dollars of extra coverage beyond what your homeowner's and auto policies cover.

TIP

Umbrella policies don't kick in until the limits of your homeowner's and automotive policies are exceeded. Because the umbrella policy doesn't pay anything until your homeowner's or auto policy's limit is topped, the rates on umbrella policies tend to be reasonable. It's common to buy $1 million of coverage for $100 or $200 a year. It's a small price to pay for such a large amount of protection and peace of mind.

How much umbrella coverage to you need? You could figure it out yourself, but I like Kiplinger's How Much Umbrella Insurance Do I Need? calculator at www.kiplinger.com/tool/insurance/T028-S002-how-much-umbrella-insurance-do-i-need/index.php. The calculator, which is shown in Figure 16-7, helps you buy just enough umbrella insurance to safeguard you from a major financial shock.

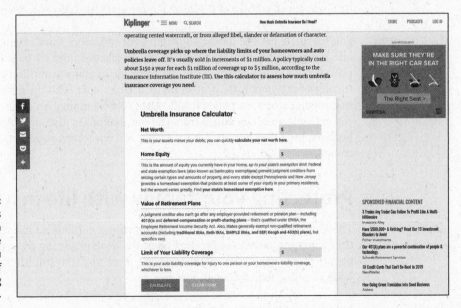

FIGURE 16-7:
Kiplinger's umbrella insurance tool helps you protect yourself without paying too much.

To use the calculator, start with your net worth and work backwards:

1. **Enter your net worth.**

Your *net worth* is the value of what you own minus what you owe.

TIP

To err on the side of safety, consider buying an umbrella policy valued at your net worth. Yes, some of your money is protected against creditors, as you'll see in Steps 2 and 3. But when you take the money out of protected accounts, such as retirement accounts, it's exposed. This approach isn't necessarily recommended, but it's a conservative way to go.

2. **Enter your home equity value.**

The *equity value* is the market value of your home minus mortgages or loans. Most states protect at least some of your home equity. The Kiplinger calculator can tabulate how much of your home equity is at risk.

3. **Enter your retirement plan balances.**

Enter the value of your retirement plans, including 401(k), IRA, Roth IRA, SIMPLE IRA, and SEP IRA. Assets held in these accounts are protected from creditors.

4. **Set a limit to your homeowner's and auto policies.**

Remember that your auto and homeowner's liability coverage pays injury claims first. Most umbrella policy insurers will require your homeowner's liability limit to be $250,000 or higher. And you'll likely need to have a per-person liability limit on your auto policy of $250,000 or more and $500,000 per accident.

TIP

You'll usually get the most bang from your insurance buck if you raise your auto and homeowner's liability limits to the lowest required by your umbrella policy provider. Because you buy umbrella coverage in giant $1 million chunks, you can usually boost your total protection at a lower cost with an umbrella than with homeowner's or auto policy limits. Also, to save money on premiums, see if you can get your umbrella policy from the same company that provides your auto and homeowner's policies. It's also easier to coordinate payments from a single company.

Protecting your family with life insurance

Thinking about all the things that can go wrong in life is no fun. That's why I left the chapter on insurance for the end of the book. Planning for retirement should be fun. It gets you thinking about what's most important in life and how to enjoy what you have for as long as possible.

But you need to prepare for unhappy events, too.

Understanding the benefits of life insurance

Life insurance isn't for you. It's for your beneficiaries. You buy a life insurance policy on your life with the idea that it will cover your financial role if you pass away. Life insurance is especially critical when you're starting a family. If you're the primary breadwinner and you die, imagine the financial hardship your family would suffer.

To combat this potentially cataclysmic crisis, you can buy a *term-life insurance* policy. By agreeing to pay an annual premium, if you were to die in a certain amount of time (or term), the insurance company agrees to pay out a pre-determined sum of money. The premium is the fee you pay to keep the policy active.

TIP

Life insurance is there only to take care of people who count on you financially, after you die. If you're not supporting anyone financially, you probably don't need life insurance. Also, other forms of life insurance wrap savings and investment plans in with the death benefit. These plans are called *whole-life plans*. Whole-life plans might make sense for a subset of people, but they're so complicated and potentially expensive that you should consult with an expert before buying one. Or you could just buy a term-life insurance policy and keep it simple.

Estimating how much life insurance you need

If you decide that you need life insurance, the next question is how much coverage you require. Some excellent online calculators, such as the following, can help you make the calculations:

>> **LifeHappens Calculate Your Needs calculator** (`https://lifehappens.org/insurance-overview/life-insurance/calculate-your-needs`)**:** Steps you through the important questions you need to answer to decide how much life insurance coverage you need. As you can see in Figure 16-8, the site shows you the two variables that determine how much money your dependents would need if you died and in the future. The site helps you measure both.

>> **LifeHappens Human Life Calculator** (`https://lifehappens.org/insurance-calculators/calculate-human-life-value/`)**:** Puts a price tag on your existence by showing how much of a financial blow your family would suffer if you died today. Putting a price tag on your life is another way to think about your life insurance needs, as you can see in the sidebar, "What's a Life Worth?" The calculator is an eye-opening tabulation of what a human life is worth.

>> **Bankrate Life Insurance Calculator** (`www.bankrate.com/calculators/insurance/life-insurance-calculator.aspx`)**:** Looks at the question of how much life insurance you need in a slightly different way. Most life insurance calculators differ in their approach, so it's a good idea to run your numbers through a few.

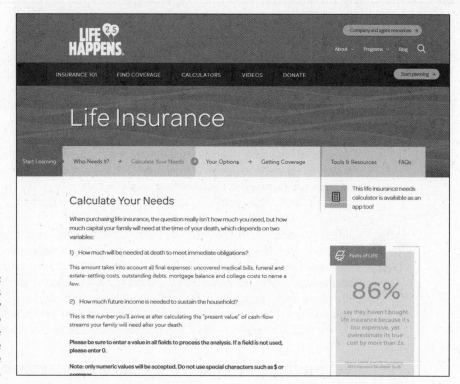

FIGURE 16-8:
LifeHappens provides many useful tools to help you see how much life insurance you need.

TIP

Don't fixate too much on how much life insurance you need. The biggest question is whether or not you need it. And if you do need it, don't waste any time. Just buy it. An easy rule-of-thumb on how much you and your spouse collectively need is to buy? You'll want a policy with a payout that's 10 times your combined household income.

Buying life insurance

Talk about a tough sell. How would you like to buy something that costs you money every year, doesn't benefit you personally, and pays out only if you die? Not exactly uplifting.

That's why the moment someone hears that you're interested in buying life insurance, sellers will come out of the woodwork to sell you a policy. Just search for *life insurance* online and you'll get life insurance ads on your screen for months.

If you do decide that you're ready to buy a policy, first check with the carrier that provides your auto, homeowner's, or umbrella coverage. Most also sell life insurance and provide a multi-policy discount. In addition, online insurance forums, such as LendingTree.com and SelectQuote, will shop your insurance needs against a network of bidders. You can then compare coverage and prices to get the best combination for you.

WHAT'S A LIFE WORTH?

You can't replace the love, caring, and non-financial support a person brings to a family. But life insurance tries to at least fill the financial hole left by a death.

But what's a life worth? It depends on your gender.

Men who have life insurance policies carry coverage amounts of $423,102, on average. This implies the value these men put on their own lives. That amount is 83 percent more than the $231,342 in coverage women with life insurance carried, according to data collected by HavenLife, an insurance agent firm.

Apparently, even men without life insurance value their lives higher than uninsured women. Men lacking life insurance said if they were to buy coverage, they'd look for limits of $355,348. That's twice the $175,423 in coverage women without life insurance said they'd buy.

A big reason for the discrepancy in the perceived value of life isn't male chauvinism. Instead, nearly 80 percent of the men described themselves as the family's primary breadwinner, earning $72,482 annually on average, versus just 37 percent of women.

Only 67 percent of women said they had life insurance, well below the 79 percent of men who did. Yet nearly 80 percent of men and women said their death would substantially injure the family's quality of life. Women, in many households, have the primary responsibility of caring for children. If something were to happen to the women in these homes, the men would likely need to pay for costly help.

Remember, life insurance protects you not only from a loss of income but also from other costs that might arise when someone dies.

4

The Part of Tens

Find solutions to the top ten retirement mistakes.

Discover the ten most common questions people ask about retirement planning.

Chapter **17**

Top Ten Retirement Mistakes

Building a comfortable retirement is up to you. If you follow sound rules by saving as much as you can and maxing out your retirement accounts, your golden years will likely be pleasant.

However, many perils can stand between you and a successful retirement. Some of these easily avoidable mistakes can severely injure your plans, resulting in the need to work longer than you expected or spend less than you'd hoped.

Waiting to Save

You might think that your earning potential is infinite and you can worry about retirement savings later. But time is an investor's top ally. If you start saving early, you will amass more than a person who saves much more but later in life.

Make life easy for yourself: Start saving now.

You should save at least 15 percent of your income as soon as you can. Make your savings plan automatic by having the money taken out of your paycheck.

The sooner you get used to living on 85 percent of your income or less, the better off your retirement plan will be.

Ignoring Fees

Fees are like termites. They nibble imperceptible amounts in the short term, they never stop, and over time, they do enormous damage. Seek out and destroy fees that don't add value to your retirement plan.

Bankrate.com's Mutual Fund Fee calculator (`www.bankrate.com/calculators/retirement/mutual-funds-fees-calculator.aspx`) will help you see how much mutual fund fees add up over time, eating away at your retirement.

Not Securing Your Information

You might think it's the responsibility of your broker and bank to safeguard your digital information. And it is. But you'll be the one suffering if your account information is stolen.

Lock all your digital information in a digital vault. Windows 10, for example, has a free digital vault. For details, go to `www.microsoft.com/en-us/microsoft-365/blog/2019/06/25/onedrive-personal-vault-added-security-onedrive-additional-storage`.

Also use a password manager such as Lastpass (`www.lastpass.com/how-lastpass-works`). A *password manager* is software that stores all your passwords in an encrypted file that's easy for you to access. And don't sign in to your bank site from a public hotspot such as Starbucks or McDonald's unless you're using a VPN (virtual private network).

Prioritizing College Savings Over Retirement

If you must choose between saving for the kids' college fund versus your retirement, your retirement wins. Your children might decide not to go to college or might be able to get a scholarship or a loan. But you can't borrow for your retirement.

Not Diversifying Your Portfolio

Your uncle says he knows about a stock that will double your retirement fund. Sure he does. Never chase after hot stocks in your retirement fund, which is your long-term money. Diversified low-cost funds are tough to beat.

With that said, don't play it too safe. Holding too many bonds or too much cash will all but doom you to subpar returns. Remember, you won't get a decent return if you don't take any risk. Even people in retirement should own stocks.

Waiting for the "Right Time" to Invest

"I'll put money in my 401(k) when the market is cheaper." Those are words spoken by people who'll never put money in a 401(k). They'll either wait and wait for a crash that never comes or get too nervous to put in money when markets do fall.

When's the best time to contribute to an IRA or 401(k)? Now.

Having Inadequate Insurance

No one likes to pay for life insurance or healthcare premiums. But skipping a key insurance plan at the wrong time could set you back so far you might never retire. Review your insurance plans, including an umbrella policy, and keep them current. You've worked too hard saving and investing to have it all wiped away by a natural disaster or accident.

Taking Money from Your Accounts Early

Retirement accounts are made for retirement, not for fixing a leaky roof or paying for an insurance deductible. Make sure you have an emergency fund to cover life's unexpected events.

Yes, you can borrow from your 401(k) or take money out of your Roth IRA. But you shouldn't. This Vanguard calculator will tell you how much borrowing money from your retirement accounts will actually cost you: https://retirementplans. vanguard.com/VGApp/pe/pubeducation/calculators/RetirementPlanLoan Calc.jsf

Not Checking Your Social Security Benefit

I hate to doubt the capability of the federal government to track the payroll deductions of millions of workers, but I do. Mistakes happen in recording contributions to Social Security. Not catching these errors can seriously reduce your benefit. It's up to you to check. And while you're at it, you can see what your Social Security payments would be so there are no surprises when you finally do collect.

Not Thinking about Income

Financial planners tell me that people are shocked the first day they don't get a paycheck. When you're working, you get accustomed to a steady income. But when you're building a retirement plan, you need to think about where you'll get the monthly income you need to pay your bills.

Building an income strategy is usually a multi-pronged approach. Your retirement accounts will likely pay interest and dividends. But for most people, that investment income will not be enough. You must also consider income you might get from a pension, and if not that, what kind of income stream you might line up by buying an immediate annuity.

Chapter **18**

Top Ten Retirement Questions

You probably have some questions about your retirement plan. And that's a good thing because rock-solid retirement plans are often built as you seek answers to your questions. For instance, the first question you likely had when you picked up this book was, "How do I start saving for retirement?" That question led you to research whether a 401(k), traditional IRA, or Roth IRA was best for you. And answering that question likely led to wondering where you should open your account. After starting with one question, you made two important steps toward setting up a retirement plan.

This chapter dives into ten questions people routinely ask about retirement planning. Each question might prompt you to learn more about your retirement plan or make the one you already have even better. Along the way, you also learn about tools to tailor your retirement plan.

So, what are you waiting for? Ask away!

How Much Money Do I Need?

The big question on every pre-retiree's mind is "How much money do I need?" Frustratingly, no one right answer exists.

Retirement plans are as unique as people's personalities and constantly evolving. Your retirement plan is a reflection, at the time, of your hopes and dreams for the future. Your retirement plan also reflects your personality. Are you a worrier? You'll probably want a bigger nest egg before you're comfortable enough to retire. Are you a planner? You'll probably start saving early.

A good rule of thumb if you retire at 65 is to have saved at least 25 times what you spend annually. If you spend $50,000 a year, try to have $1.25 million saved. That way, you should be able to take out 4 percent the first year, adjusted annually, for 30 years without running out. If you want to retire younger, shoot for at least 30 times what you spend annually. That's $1.5 million in this example.

In addition, online calculators do a good job estimating with more precision how much you'll need. For details, flip back to Chapter 3.

Is Medicare Enough?

Healthcare costs are a giant wild card faced for anyone thinking about retirement. Given the magnitude of potential costs, you don't have a retirement plan until you have a healthcare plan.

For most people, Medicare is not enough. With Medicare Part A, you get hospital coverage. Part B, which costs most people $135.50 a month, covers doctor visits and lab tests (www.medicare.gov/your-medicare-costs/part-b-costs). You can also pay to get drug coverage with Part D.

Many people find that they need more coverage and buy a Medigap policy. Others purchase a Medicare Advantage plan, offered by private insurers, which combines Parts A, B, and C.

Medicare provides information to help you sort out all these plans: at www.medicare.gov/index.php/your-medicare-costs.

What Will I Do with My Free Time?

More pre-retirees should ask themselves how they will fill their free time. Although you might be able to afford retirement financially, are you ready to step away from your work life emotionally? Many people tie their identities to and structure their days and social circles around office life. If you love what you do and are good at it, retirement might not be the goal you think it is.

A good friend of mine who considered taking an early retirement package figured that he needed at least three new activities or goals to fill up his time if he was no longer working. Unable to come up with them, he passed on the buyout and stayed at work.

What three activities or goals do you have?

Will I Run Out of Money?

After you retire, you might wonder how long your money will last. You can measure the likelihood of your money going the distance, given a number of reasonable assumptions.

Vanguard's Nest Egg Calculator (https://retirementplans.vanguard.com/VGApp/pe/pubeducation/calculators/RetirementNestEggCalc.jsf) provides a quick and easy estimate of how long you might expect your money to last. It also shows you how to make adjustments, if needed.

For instance, suppose you are still working and have saved $1 million, spend $45,000 a year, and plan to need the money for 30 years after you retire. If you invest 60 percent of the $1 million in stocks and 40 percent in bonds, Vanguard estimates that you have an 85 percent chance of having enough. If you cut spending to $40,000 a year, the probability of having enough jumps to 91 percent. Or if you hold spending at $45,000 annually but work longer and save another $300,000, the odds of success jumps to 96 percent.

Should I Have a Roth or Traditional IRA?

You'll read lots of opinions regarding whether a Roth IRA is better than a traditional IRA. For me, it boils down to whether you think your tax rate will be higher or lower in the future.

If you think your tax rate will be higher, the Roth IRA is for you. If you're in a low tax bracket now, why not pay your taxes now? If you think your tax rate will be lower in the future, skip the Roth and go with the traditional IRA. Perhaps right out of college you got a high-paying job that you plan to do for only a few years before joining the Peace Corps. You might as well pay taxes when they're likely lower in the future.

TIP

If you think your tax rate will be the same, the Roth and traditional IRA plans are the same, taxwise. The Roth does have the advantage of not requiring you to take distributions when you turn 70½.

How Good Is My 401(k)?

If your 401(k) offers a match of any kind, it's good. You should contribute at least enough to get the maximum match. Beyond that, deciding whether the 401(k) is the best place to put your retirement money gets trickier.

To find out, look at the funds in the plan. If you can choose low-cost funds and a sampling of low-cost index funds, the plan is likely good. If you're not sure whether the plan is suitable, head over to BrightScope (`www.brightscope.com`) and enter the plan's name. The site will analyze your 401(k) and help you decide if you could do better setting up your own IRA.

What's an RMD?

Deferred taxes on retirement accounts are good while they last. But eventually, the taxman will want his cut. Enter the required minimum distribution, or RMD. With traditional IRAs and 401(k) plans, when you turn 70½, you must start taking money out of your retirement accounts by April 1 of the following year. Going forward, you must take money out by December 31. And yes, you must pay taxes on the money you're taking out.

The amount you must take out varies based on your age. Vanguard can estimate your RMD at `https://personal.vanguard.com/us/insights/retirement/living/estimate-your-rmd-tool`.

WARNING

Failing to take an RMD is a massive fail. If you take out less than your minimum RMD, you owe a 50 percent tax on the shortfall. Yes, 50 percent. That pretty much wipes out any tax benefit of putting money in a tax-deferred account in the first place.

Remember, you don't have to take a required minimum distribution from a Roth 401(k) or Roth IRA. That's a big advantage of those types of accounts.

Can Retirement Rules Change?

Retirement rules can change. In May 2019, for example, the U.S. House of Representatives passed the Setting Every Community Up for Retirement Enhancement (SECURE) Act. The SECURE Act is poised to revise many important aspects of retirement planning.

At press time, it was unclear which changes to retirement planning the Senate would adopt, but the sweeping nature of the House version showed that lawmakers weren't afraid to make some major changes. Specifically, the House version went after Stretch IRAs, which are given to non-spousal beneficiaries after you die. The House wants to force the money to be taken out — and taxed — more rapidly.

Other rules open to revision include pushing back the age at which you must take RMDs and allowing annuity products to be offered in retirement plans.

WARNING

The fact that Congress can change the rules around the tax status of retirement accounts is one reason why some critics are opposed to Roth IRAs and Roth 401(k) plans. Some fear that Congress might try to tax distributions taken from Roth accounts in the future. If so, this would result in double-taxation of the money. This scenario is unlikely, but the possibility argues for tax diversification. Using the tax diversification idea, why choose between a Roth or traditional account? Why not have both? That way, no matter how retirement accounts change in the future, you can maximize your tax benefit (or at least minimize the cost).

What Can I Do If I'm Near Retirement Age and Don't Have a Plan?

Are you getting close to retirement age but still don't have a retirement plan? You've picked up this book, which is a good start. The key thing is to not panic.

You need a retirement plan, of course. However, you might first need to adjust your expectations. Rather than targeting retirement at age 65, you'll want instead to find ways to boost your savings rate and lengthen your time in the workforce.

The key for you is recognizing that your employment income is your top asset and should be protected. Make sure your skills remain relevant in your field. Get disability insurance. You'll want to maintain your enthusiasm for your work, too, because you'll likely be working longer than many of your similarly aged friends.

Also do your best to not take Social Security until after your full retirement age. For every year after your full retirement age that you wait to claim Social Security, your benefit goes up by 8 percent, according to Charles Schwab (www.schwab.com/resource-center/insights/content/social-security-should-you-wait-until-age-70-to-collect). You'll rely on Social Security more than others, so you should try to maximize your benefit from it.

Do I Need a Financial Advisor?

You don't need a financial planner. You can do all your retirement planning yourself. The question, though, is will your retirement plan improve if you hire a planner? Consider the following factors:

» **Do you have time to monitor your portfolio and developments in financial planning?** If you're busy with other obligations, it might be worthwhile to have someone watching over your financial affairs.

» **Are you interested in personal finance?** If you find personal finance topics interesting, managing your own money might not only save you money on fees but also give you something to do in retirement.

» **Do you know a financial planner you're comfortable with?** A skilled advisor who has experience optimizing plans like yours can add value. Do you know a planner like this? Do the fees the planner charges fit into your plan? Have you looked up the planner on BrokerCheck (https://brokercheck.finra.org/) to make sure he or she has the proper licenses and a clean record?

» **Is your financial situation complicated?** If you're a multi-millionaire or a divorced business owner with interests in multiple partnerships, the complexity of your situation might warrant getting help. With large estates, one major smart move can save enough money to justify the fees.

» **Are you comfortable with technology?** If you're comfortable with apps and online tools, you might want to sign up for a robo-advisor service. This type of service can help you optimize your plan at a reasonable cost. If you're not comfortable with technology, or just want someone to talk to about your financial goals, it makes more sense to hire a human advisor.

Index

D

Dashlane (password manager), 121, 122

debt
coming up with debt-busting plan, 208–209
cutting debt anchor loose, 206
types of, 206
understanding how it derails your retirement savings plan, 206–207

deductibility, 70–71

deductible, defined, 296, 304

deferred annuities, 267

defined benefit plan, 13, 63, 64, 277

defined contribution plans, 14, 16, 63, 64, 277

Depop, 209

deposits, setting up IRA deposits, 150–153

"Determining withdrawal rates using historical data" (Bengen), 48

digital vault, 314

DinkyTown, retirement calculators, 55

disability coverage (SSDI), 178–180

discount brokers, use of, 99

Discover Bank, 202

discretionary money, as expense category, 23

diversification, 145, 273, 315

dividends, defined, 75

Dow Jones Industrial Average, 82

downside capture ratio, 166

duration (of bonds), 229

E

Early Earl (fictional character), 57–58

earned income, 153

earnings statement, sample of, 183

eBay, 209

efficient frontier, 227

80 percent rule, 34

Einstein, Albert (theoretical physicist), 57

elections, changing yours, 131

Electronic Deposit Insurance Estimator (FDIC), 204

emergency fund, 199–205, 315

Emergency Fund Calculator (PNC Bank), 201

emerging markets, 91, 225, 226–227

Employee Retirement Income Security Act (ERISA), 279

employer matching
as advantage of 401(k) plans, 66
example of, 18, 65, 134
limited availability of for 401(k) plans, 67
qualifying for, 38, 68, 94, 118, 171, 207, 295, 320
in retirement plans, 15–16, 62, 97, 282
SIMPLE (Savings Incentive Match Plan for Employees), 74–75, 77
statistic on percent of large companies offering, 65
in traditional 401(k) plans, 14

entry date, for 401(k) plans, 97

equity, as another name for stocks, 82, 126

equity value, defined, 306

ERISA (Employee Retirement Income Security Act), 279

ESG (environmental, social, and governance) investing, 168, 222, 235–239

Estate & Trust Administration For Dummies, 2nd Edition (Munro and Murphy), 155

ETF.com, 239

E-Trade, 104–105

Etsy, 209

Excel (Microsoft), 28, 29, 250

exchange-traded funds (ETF)
described, 98
use of by IRA providers, 104, 105
use of by mutual fund companies, 99, 100

expected return, 50–51, 87

expense ratio, 101, 160, 164

expenses
classifying of, 22, 23
determining how much you spend, 21–40
finding out where your money goes, 22–24
how they change as you age, 34
tax deductibility of, 22
tracking of, 22–24

Exposure section (Morningstar), 168

F

Facebook, market value of, 225

Facebook Marketplace, 209

FDIC insurance, 203

Federal Deposit Insurance Corporation (FDIC), 204

Federal Housing Administration (FHA), 274, 275

Federal Insurance Contributions Act (FICA), 182

risk

 assessment tools for, 85

 gauging your appetite for, 79–92

 in investing in corporate bonds, 84

 in investing in stocks, 84

 in investing in Treasury bills, 84

Risk Capacity Survey (Index Fund Advisors), 85–86

risk questionnaires, as 401(k) tool, 123–124, 130–131

Risk Return scatter plot (IFA.com), 226

Risk tab (Morningstar Research), 164–166

risk tolerance, 80–86, 91–92

RMD (required minimum distribution), 70, 138, 154–155, 320–321

RMD calculator (Vanguard), 154, 155, 320

robo-advisors

 advantages of, 106

 companies who provide, 103, 105

 comparison of, 109

 defined, 149

 described, 106–109

 determining if one is best for you, 114

 disadvantages of, 107

 as making waves in IRA business, 99

 as offering high-yield cash vehicles for parking cash, 202

roll over (of 401(k) plan), 16, 136

rolling over, of pension plan, 278, 291–292

rollover IRAs, 72, 137, 140, 152, 292

Roth Conversion Calculator (CalcXML), 153

Roth IRA conversion, 72, 152–153

Roth IRA (Roth 401(k) plan)

 benefits of, 70, 152

 conversions to, 72, 152–153

 deciding if you should have Roth or traditional IRA, 319–320

 eligibility (2020), 72

 as exempt from RMD rules, 70

 income-based limits on contributions to, 71

 as interesting twist on retirement savings, 68

 tapping of to pay for college, 218

 as taxing retirement contributions immediately, 16

 use of to help buy house, 212

rules

 about retirement, can they change? 321

 early distribution rules, 97

 80 percent rule, 34

 4 percent rule. *See* 4 percent rule

 legislative rules, impact of, 243

 loan rules, 97, 136

 required minimum distribution (RMD). *See* required minimum distribution (RMD)

 restrictive inclusion rules in pension plans, 16

run rate

 calculation of, 25–31

 defined, 21

Russell 2000, 90

S

S&P Down Jones Indices, on defining company size, 224

S&P Global Market Intelligence, ranking of largest companies by, 225

S&P/Case-Shiller U.S. National Home Price Index, 211

Save for Retirement tool (Vanguard), 53

Savingforcollege.com, 218, 219, 220, 256

savings

 according to BLS data, 32

 average retirement savings, 257

 balancing retirement savings with other needs, 197–220

 for college, 215–220

 as expense category, 23

 guidelines for spending on, 24

 high-yield online savings accounts, 202

 for homeownership, 69, 211–215

 HSA (health savings account), 264, 294–298

 importance of "save first," 38

 keeping track of, 23

 mistake to prioritize college savings over retirement, 314

Savings Incentive Match Plan for Employees (SIMPLE), 74–75, 77

Schedule SE (Self Employment), 184

Sears, pension plan of, 285

SEC yield, defined, 163

Securities and Exchange Commission, 112, 160, 278

self-directed IRA, 149–150

self-employed, deductions by for Social Security and Medicare taxes, 184–185

self-employed options/plans, 63, 73–75

senior intern, 265

SEP-IRA plans, 63, 70, 73–75, 77

X

Y

Z

About the Author

Matt Krantz is a nationally known financial journalist who specializes in investment topics as personal finance and management editor for *Investor's Business Daily (IBD)*. In addition to writing for IBD, his work has appeared in *USA TODAY* and *Money* magazine. He's covered financial markets and Wall Street for decades, concentrating on developments affecting individual investors and their portfolios. His stories routinely signal trends that investors can profit from and point out ways to improve investment success. Krantz has written or co-written several books in addition to this one, including *Fundamental Analysis For Dummies* and *Investment Banking For Dummies.*

Readers often tell Matt he's the only one who has been able to finally solve investing questions they've sought answers to for years.

Matt has been investing since the 1980s and has studied dozens of investment techniques while forming his own. And as a financial journalist, Matt has interviewed some of the most famous and infamous investment minds in modern history.

He earned a bachelor's degree in business administration at Miami University in Oxford, Ohio. He has also spoken for investing groups, including at the national convention of National Association of Investors Corporation, and has appeared on various financial TV programs.

Matt is based in Los Angeles. When he's not writing, he spends time with his wife and young daughter, running, playing tennis, mountain biking, or playing Xbox games.

Dedication

This book is dedicated to my wife, Nancy, and daughter, Leilani, who are always available to help me come up with a better word or a new way of thinking.

Author's Acknowledgments

Wiley personnel have been tremendous to work with on this project, including senior acquisitions editor Katie Mohr, and project and copy editor editor Susan Pink, who found ways to make this book even more useful to readers with great edits and suggestions, and technical editor Bill Hughes.

A big thanks to Matt Wagner, my literary agent, for thinking of me for the project and first presenting it to me.

Thanks to my mom and dad for instilling, at a very young age, a curiosity in investing, writing, and computers (and for buying me my first computer well before having a PC was common). And thanks to my grandparents for teaching me the power of saving and investing.

And thank you, readers, for picking up this book.

Publisher's Acknowledgments

Associate Publisher: Katie Mohr

Project Editor: Susan Pink

Copy Editor: Susan Pink

Technical Editor: Bill Hughes

Editorial Assistant: Matt Lowe

Sr. Editorial Assistant: Cherie Case

Production Editor: Mohammed Zafar Ali

Cover Image: © ac productions/Getty Images